COLORS AND CHORDS

THE ART OF JOHNNY OTIS

Biographical essay and discography by LEE HILDEBRAND

Art commentary by MARY LOVELACE O'NEAL

POMEGRANATE ARTBOOKS *San Francisco*

Published by Pomegranate Artbooks
Box 6099 Rohnert Park, California 94927

Pomegranate Europe Ltd.
Fullbridge House, Fullbridge
Maldon, Essex CM9 7LE, England

Library of Congress Cataloging-in-Publication Data

Colors and chords : the art of Johnny Otis / biographical essay by
Lee Hildebrand : art commentary by Mary Lovelace O'Neal :
foreword by John Outterbridge. — 1st ed.
p. cm.
Discography : p.
ISBN 0-87654-359-X (pb)
1. Otis, Johnny, 1921– —Criticism and interpretation.
2. Afro-Americans in art. I. Otis, Johnny, 1921–
II. Hildebrand, Lee. III. O'Neal, Mary Lovelace.
N6537.082C66 1995
709' .2—dc20 94-49446
CIP

Pomegranate Catalog No. A779

Designed by Peter Howells

Printed in Korea
00 99 98 97 96 95 6 5 4 3 2 1

First Edition

To my loving wife, Phyllis
J.O.

FOREWORD
THE VISUALIST JOHNNY OTIS

I WAS ABSOLUTELY ASTONISHED when first introduced to the visual images and uncaged thoughts of the legendary Godfather of West Coast rhythm-and-blues music. He expresses with well-forged confidence and a rather personal language of line, form, craftsmanship, and color, obviously nurtured over a period of many, many years. Johnny Otis is a natural humorist, with a backlog of skillfully rendered drawings, quick sketch notes of merit—loads of original archival stuff that most serious collectors would give up land for. He creates in the genre of the Harlem Renaissance masters, only with the touch of a freshly stylized, multihued palette, bold surrealistic characterizations, and the tonal audacity found in his disciplined, deeply rooted musical heritage. With a pronounced curiosity and thirst for life, with penetrating substance, this visual acuity of the artist has tooled a stage of excitement in his innovative use of found objects, mixed media, color, image, form, and presentation. Animated sculptural gestures reach, sit, stare, perform, gyrate, interweave, and suggest allegorical narrations of soul-shaped spiritual awareness.

There are truly any number of reasons why the art of Johnny Otis bestows upon us such a brilliant kaleidoscope of entertainment and metaphor. The most compelling is that he is the originator who agitates his own sense of poetic narrative, philosophy, and idea pool. By confronting himself with such pedigree challenges, he shares with us facet after facet of magnificent storytelling. One other reason to celebrate the inventive nature of this fine talent has much to do with the fact that he is constantly dealing with notions that parallel those universal equivalents of what it means to be human. A need to hear and to examine the tales of life is essential to the Homo sapien, following in no less importance after acknowledging the need for nourishment, love, and shelter. Millions survive void of love and home, none in silence, none without tale. The Otis visual narratives are the dominant sounds and motions of our lives, from the small accounts of each day's events to the vast incommunicable sagas that beset us all.

JOHN OUTTERBRIDGE, 1995

This book would not have been realized without the tireless coordination of my publicist, art agent, and friend Veronica Aiken.

Fellow drummer Hal Kronick has been a kindred spirit since we met in Berkeley as teenagers. He not only put up with and responded to my meandering midnight cartoons over the years, but saved them and loaned many for these pages.

JOHNNY OTIS

Veronica Aiken has been a constant source of inspiration through this project. Many thanks also to Opal Louis Nations, Chris Strachwitz, Heath Finnell, and Curtis Fukada for their help.

LEE HILDEBRAND

My very special thanks to Patricio Moreno Toro and Veronica Aiken for being there to bounce ideas off of into the wee, wee hours.

MARY LOVELACE O'NEAL

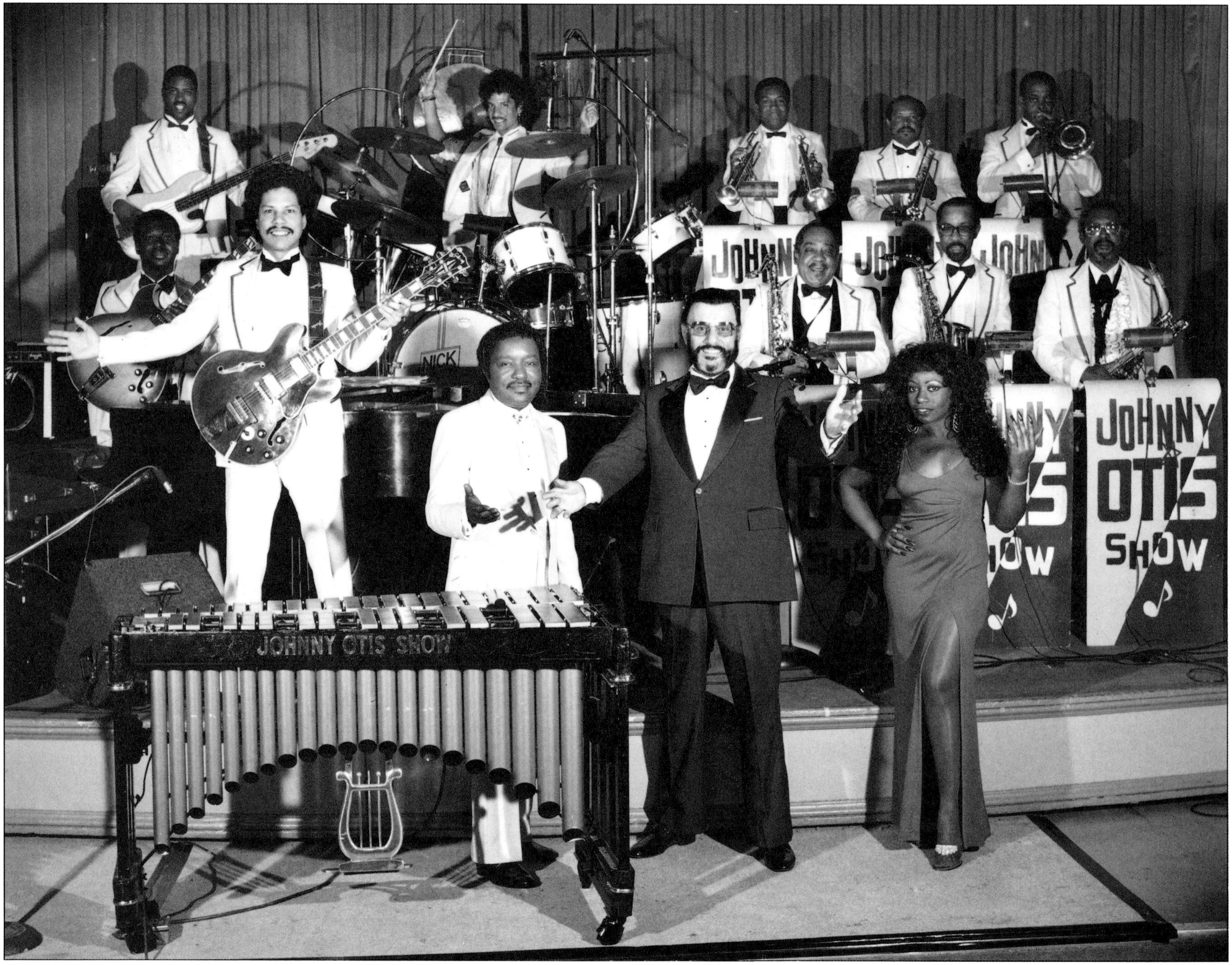

The Johnny Otis Show, 1988

A Unique American Life

By Lee Hildebrand

ALTHOUGH THE GREEN-AND-WHITE- neon sign along Highway 116 in downtown Sebastopol still reads "Johnny Otis Market," the fruit, vegetables, and other edible goods that once filled the store's shelves are long gone. After opening the establishment in 1993, its proprietor discovered that people of the quiet northern California town, famous for its apples, weren't in need of any more fresh produce. It seemed, however, that the predominantly Caucasian populace did have an appetite for the product for which this Greek grocer's son is most renowned: African-American music.

All that remains of the former furnishings are a deli counter and a shelf near the front door that stocks CDs and cassettes and bottles of Johnny Otis Apple Juice, an organic, two-thirds-sweet, one-third-tart blend squeezed from plump red apples harvested at Johnny's own orchard and those of several of his Sebastopol neighbors. The market now operates as a restaurant and cabaret, serving up sandwiches daily and live music five nights a week. When they're not off performing at a blues festival in Chicago or a San Francisco night club, Johnny and the ten instrumentalists and vocalists who form the core of the Johnny Otis Show are the main course on Fridays and Saturdays.

In keeping with Otis's philosophy of making little distinction between the various subgenres of African-American music, the band's repertoire—like the records he selects for his weekly radio program, broadcast Saturday mornings over KPFA in Berkeley via remote from the market—juxtaposes blues, jazz, early R&B and rock 'n' roll, and classic soul. The band is anchored by Johnny's son Nicky on drums and grandsons Lucky on electric bass and Eric on electric guitar (their father is the brilliant guitarist Shuggie Otis, now also a Sonoma County resident), making it a three-generation family affair. Directing the revue from behind a grand piano and sometimes while standing in front of a vibraharp, the seventy-three-year-old, tuxedo-clad leader jumps from decade to decade as he mixes songs made famous by Wilson Pickett, Jackie Wilson, Ike and Tina Turner, Ray Sharpe, Billie Holiday, the Supremes, Duke Ellington, Lionel Hampton, the Temptations, B. B. King, Bobby Bland, Louis Armstrong, Sly and the Family Stone, Otis Redding, and Aretha Franklin—as well as his own greatest hit, 1958's "Willie and the Hand Jive"—to create a rich African-American musical pastiche.

While veteran soul singer Jackie Payne applies his gravely low tenor to a treatment of the old standard "All of Me," trumpeter Larry Douglas, trombonist Danny Armstrong, and clarinetist Ronald Wilson (who also plays alto, tenor, and baritone saxophones with the band) produce Mardi Gras-like polyphony as they stroll through a near-capacity crowd of around a hundred that's waving paper napkins in time to the song's two-beat bounce. The three musicians then return to the stage and stand still to blend their horns in sinewy harmony for a haunting rendition of Ellington's 1927 blues, "Creole Love Call."

Wearing a square-box hat that's cocked to one side, a fourth horn player is perched on a ledge above the bandstand. He sits on a tiny white chair, his cone-shaped horn pointed upward as if adding another hue to the orchestral palette. His horn is silent, however. Joining him on the ledge are two other of Johnny's plaster, acrylic, and wood sculptures: a girl seated on a bench feeding her younger brother watermelon with a fork, and a monster with another monster coming out of its mouth, which has a third coming out of its mouth—a head begetting a head begetting a head, each more whimsical than the last—known as *Humongous and Friends.*

The room's electric baby blue walls are washed in the bright primary colors of some of Johnny's other sculptures and paintings, though the wall opposite the stage is devoted to a rotating exhibit of works by other Sonoma County artists. Some of Johnny's, like the sculpture *Mom and Pop Store* in which the 7-Up sign above the counter is fixed at 3:20 (the time at which he and his childhood chums in Berkeley would arrive after school to purchase candy and sodas), draw on his life experiences. Others, such as *Humongous and Friends* and a mural—in which familiar cartoon characters, a dancing plate, spoon, and knife, and Dizzy Gillespie, wearing a red-and-green dashiki, his cheeks puffed as he blows his bent trumpet, march in a merry parade—are the product of vivid fantasy.

A lithograph of *Jazz,* the best known of his paintings, is mounted in a place of prominence above the deli counter, and above that a mural titled *Artists and Models Ball.* Leonardo Da Vinci and Mona Lisa sit arm and arm next to Picasso and a cubist woman, while Matisse frolics with a figure from *The Dance* and Gauguin strums a ukulele for a beautiful Polynesian dancing girl. To their left is a West African–style ebony wood carving of a female figure with a statuesque Masai warrior carrying a spear in one hand, a boom-box in the other.

Such subtle, humorous social commentary is at the core of much of Johnny's visual art. As a white man who decided over sixty years ago that he'd rather be black—and has lived as such ever since—he has come face to face with racism throughout his prolific, astonishingly varied career. Besides leading his own bands for half a century, he has distinguished himself as a songwriter, record producer, disc jockey, television show host, civil rights activist, preacher, cartoonist, painter, and sculptor.

Unlike many white musicians who were drawn to African-American culture through music, Johnny adopted the culture first, the music later. Born on December 28, 1921, in Vallejo, California, to Greek immigrants Alexander and Irene Veliotes, he is the oldest of their three children. (The youngest, Nicholas, born in 1928, served as American ambassador to Egypt and is currently president of the American Publishers Association.) When Johnny was two, the family moved to the corner of Dohr and Ward streets in west Berkeley.

In *Listen to the Lambs,* a combination autobiography and political treatise on the 1965 Watts uprising published in 1968 by W.W.Norton, Johnny wrote:

> Until the late '30s, when the Depression forced him out of business, my father had a grocery store in Berkeley. We lived above the store in an integrated neighborhood that soon was to become an almost entirely Negro community. There were a few white and Oriental children in the neighborhood but the bulk of my childhood playmates, especially those with whom I had the most constant and intimate contact, were black. There was nothing particularly unique, I suppose, about a white child being raised among black folk in America. The difference in my case was that during my preteen years and adolescence I didn't veer off into the white world. As a kid I decided that if our society dictated that one had to be either black or white, I would be black. I did not become black because I was attracted to Negro music. My attitude was formed long before I moved into the music field. Nor did I become a member of the Negro community because I married a Negro girl. These eventualities were outgrowths of my life among black people. I became what I am because as a child I reacted to the way of life, the special vitality, the atmosphere of the black community. . . . No number of objections such as, "You were born white . . . you can never be black," on the part of whites, or, "You sure are a fool to be colored when you could be white," from Negroes, can alter the fact that I cannot think of myself as white.

Johnny's best friend was a black neighbor named Rudy Jordan. They had plans of opening an auto-wrecking yard when they grew up. Driving around Berkeley and Oakland in a Model T Ford that Johnny's father had given him, they spent their spare time cruising for girls and abandoned cars. And they attended black Pentecostal churches in their neighborhood, something Johnny found more appealing than the Greek Orthodox one he occasionally attended with his parents.

"Rudy and I frequented one of them the most because they gave away graham crackers and chocolate milk to the kids," Johnny recalls. "During the Depression that was a real delicacy, but we really went to meet the little sisters. And then the gospel music started to become an attraction—and even the gospel preaching. It was really marvelous."

Two incidents with adult authorities, both involving Rudy, were central to Johnny's decision to break with the white world. To please his mother, he had joined the Boy Scouts, but when he submitted Rudy's name for membership, he learned that blacks were not eligible for admission to the troop. And then a school counselor called Johnny into the office one day. "He told me he thought it was an unhealthy thing for me to hang around black kids," Johnny remembers. "He had trouble explaining it to me because he didn't want to come out with any harsh language. My answer to him was that I was really confused because we had just left a lecture on brotherhood and democracy, and you're telling me that I shouldn't associate with black kids? He got real red in the face. He was really frustrated then."

Johnny's involvement with music began in junior high school when a music teacher assigned him a tuba. "I carried it home one day," he explains. "Walked down the Santa Fe tracks, which was over a mile. I had great fun 'cause I was tooting and the girls followed me. But the next morning, when I carried that big, heavy motherfucker all the way back, it was tiresome." He turned in the cumbersome instrument and bought a pair of drumsticks. Though he had received no lessons, he joined the school band playing a snare drum and managed to keep up on marches like "Under the Double Eagle" by watching other drummers and playing by ear.

Johnny was eighteen when he entered Berkeley High School as a freshman. Asthma, combined with growing disinterest, had caused him to fall behind in school. Music soon became a consuming passion. He soaked up the sounds around him like a sponge, as when a Pullman porter who lived across the street brought home from one of his trips a copy of Mississippi Delta bluesman Robert Johnson's "Terraplane Blues," a tune that built its double entendres around the functions of an automobile. "He had a Cord—you know, that beautiful car—and lovely ladies," Johnny says of the neighbor. "He would have parties, and we would go to the window. That's where I heard that record. You'd be surprised how youngsters react to the sexual, kinda naughty lines like 'Your carburetor needs adjusting.'"

He and his friends began making trips to 7th Street, the bustling boulevard in West Oakland that was the hub of commerce and social life for African-Americans in the area. "We used to slip down to West Oakland and hear people," Johnny remembers. "There was Slim Jenkins', where we'd hear more sophisticated jazz styles, and we'd go in there 'cause we were interested in jazz, but where we really liked to go was down the street a little bit to the buckets of blood—there were about three of 'em."

He also caught the big bands when they passed through the area. He says that after seeing Count Basie's, which included tenor saxophonist Lester Young and drummer Jo Jones, at the 1939 World's Fair on Treasure Island in the middle of San Francisco Bay, "my life was never the same." Duke Ellington had a similar impact. "When I stood as a kid at Sweets' Ballroom in Oakland in front of that Duke Ellington band and looked up at those exotic, powerful men in that band, it was hard to believe it was real," he explains. "It was like a fantasy. There were black men, brown men, lighter-colored men. Each one of these people had been hand-picked by the great Duke Ellington, and how unlikely, just as in the case of Count Basie, that these giants would gather on one bandstand and become a family and jell the way they did and send those atomic missiles across the footlights at us." Also at Sweets', Johnny saw Lionel Hampton, who would become the major influence on his vibraharp style.

When a piano-playing friend named Otis Matthews asked Johnny to be the drummer in a combo he was forming, Johnny jumped at the job. He dropped out of school after the ninth grade, went to a music store, and forged his father's signature on a contract to buy a set of traps—and a cheap vibraharp.

Otis Matthews billed himself as "Count" after Basie, though his style was far from refined. "Count Otis Matthews was a year or two older than myself," Johnny states. "His people were from the Mississippi Delta. He was really from that environment. He was steeped in boogie and blues. It was just hard, boogie-woogie blues style—very rough, very unsophisticated."

Johnny made his professional debut in 1939 with Count Otis Matthews' West Oakland Houserockers, a sextet comprising piano, trumpet, clarinet, guitar, bass, and drums. Too young to play in clubs, they performed for little or no money at a gym in West Oakland and at house-rent parties at which people would charge their friends and neighbors admission in exchange for food and entertainment. "They were blues and boogie affairs with chitlins in the kitchen," Johnny fondly recalls. "Playing with that band was not a matter of making money because we almost never made any, but we got all we wanted to drink

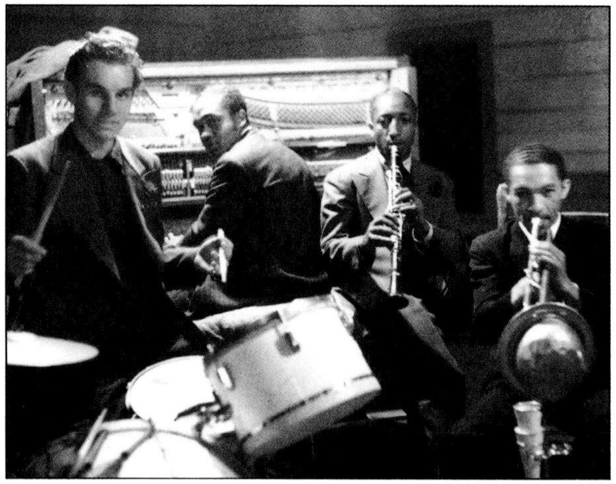

Count Otis Matthews and the West Oakland Houserockers, 1941

and all we wanted to eat and we had plenty of pretty little chicks around."

Among the most-requested tunes in Matthews's repertoire were the risqué blues he sang. "He had some naughty verses," Johnny recalls. "Like he would sing, 'Ooh wee, baby, I ain't gonna do it no more, 'cause every time I do it, it makes my wee-wee sore.' In 1939 and '40 that was very daring. The song that everyone waited for was 'Mama bought a chicken, thought it was a duck, put him on the table, with his legs stuck up.' He had about twenty verses and some of those were naughty—naughty, not ugly."

Another song was "The Signifying Monkey," but the band performed it only at private parties, not public dances at the gym. "If you sang, 'Signifying monkey told the lion one day, there's a big, bad motherfucker comin' your way,' you could go to jail for that in those days," Johnny explains. Thirty years later, in more liberal times, Johnny and his band recorded "The Signifying Monkey" and other nasty boogies from the Matthews book under the group pseudonym "Snatch and the Poontangs." And a rhythm that Johnny had learned from Matthews, the African-derived "shave and a haircut, six bits" beat that came to be associated with Bo Diddley, was revived in 1958 for Johnny's "Willie and the Hand Jive."

In 1941, Johnny married Phyllis Walker, whom he had known since he was a child, though not closely, as she lived about a mile away on the Oakland side of the border and attended Oakland schools. While Johnny's father was not much concerned about race, it took his mother eighteen years before she agreed to meet and accept her son's black bride. He wrote in *Listen to the Lambs*:

> It is a tribute to my wife's sweet forgiving nature—typical of so many black people—that she could welcome my mother with love and understanding after such an incredible period of time. I resented the situation then, and I find it difficult to erase from my heart now, because it was an affront to my wife, my children, and my adopted people. But I suppose I lack some of Phyllis's compassionate nature.

They were married in Reno, where Johnny and West Oakland Houserockers bassist Robert Johnson had found a better-paying gig. When the engagement fell apart, they headed to Denver. "Bob Johnson's uncle lived there, and he told us he'd make Pullman porters out of us," Johnny explains. "I came within one day of becoming a Pullman porter. I probably would have loused up my whole musical future."

Johnny was instead recruited by Denver bandleader George Morrison, a vocalist and violinist whose specialty was singing and playing Al Jolson's "Sonny Boy" in a bellhop uniform. After a year with Morrison, the drummer joined trumpeter Lloyd Hunter's Omaha-based orchestra, with which he remained for a year and a half. "There was no Uncle Tomming in that band," he boasts.

The Morrison and Hunter bands entertained mostly white audiences. "We had to play 'Moonlight Serenade,' 'String of Pearls,' and all that stuff that we didn't care for," Johnny remembers, "but occasionally we'd go to a bigger city and play for a black dance and we were really ready because we had the Basie and Duke arrangements, along with the Tommy Dorsey and Glen Miller things. Then we were able to go out and play 'Moten Swing' and 'Swinging the Blues' and have fun." The Hunter band included alto saxophonist Preston Love, with whom Johnny formed a lifelong friendship.

At the recommendation of Nat "King" Cole and Jimmy Witherspoon, Johnny moved to Los Angeles in 1943 to join saxophonist Harlan Leonard's Kansas City Rockets at the Club Alabam. A legendary Midwestern outfit that was initially formed from remnants of Bennie Moten's orchestra (Count Basie took the rest) and had briefly included Charlie Parker in its ranks, the Rockets had relocated to southern California during World War II. "That was a fine band," Johnny says, "and we were playing for black audiences exclusively, so every night was wonderful." Johnny supplied Hunter's big band with four-to-the-bar swing beats in the manner of his idol, Jo Jones, the great Basie drummer.

The Morrison, Hunter, and Leonard aggregations were known as "territory" bands, because, unlike "name" bands, they did not tour beyond given geographical regions. But, Johnny explains, "a territory band could become a name band overnight. The minute you got a hit record, you had a national reputation. How well you did from that point depended on how deeply you moved the crowds you played for. Some bands would get a hit and never he heard from again, and others would get a hit, maybe no more than one, and be remembered forever."

After leaving the Rockets, Johnny began making a name for himself around Los Angeles recording studios as a sideman, playing drums on sessions by saxophonists Illinois Jacquet and Lester Young and on "Drifting Blues," a seminal West Coast blues hit by guitarist Johnny Moore's Three Blazers featuring singer-pianist Charles Brown. Johnny also worked briefly with the bands of vocalist Bardu Ali (formerly with Chick Webb), tenor saxophonist Jack McVea, and trumpeter Jake Porter and even substituted for an ailing Jo Jones with the Basie orchestra at the Plantation Club.

In late 1945, at the instigation of Club Alabam owner Curtis Mosby, Johnny organized his own big band and borrowed some charts from Basie until he could get original material written. "We didn't stay a territory band long," he states. Johnny quickly landed a contract with Excelsior Records, one of many independently owned labels that emerged toward the end of World War II to fill the void left when the three dominant companies—Columbia, Decca, and RCA Victor—cut back on making "race" records due to the shortage of shellac (import from India of this material, which gives records their hard surface, was disrupted by the war). Excelsior, which already included the King Cole Trio on its roster, was

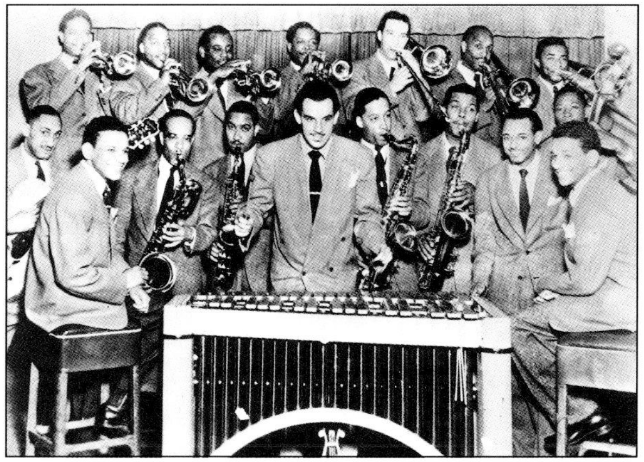

Club Alabam, 1946

owned by Otis Rene, an African-American songwriter who earlier had penned the standards "When the Swallows Come Back to Capistrano" and "When It's Sleepy Time Down South" with his brother Leon. The brothers were now in competition, with Leon running his own label, Exclusive Records, but they shared a pressing plant. "The trick in those days," Johnny explains, "was not in getting a record recorded or even getting it promoted, but in getting it pressed, because of the shellac shortage."

Having prepared one number too few for its first recording session, the Johnny Otis orchestra cut "Harlem Nocturne," a stock arrangement of an Earle Hagen composition that previously had been recorded by two white bands, Ray Noble's and Randy Brooks's. While retaining the Ellingtonesque voicings of the chart—the song originally had been titled "Duke's Mixture"—Johnny altered the phrasing, making it "blacker," and with his own tom-toms and Curtis Counce's bass, gave it a more pronounced lope.

Although predominantly African-American, the Otis band included a few nonblack players, among them Rene Block, a saxophonist of Mexican and Argentine ancestry whose creamy, Johnny Hodges–inspired alto led "Harlem Nocturne." At the time, it was not against the law in Los Angeles—as it was in the South—for musicians of different races to perform together on stage, yet Johnny recalls a 1946 visit by an FBI agent to the Club Alabam: "He came to me and asked, 'Do you have a mixed band?' I got smart and said, 'Yeah, I've got men and women.' He was confronting me as if it were a crime. I don't know how he wound up on Central Avenue asking me that question. To his eyes, he thought that Rene Block looked like a white boy on the bandstand. I think Allen Eager [a white bebop tenor saxophonist] was in the band then, too."

Johnny's rendition of "Harlem Nocturne" became a hit throughout the country, outselling the earlier Noble and Brooks versions, and established his band as a national attraction. "Harlem Nocturne" took the orchestra to Harlem itself, where Johnny made the first of what would be many appearances at the Apollo Theater. He and his fifteen musicians (which included, at various times, trumpeters Teddy Buckner, Art Farmer, and Dootsie Williams; trombonists Henry Coker and George Washington; saxophonists Rene Block, Allen Eager, Preston Love, Paul Quinichette, Lem Tally, and James Von Streeter; pianists Bill Doggett and Gene Gilbeaux; bassists Curtis Counce and Junior Raglin; and vocalist Ernestine Anderson) stayed on the road for much of the next year and a half, appearing at other major black theaters, as well as some white ones, often on shows with such stars as the Ink Spots, Louis Jordan and His Tympany Five, and the King Cole Trio.

The orchestra lasted until 1947, when the economy forced Johnny, along with countless other bandleaders, to pare down. And when he did, his new group had a different sound, one that was instrumental in giving birth to a new style that would soon be dubbed "rhythm and blues," later "rock 'n' roll."

"My case is kinda typical, along with Joe Liggins, Roy Milton, Sonny Thompson—I'm trying to think of some of the people who went through the same experience—T-Bone Walker, and a few others," he explains. "We all had big-band experience, and we all longed for that big-band sound, but the day came and the money wasn't there. People's tastes changed; the war was over and the economy took a big tumble. We were faced with having to survive in music, so I did what a lot of us did: Instead of seven or eight brass, I cut it down to two brass, and instead of five reeds, I cut it down to two reeds. So right there, I chopped off a whole lotta salaries, and I made quite a change in the drums, piano, and guitar. In the big band I used a rhythm guitar. In the little band I used a twangy, T-Bone Walker–type guitar player—a bluesman, Pete Lewis. On the piano I made sure I got somebody who could play boogie-woogies and blues—Lady Dee Williams. And the average jazz drummer was a little busy and quite reluctant to play what I wanted him to play, so I got a man who was not so sophisticated, with not so much technique, but he didn't mind doing this. [Johnny pounds out a hard backbeat on his coffee table.] He was a strong guy and he could do it all night—Kansas City Bell.

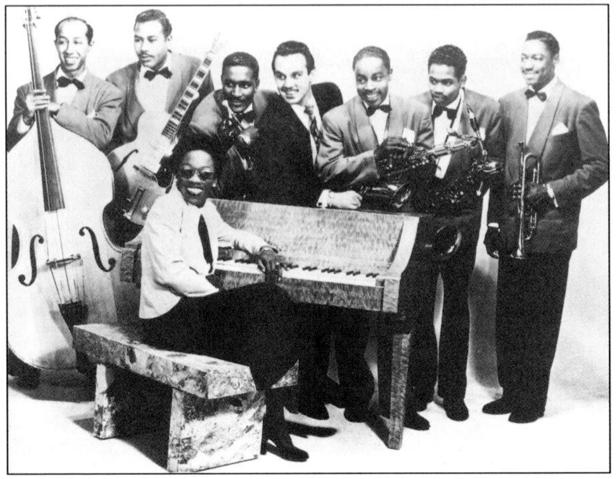

Johnny Otis Band (Lady Dee Williams on piano), 1950

"I had noticed in the years previous with my big band that while the people loved jazz—after all, it was their music, black music—they really came to life when we played 'After Hours' or boogie woogies and jumps. That's what really moved them, so when I started recording with the smaller band, I moved in that direction and so did the other guys. It was a commercial move. Some of my friends in jazz thought I had sold out, but I was proud of that. I loved what we were doing. I never felt ashamed of it. To begin with, I wasn't Max Roach or Jo Jones. Suddenly, I realized that my time with Count Otis Matthews' Houserockers was gonna come in real handy because I hearkened back to that day and included those elements in our music. We began a synthesis by bringing together swing big-band flavors, country blues, a touch of gospel, and even a little bebop from time to time. That's how rhythm and blues was born."

Headquarters for this melding of musical styles was the Barrelhouse Club, opened in Watts in 1948 by Otis in partnership with Barbu Ali and his wife, Tila Ali, and King Cole Trio bassist Johnny Miller. It was there that Johnny honed the skills of the Robins and Little Esther, vocalists who would propel his name to the top of the rhythm-and-blues charts in 1950.

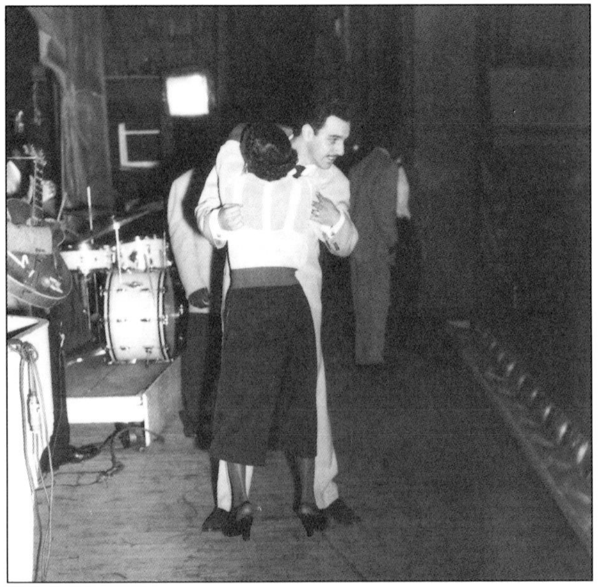

Johnny Otis with Lady Dee Williams, 1950

Besides running the Barrelhouse, he operated a chicken farm in Watts—the Progressive Poultry Company—with bassist Mario Delagarde. "People could come and pick out the chicken they wanted, which appealed to Southern people a lot," Johnny explains. One day, while promoting the Barrelhouse on radio station KFVD, he and disc jockey Hunter Hancock (who emceed the club's Thursday night talent shows) got to talking about the chicken farm over the air.

"When I got home," Johnny remembers, "people were lined up for two blocks. I sold everything that afternoon. The next day, Lady Dee, myself, Mario, Little Esther, and a couple of other people piled into three big cars and three big trailers I rented and went up into the foothills where there were chicken ranches, about fifty miles away from L.A. I bought all their seconds, which are chickens that either are not big enough or a wing is just not right. From then on, I was really in business with the chicken ranch."

One day, while building coops for his birds, Johnny suffered an accident that ended his career as a serious drummer. He cut the index and middle fingers of his right hand down to the bones, severing tendons. He recalls that the doctor, "instead of putting them back in an extended position, put them in a flexed position, which was a real quick way to get rid of me." This left him unable to properly grip the right stick. "You have to have delicate control to really play the drums," he explains. "I was trying to play jazz drums, swing drums. I could never play that way again, but I could bang that rock 'n' roll pretty good." Vibes then became his main instrument, and in the mid-'50s, when illness forced Lady Dee Williams's departure from the band, he taught himself to play piano. "I knew the keyboard because of the vibes, so I started fooling around and I never left the piano." he says. "I tried to learn little boogies and things so I could function."

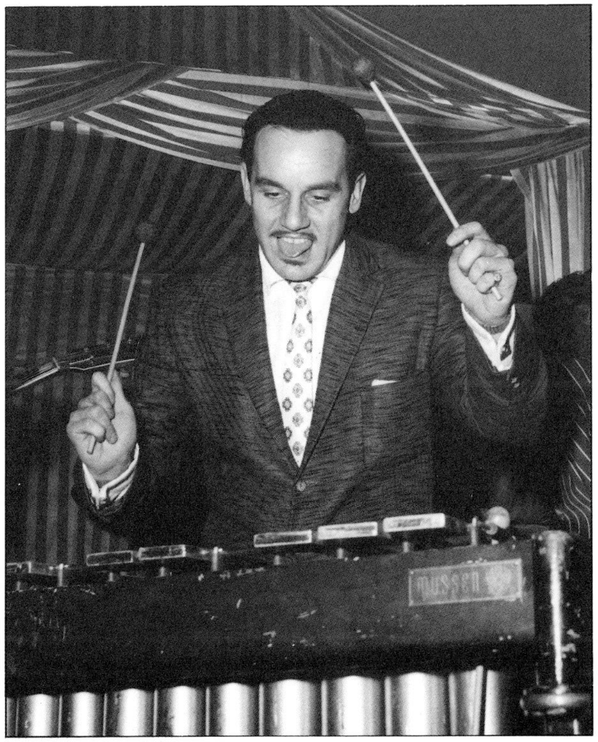
Johnny Otis, c. 1956

Johnny also quit the poultry business, in 1950, when his composition "Double Crossing Blues" took him and his band back out on the road for a run of black theaters, dance halls, and tobacco barns across the United States that lasted three years. Johnny's second release under a new contract with the New Jersey-based Savoy label, that had been secured through Los Angeles A&R man Ralph Bass, featured vocals by two of his regular Barrelhouse Club attractions: Little Esther and the Robins.

Little Esther (born Esther Mae Jones and known as Esther Phillips later in her career) was all of thirteen when Johnny first heard her singing at an amateur contest at the Largo Theater in Los Angeles. Although short, she was quite bosomy for her age, and her scratchy, melisma-dripping alto voice was also mature, a cross between those of Little Miss Cornshucks and Esther's main idol, Dinah Washington. Impressed by the young singer's Largo Theater rendition with saxophonist Big Jay McNeely's band of the Washington hit "Baby, Get Lost," Johnny invited Esther to the Barrelhouse amateur show and soon produced her first two singles, "I Gotta Guy" and "Mean Ole Gal," for the Modern label. Neither were hits.

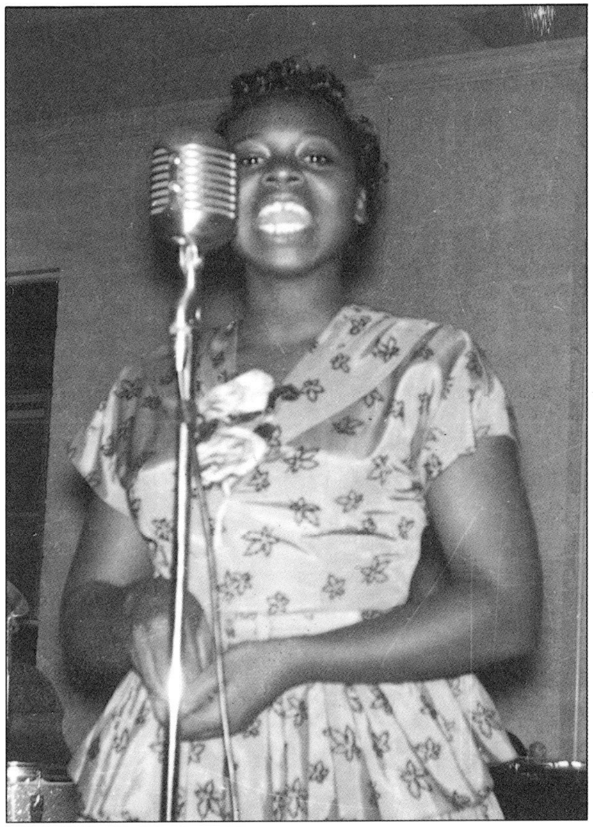
Little Esther, 1950

The Robins evolved from the A Sharp Trio, which was formed in 1947 and comprised Ty Terrell and brothers Billy and Roy Richards. The trio became the Bluebirds after joining the Barrelhouse crew and, at Johnny's suggestion, adding bass singer Bobby Nunn. Rechristened the Robins, the quartet joined Little Esther on "Double Crossing Blues," with Nunn sharing the lead in deep, resonant tones similar to those of Jimmy Ricks, the famous basso of the Ravens.

Johnny based the song's lyrics, in part, on a vaudeville routine by comedians Apus and Estrelita, about whom he told writer Norbert Hess:

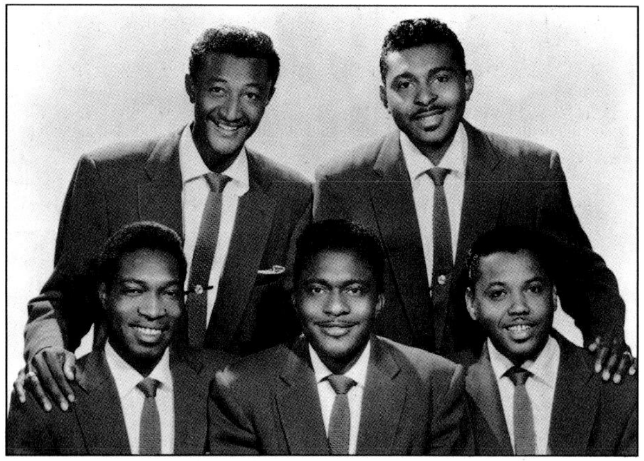

The Robins, c. 1952

She was very attractive and he was a very homely dude. In the middle of this act she'd say to him, "You should be out in the forest fightin' a grizzly bear," and he would say, "How come you ain't out there?" She'd say, "'Cause I'm a lady," and he would say, "Hell, they got lady bears out there, too." The audience would crack up.

The song, with its comic punch line, shot to No. 1 on *Billboard* magazine's Best Selling Retail Rhythm & Blues Records list in early 1950 and remained in that position for nine weeks. It was the first of ten Top 10 R&B hits for Johnny that year. Others included "Cry Baby," "Cupid's Boogie," "Deceivin' Blues," "Wedding Boogie," "Faraway Blues," and "Rockin' Blues," most featuring Little Esther, often in duet with fellow band vocalist Mel Walker.

The success of "Double Crossing Blues" and its follow-ups made Johnny the hottest musical attraction in black America. Fronting the band on vibes, he hit the road with his California Rhythm and Blues Caravan, featuring Little Esther and Mel Walker. The Robins had chosen to remain in Los Angeles and struggled on for several years before evolving into the hugely successful Coasters.

Racism again raised its ugly head while the band was on tour. Johnny recalls a 1950 incident in the deep South: "We pulled up to a large, wooden, raggedy lodge hall in Biloxi. Our bus was painted like a minstrel show—a lot of colors and 'Little Esther and Johnny Otis.' It was in the black community, but there was this old white policeman sitting on the porch. He was the officer for the dance that night. He ran up to me and shook my hand and said, 'Your name?' I said, 'Johnny Otis.' Then he kept calling me 'Mr. Otis' and 'sir.' I kept trying to show him the bus and my name, because I knew the moment of truth was gonna arrive sooner of later. My road manager, [former Basie saxophonist] Earle Warren, who was black and looked white, pulled me aside and said, 'Do you know what's going on?'

"That night, when we came to work, the place was packed. Little Esther was the star of the show. As I came in, the policeman said, 'I'm gonna take care of things for you tonight, Mr. Otis.' Then I went up and started playing. I saw him get up on a chair, and he looked up at the stage. There were laws then against whites and blacks playing together. Earle told me later that he said, 'What's that white boy doin' playin' with them niggers up there?' Earle said, 'Oh, no, sir, he's colored.' He thought that over, and as soon as I came off the bandstand at intermission, he got even with me immediately. He said, 'Listen, boy, you cut that goddamn music off at one o'clock, you hear me?' He waited to hear me say, 'Yes, sir,' and I did, too, 'cause I was in Mississippi."

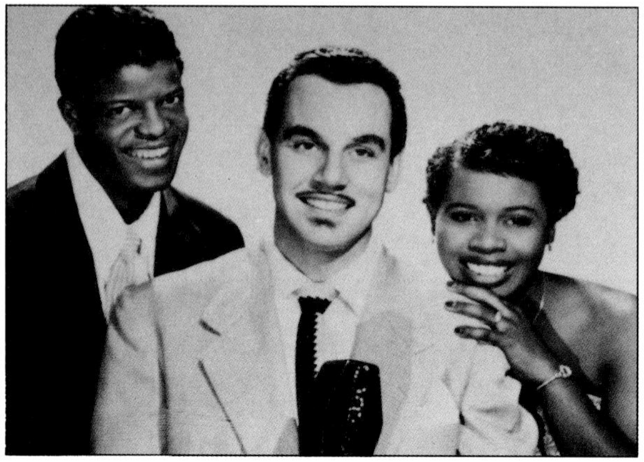

Johnny Otis with Little Esther and Mel Walker, 1950

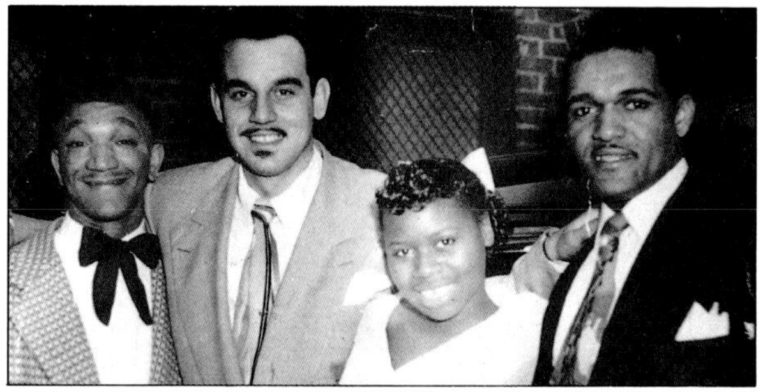

Redd Foxx, Johnny Otis, Little Esther, Slappy White, 1950

Johnny's hit streak ended in 1952—he wouldn't have another of his own in the U.S. until 1958's "Willie and the Hand Jive"—and he discontinued regular touring the following year, but he continued to perform around southern California, write songs, produce records, and discover new talent throughout the '50s. Besides Little Esther and the Robins, his discoveries included Linda Hopkins, Willie Mae "Big Mama" Thornton (Johnny produced her original 1953 hit recording of "Hound Dog" and supplied its decidedly down-home drum beats), Jackie Wilson, Little Willie John, the Royals (later to become Hank Ballard and the Midnighters), Etta

James, and Sugar Pie DeSanto. His band also played on record dates by Johnny Ace (including the 1955 smash "Pleading My Love") and Little Richard. Among the most famous Otis compositions are "Every Beat of My Heart" (first recorded in 1952 by the Royals and successfully revived nine years later by Gladys Knight and the Pips), "The Wallflower" (a No. 1 R&B hit by cowriter Etta James in 1955 and a No. 1 pop charter, also that year, for Georgia Gibbs under the title "Dance with Me Henry"), "So Fine" (originally recorded by the Sheiks in 1955 and turned into a 1959 hit by the Fiestas), and "Willie and the Hand Jive" (the only record by Johnny himself to crack the pop Top 10).

In 1953, after his final national tour, Johnny decided to take up Apollo Theater owner Frank Schiffman's suggestion that he try his hand at radio. Opening the Los Angeles phone book, Johnny randomly selected KFOX in Long Beach. Luckily when he phoned, program director Hal Scheidler answered.

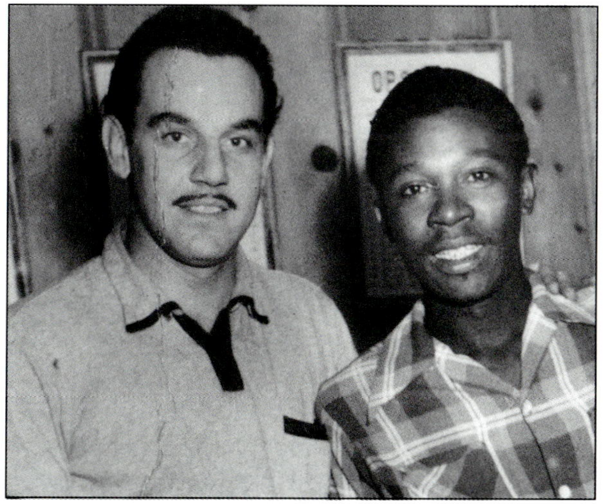

Johnny Otis with B. B. King, 1950

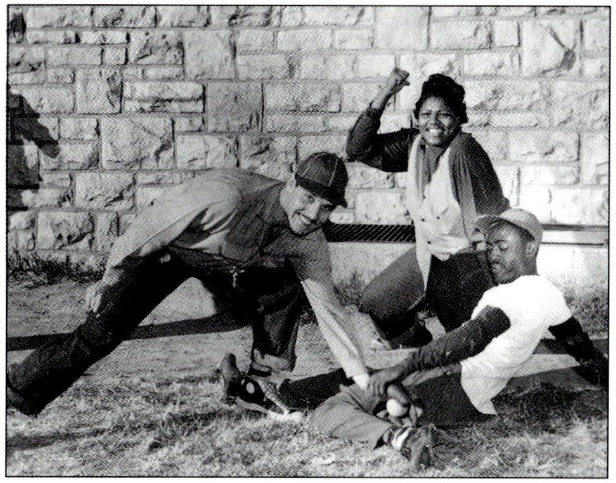

Johnny Otis with Big Mama Thornton and Little Arthur Matthews, 1953

"My name is Johnny Otis," the bandleader said. "I'd like to become a disc jockey."

"Johnny Otis, the Duke Ellington of Watts?" Scheidler responded. "Are you serious?"

Despite the station owner's initial remarks to Johnny—"I don't wanna hear none of that goddamn nigger music"—Scheidler managed to get Johnny a one-hour evening slot on KFOX. When the station was sold six months later, there were no more racist complaints. The program, which was first done remote from a black drive-in restaurant and later from a record shop Johnny owned (and sometimes even from his home), was expanded to three hours and lasted seven years. Along with Hunter Hancock, Huggie Boy, and Lonnie Johnson (a nephew of the great blues and jazz guitarist of the same name), Johnny became one of the leading southern California rhythm-and-blues deejays of the '50s. Comedian Redd Foxx, a frequent attraction on Johnny's live musical revues since the late '40s, served as his assistant on the KFOX broadcasts.

At KFOX, Johnny played the hits of the day—but only those he liked. He admits, however, that he accepted payola from time to time. "I did not understand then that the airwaves belong to the people and are a trust and that you should not prostitute it that way," he explains. "The total amount of money that I took during those years was seven hundred and some dollars, and that's not much. I remember that when they'd come and the record wasn't any good, you'd ruin your programming if you played that. I wasn't hungry, so I wouldn't take it. I thought it was a perfectly legitimate thing, though, until the payola probes came."

The radio program's success led to a weekly variety show on Los Angeles television. The Johnny Otis

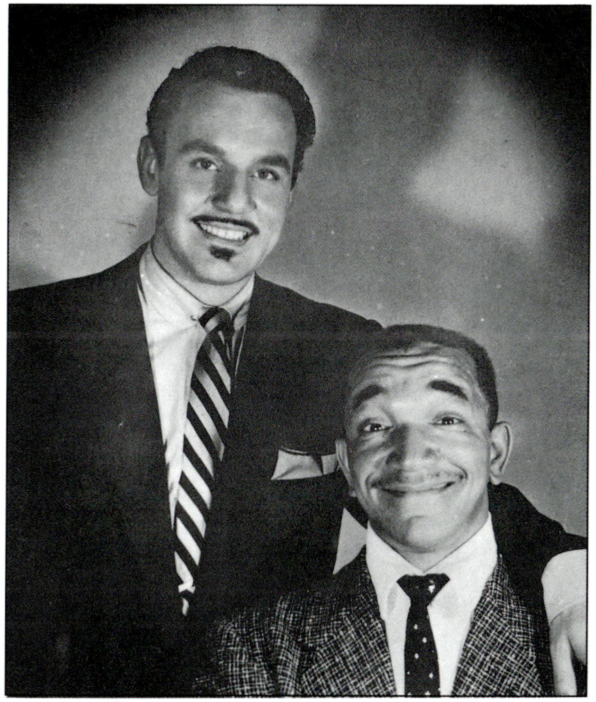

Johnny Otis and Redd Foxx, 1956

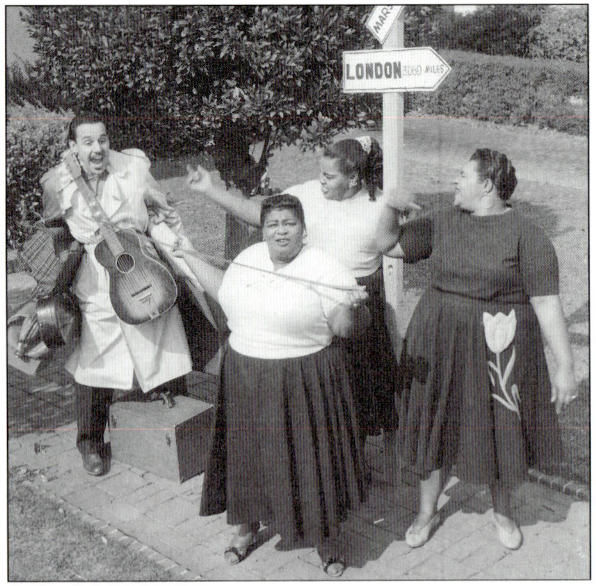

Johnny Otis with Three Tons of Joy, 1957

Show, as it was known, featured members of his own large revue, in addition to such guest artists as Ray Charles, James Brown, Sam Cooke, Little Richard, Fats Domino, the Moonglows, the Drifters, and the Everly Brothers. It stayed on the air seven years, first on KTTV (Channel 11), then moved to KTLA (Channel 5), and finally to KCOP (Channel 13).

After Savoy, Johnny recorded for Mercury (which included sessions featuring the great former Duke Ellington tenor saxophonist Ben Webster), Peacock, and his own Dig label before signing with Capitol in 1957. His revue at the time featured a trio of rotund female singers known as the Three Tons of Joy. "Ma, He's Making Eyes at Me," Johnny's first release for the Hollywood-based major label, spotlighted the robust vocals of Marie Adams and her full-figured cohorts. It became a No. 2 pop hit in England, but failed to make much of an impression at home. The situation reversed the next year when "Willie and the Hand Jive," with vocals by Johnny himself, rose to No. 3 R&B and to No. 9 pop in the U.S., but didn't click in the U.K., although it subsequently became a favorite of numerous British rock artists. Supplying the distinctively percussive rhythm-guitar parts to "Willie and the Hand Jive" was band member Jimmy Nolen, who went on to play a key role in the development of James Brown's funk style and to influence countless guitarists around the world.

Scoring no more substantial hits after "Willie and the Hand Jive," Johnny increasingly turned his attention to politics. With Mervin Dymally (whom he had first met at the Apollo Theater in 1946, shortly after Dymally had arrived in the U.S. from Trinidad) and other African-American Democrats, Johnny organized a black political awareness group in his living room. It was called ATTACK. The group at first organized picket lines around businesses in the black

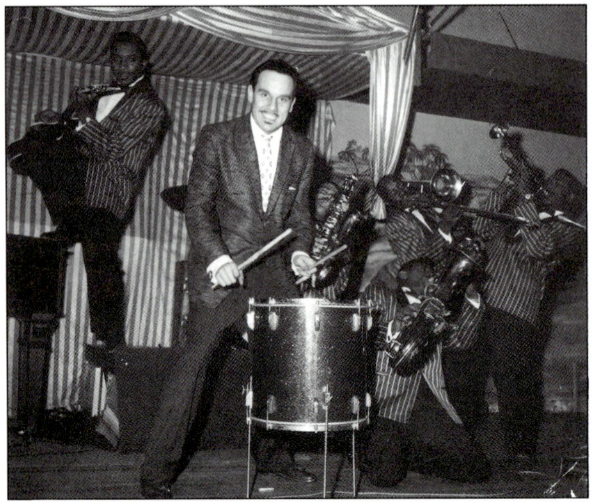

Johnny Otis and band, 1956

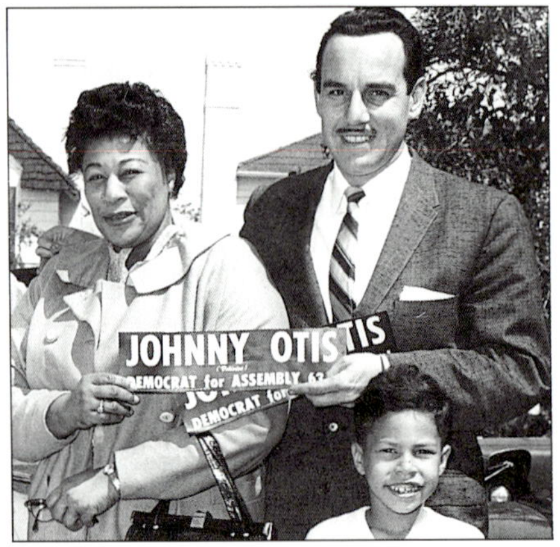

Johnny Otis with Ella Fitzgerald and Shuggie Otis, 1961

community that would not hire black workers, then focused on getting blacks elected to public office. Johnny credits ATTACK with having helped to elect Dymally to the California Assembly and Tom Bradley—who was not a member of the group but attended meetings—to the Los Angeles City Council. Johnny served as Dymally's deputy chief of staff for over a decade, following him from the state assembly through the state senate and the California lieutenant governorship to the U.S. Congress. Johnny even ran for state assembly seats twice himself; he says he came close to winning the first time, but fell short because his legal name—John Veliotes—was on the ballot rather than the one by which most people knew him.

Between 1962 and '68, Johnny made only a few recordings (mainly on his own Eldo label, for which he had produced "Image of a Girl" by the Safaris, a Top 10 pop hit in 1960) and performed infrequently. "The black audience was no longer interested in us, and the white audience had moved on to the Beatles and things," he explains. He became especially disturbed by the way audiences embraced the music of the Beatles, the Rolling Stones, and other British rock groups that had borrowed heavily from African-American sources. "It was a little dismaying to see acts come along and recycle our music and make tons of money with it, and we couldn't even get a job," he states. To occupy his time when he wasn't holding political meetings, working on Dymally's campaigns, writing a weekly sociopolitical column for the *Los Angeles Sentinel,* and walking picket lines, Johnny took up painting. His interest in performing finally returned, however, sparked by his eldest son, John Otis, Jr., better known as Shuggie.

When Shuggie was twelve, his dad overheard him playing along to a Motown song on a guitar so beat-up it had only two strings. Trading in some of his drum equipment, Johnny bought Shuggie a cheap Japanese electric guitar and an amplifier. "He disappeared into his room and, in six days, it sounded like B. B. King," Johnny recalls. He then took his son to a teacher in Hollywood. "Mr. Otis," Johnny remembers the instructor saying, "I can't teach him anything. I teach beginners and he's way advanced." At the suggestion of legendary saxophonist-composer-arranger Benny Carter, however, Shuggie did study composition and arranging, lessons that paid off handsomely, especially when the Brothers Johnson took Shuggie's song "Strawberry Letter 23" to the top of *Billboard*'s soul chart (and to No. 5 on the pop list) in 1977.

"When I found out this little kid of mine could play guitar, I put a band together," Johnny says. The new group consisted of little more than Johnny, Shuggie, and vocalist Delmar "Mighty Mouth" Evans. In 1968, through iconoclastic rock star Frank Zappa, Johnny learned that the Bihari brothers (for whom he'd recorded on the Modern label in the late '40s) were interested in recording him for their Kent label. The resulting album, titled *Cold Shot,* was a low-budget affair on which father and son played most of the instruments through overdubbing (Johnny on vibes, piano, and drums, Shuggie on guitar and electric bass), but drew raves from *Rolling Stone* and other periodicals of the emerging youth counterculture. Johnny was suddenly hip again, and his son was hailed as the hottest thing since B. B. King.

Writing about *Cold Shot* twenty-six years later, in his notes to an Epic/Legacy compact disc reissue compilation titled *Shuggie's Boogie: Shuggie Otis Plays the Blues,* critic Pete Welding observed:

> Something of a left-field sensation, the album was one of the most widely praised of the year, virtually every reviewer commenting on the singular freshness, audacity, and confident assurance of Shuggie's playing, both on bass and guitar, but especially on the latter. Many . . . proclaimed that a major new blues guitar talent had arrived. And the fact that Shuggie was fourteen at the time he made the recordings didn't hurt either. Certainly it made for colorful copy. But given the power and maturity of his playing, it was beside the point. Even if he had been twice his age, it would have been considered an impressive debut—his playing was that fluent and inventive.

The following year, Columbia Records executive John Hammond, the man responsible for signing such artists as Count Basie, Billie Holiday, Charlie Christian, Aretha Franklin, Bob Dylan, George Benson, and Bruce Springsteen over the years, suggested to Larry Cohn, then head of A&R for the company's Epic subsidiary, that he sign the teen guitar sensation, only to learn that Cohn not only had already signed Shuggie, but also Johnny and Don "Sugarcane" Harris, the brilliant singer-violinist who had appeared on several tracks of *Cold Shot.*

The Epic deal led to two albums for Shuggie, two for Johnny, and one for Sugarcane. Johnny's crowning achievement of this period was his 1970 appearance at the Monterey Jazz Festival, where he and his band were joined by such other rhythm-and-blues pioneers as Ivory Joe Hunter, Roy Milton, Esther Phillips, Joe Turner, and Eddie "Cleanhead" Vinson. Highlights of the three-hour Saturday afternoon performance were captured on a two-disc Epic album (now available on CD) and used in a scene of the Clint Eastwood motion picture *Play Misty for Me.*

The Johnny Otis revival was shortlived, however. He kept the band (with Shuggie on guitar) together during the '70s but was again recording for small labels and performing sporadically. He continued working for Mervin Dymally—and became a minister.

In 1978, after being ordained three years earlier by blues singer-turned-preacher Gatemouth Moore, Johnny opened his his own nondenominational Landmark Community Church. Its members included Esther Phillps, Etta James, jazz organist Jimmy Smith, and actor-comedian LaWanda Page (whose risqué comedy albums Johnny had produced prior to her rise to greater stardom as Aunt Esther on "Sanford and Son"). The congregation was predominantly African-American, but also included some whites, Latinos, Asians, and even a few Jews and Buddhists. He closed the church in 1985, due to increased crime—car break-ins, purse snatchings, rapes—in the westside Los Angeles neighborhood where it was located.

Even without a building, the congregation remained active for a few more years, distributing free food—sandwiches, fruit, cookies, orange juice—to about a thousand people every Saturday morning in downtown L.A. Donations were solicited over listener-supported radio station KPFK, where Johnny continued his disc jockey career after stints on KDAY, XERB (with a studio in Los Angeles and transmitter in Rosarito, Baja California), and KPPC.

"We began to reevaluate what the Landmark Community Church was really doing of any substance, and we felt we weren't doing much of real substance," he explains. "We were having a marvelous time on Sunday mornings praying, shouting and singing gospel music, going to other churches and fellowships and having big social affairs at the Hilton downtown and having fashion shows and the rest of the stuff that churches fall into, but we weren't doing much of anything that had to do with what Jesus asked us to do: to love one another." The distribution of food to the homeless, he says, "became more important to us than the church services themselves."

Johnny's break with established black religion had begun during the late '50s. "Sam Cooke and I were members of one of the largest Baptist churches in Los Angeles," he explains, "and we came in and sat together one Sunday. The minister spotted us. He didn't mean any harm, but it's typical of the fundamentalist mentality. He said, 'I see Johnny Otis and Sam Cooke. Brother Johnny and Brother Sam have been out on the road, but one of these days they're gonna leave the devil's music alone and come back home.' Sam said, 'Did he really say that?' I said, 'Yes.' He said, 'Well, I'm never coming back here again.' And I didn't either. I was really embarrassed and offended, and so was Sam.

"Then I found this little church deep on the east side where Dr. Bernice Smith was the pastor. Here was a woman pastor, which appealed to me because that indicated that there might have been a little freer feeling there." Dr. Smith suggested that Johnny become a minister himself, but he resisted the idea for years, fearing that people might laugh at him. He imagined himself being referred to as "Reverend Hand Jive," but she kept encouraging him. "She told me I was right about [being tired of] all that 'ain't nobody goin' to heaven but us' nonsense," he says. "She felt we should be dealing with things other than how to build a pedestal to stand taller than someone else, and maybe we should be reaching down to those folk who need some help."

On his radio programs, currently heard over KPFA in Berkeley and KPFK in Los Angeles, Johnny mixes idioms, playing blues, soul, jazz, gospel, and even an occasional Hank Williams country classic. He finds no problem in going from a gospel to a blues record. "The Swan Silvertones and Lightnin' Hopkins have a lot in common," he states. "All you have to do is change 'Jesus' to 'baby.' I did a song once called 'Rock Me Baby' that was based on 'Thank You Jesus.' I wasn't a minister then, but I'd do it today. What's wrong with that? Nothing.

"We've been told that it's the devil's music and all that. That's unfortunate 'cause I wonder how many Ray Charleses and Aretha Franklins and Otis Reddings and Dinah Washingtons and Lester Youngs we have been deprived of by the fundamentalist preachers who have intimidated the black community.

"Wynton Marsalis has a theory. He says the black church is a carbon copy of the white Southern fundamentalist church. I think he's right. He said that somewhere back in history, during slavery times, a white preacher must have gone to the black preacher and said, 'That stuff is the devil's music.'"

The music business picked up again for Johnny in the early '80s. *The New Johnny Otis Show,* a 1981 album for Alligator, the highly respected Chicago blues label, received a Grammy nomination—Johnny's first. By mid-decade, he and the band were touring regularly. They appeared at major clubs and jazz and blues festivals throughout the United States, including extended runs at the Fairmont Hotel chain's elegant showrooms in San Francisco, San Jose, Denver, Houston, and New Orleans, and traveled to Europe, Africa, and Japan. He also became more prolific as a visual artist during the '80s, and his paintings and sculptures were exhibited for the first time in art galleries.

If he's finally getting some long-overdue respect, Johnny feels that conditions for African Americans haven't changed substantially since he began performing over a half century ago. "In many ways, it's beginning to feel to me like the country's going back to the 1940s," he says. "How long has it been since we'd go down South and the signs were up? We couldn't use the bathrooms. We couldn't eat. We couldn't get a hotel room. I don't think the attitudes of everybody have changed. The laws probably allowed a lot of people who had a decent outlook to relax and just be decent, but the hard-core racists are still among us. In Dallas a few years ago, Bob Frazier, my trumpet player, and I would shoot pool after the last show at the Fairmont Hotel at a nice little bar downtown. I had an occasion to use the restroom, and restrooms usually have kinds of poems on the wall. Some of those poems really took me back to the '40s. They were so ugly and extremely racist. They were awful. I hadn't seen that stuff in a number of years, but it's still around. Of course, thirty years ago, Bob and I couldn't have gone in there and played pool.

"A lot of things have changed. When we go down South now, we stay in the finest hotels and eat anywhere we want to eat. In that sense, things are different. We don't feel that bitter iciness. And there's no doubt that we have built a black middle class; it's small and fragile, but it's there. We have black men and women in positions that we never had. We have black elected officials. All this has made a change. But in another way, things are even worse. First of all, the disparity gap between white and black incomes continues to widen. The infant mortality rate in Watts is four times what it is in the majority community. Unemployment is horrendous, especially among young black men. These are the statistics that tell the real story about what's going on in America."

Johnny is especially dismayed by the recent takeover of the U.S. Senate and House of Representatives by the Republican Party. "There are some Republicans who have decent social attitudes," he says. "They're fine. There's still a few of 'em around, but they can hardly function because the party is being held hostage by the right-wing fascists who have taken over. They will throw their weight around, and they will affect all the legislation to cut the ground from under poor people. In time, they will ruin the economy of this country. At that point, all of the rest of us will see what has happened to us, hopefully, and join forces and start really working toward realizing the American dream. But something worse could happen. Maybe these bastards will actually affect a form of American fascism and keep us all in chains forever and ever. But I don't think that could happen here because there are too many people who wouldn't stand for it.

"In the short run, I'm very pessimistic. But in the long run, I'm totally convinced that the average American is a good person. They're products of their environment, and you have this materialistic, money-grabbing philosophy that infects our people and makes them perform less than decently, but they are at heart good people. Their racist tendencies are fed by this society; still, I don't think Americans are going to stand still for their fellow citizens, even if they don't care too much about 'em, being ground into dust. Maybe I'm being unduly optimistic, but I think that at a certain point, they're gonna say, 'Hold on, now! Wait a minute! We're not that mean-spirited. We can't do that to people, no matter what color they are.' By then, many of them will have dropped from the middle class into the underclass, and they'll realize it's our collective battle. It might take the average American getting his ass kicked real good. I'm not saying it's gonna take a big, bloody revolution. I don't think it's gonna take that. But at a certain point they'll say, 'Hey, wait! Two percent of our people control all the wealth. We don't have a Congress. We don't have a representative Senate. We have people who are bought and sold. Might as well privatize the goddamn Congress and let the big corporations buy the Congress outright!'"

In 1991, after forty-eight years in southern California, Johnny and Phyllis Otis moved to a rural section of Sebastopol. With five acres, Johnny has plenty of space to pursue his seemingly limitless activities. Behind the house—a center of near-constant activity by family, friends, musicians, dogs, and cats—are coops stocked with chickens, pigeons, and parrots, and three small barns. One serves as Johnny's art studio, another as the Johnny Otis Music School (where a dozen teachers, including son Nicky, grandson Lucky, and three other members of the band, give private lessons to a number of local students); the third houses a recently installed sixteen-track recording studio.

Most of the property is given over to the growing of fruits, nuts, and vegetables. Besides pears, plums, cherries, walnuts, and grapes, there are fifty varieties of apples on two hundred trees. "It's just fun to see them grow and to taste the different flavors and textures," Johnny says.

Everything is grown organically. Inspired by Nicky, a vegetarian, Johnny began experimenting with organic farming while living in southern California, but found the soil on his property there to be too hard. "Here," he says, "I have sandy soil. It's so nice, but it's lacking in nutriments. That's why we have to compost, compost, compost. Nicky began

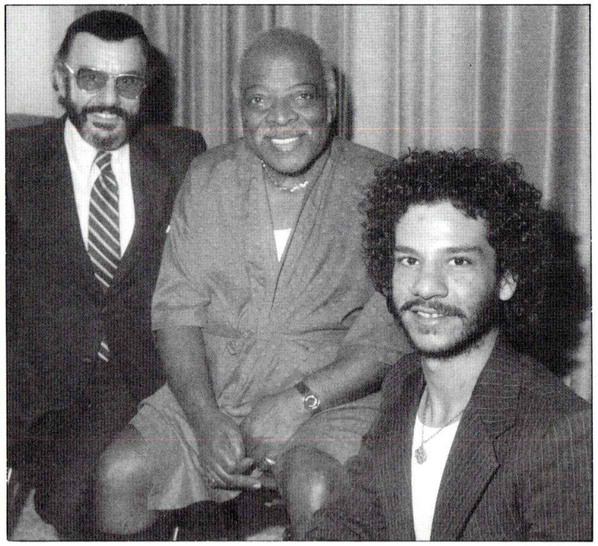

Johnny Otis with Count Basie and Nicky Otis, c. 1975

building giant compost piles. Now, after four years, we've got tons of rich compost, and we've built up the texture of the soil by constantly putting organic material in.

"Composting is a must. If you're going to attempt to do organic farming, you have a difficult job ahead of you because the insects are so difficult to control. You're not going to eradicate them; you hope just to control 'em. If you don't use insecticides, they'll eat you up. Nicky and I found out that if you use compost—rich soil that has within it all the components—then all the little critters that thrive in the soil will come—little grubs, earthworms, and certain beneficial bacteria. When you use rich compost and irrigate, the plant gets so healthy. It creates its own insecticide and it builds up resistance to other kinds of problems, various diseases also. You keep it under control that way. They're probably still gonna take some of your harvest, but we're willing to give that up to have a good, clean food."

At the end of the summer of 1995, following a European tour, Johnny plans to close his cabaret/deli and move into a larger venue, Rhythm & Brews, a three hundred–seat showroom, restaurant, and microbrewery being opened by the Sebastopol Brewing Company. He and the band will be appearing there on Fridays and Saturdays; when they're on tour, he hopes to book such classic rhythm-and-blues acts as the Penguins, Hank Ballard and the Midnighters, and Richard Berry. Johnny plans to use a building behind the property to house the newly established Johnny Otis Children's Center for the Arts, a nonprofit, tax-exempt coropration that will offer free classes in painting, sculpture, dance, drama, and poetry, as well as health education and medical care provided by local doctors, nurses, and pharmacists.

When it comes to music, however, Johnny feels that too much formal training often can be a detriment. "My experience in music tells me that there are two dangers: If you're completely unschooled, you're

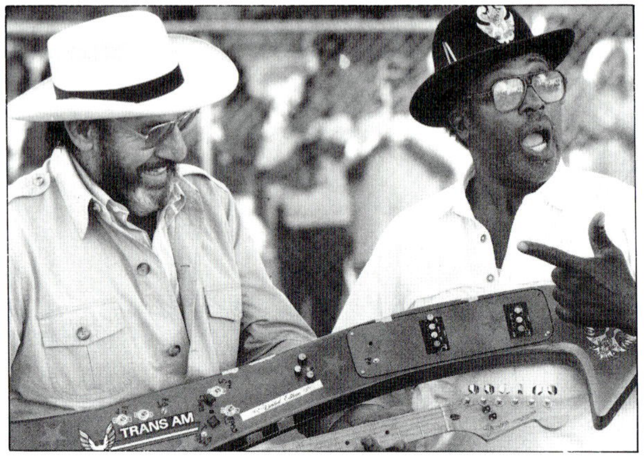

Johnny Otis and Bo Diddley, 1989

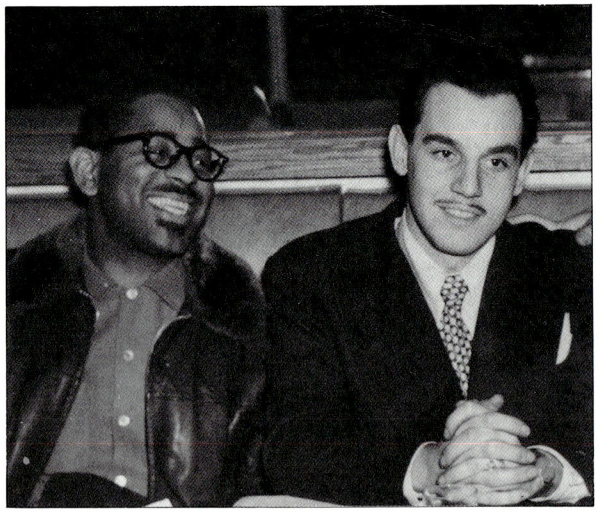

Dizzy Gillespie and Johnny Otis, 1947

at a disadvantage, but sometimes if you're overschooled, you're at a disadvantage," he says. "The people who I think are great in the music that I've been privileged to be a part of are people like Duke Ellington, Count Basie, Lester Young, Dizzy Gillespie, Charlie Parker, Max Roach, and Jo Jones, and I don't think any of them were conservatory trained. Yes, they had training, but they trained themselves.

"I've learned that the brothers and sisters who have come through my band from conservatories were the least effective people in my band. Some of them, in addition to the academic background, had perfect pitch—and that made it even worse. Every two minutes, they wanna tune up. They're distressed. They want it to be perfectly on pitch. I can't understand it because I don't have perfect pitch. I'd rather have somebody with relative pitch, with a lot of feeling."

Johnny admits that the rhythm and blues, jazz, blues, and soul that he and the band play "have a few little warts and blemishes, but that's okay. We like to leave it loose. I saw a Picasso exhibit once, and I saw this big painting and it had drips and splatters on it, not mistakes, but the paint had run and he just left it there. I thought, 'Hell, yeah!' The total impact is what's important, not the little piece of paint that dropped off."

A twelve-year-old African-American boy that Johnny once saw playing a battered horn on a New Orleans street left a strong impression. "He was a jaunty, cocky little dude," Johnny recalls. "He had no training, but he was playing that trumpet, baby, and he was playing it, at least for me, in a much more meaningful way than a man with super training and a beautiful instrument and no feeling.

"That was genius. When you put the two together—virtuosity and genius—you've got Dizzy Gillespie and Charlie Parker. But more important, as Nijinsky once said, 'Art is greater than technique,' and it is."

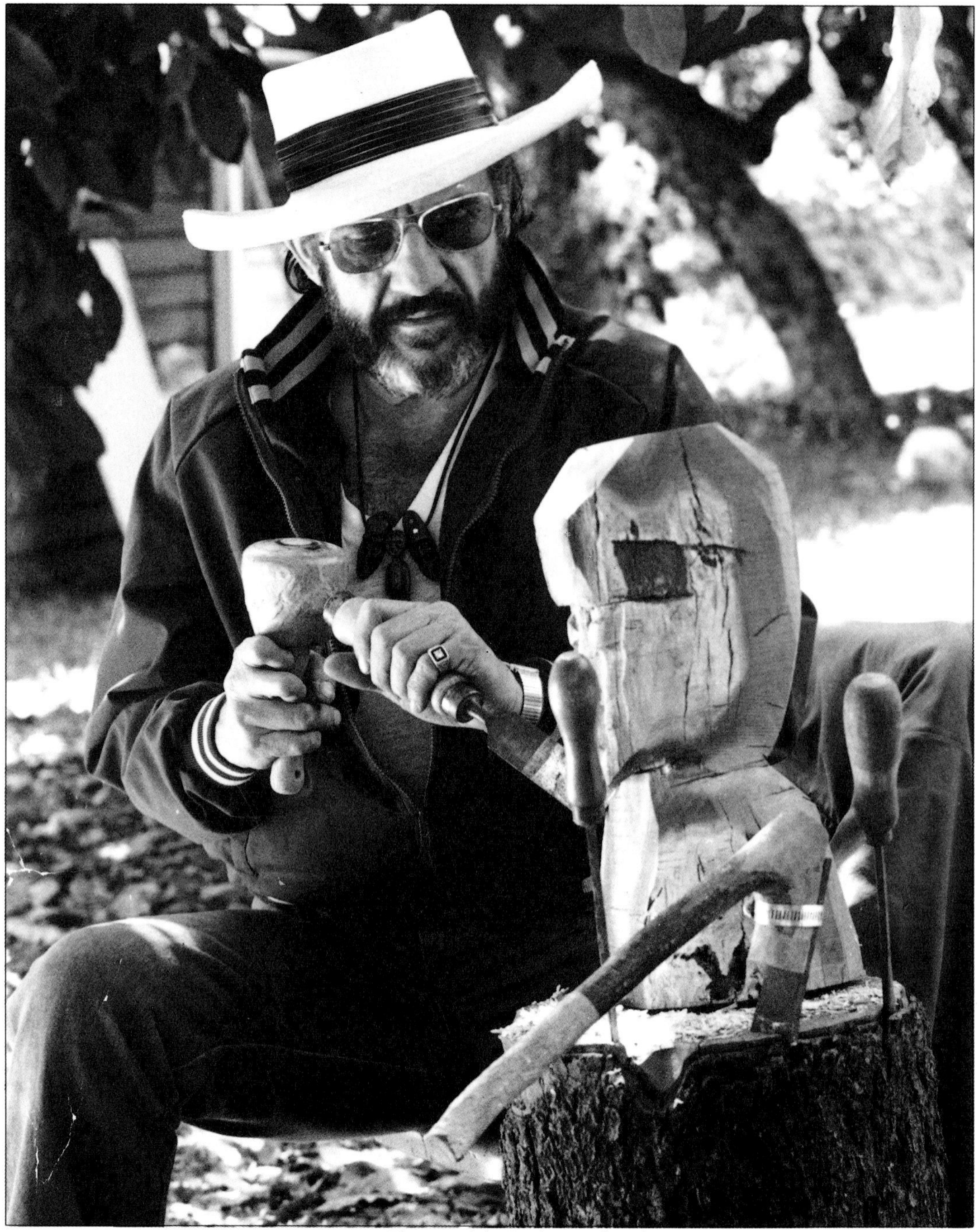

c. 1988. Photograph by Stephan Rockwerk.

Colors and Chords

By Mary Lovelace O'Neal

Looking at the work of Otis, one might assume he is either African American or an African in the diaspora, or consider him to be a follower of Picasso, Braque, and cubism. Any of these conclusions is reasonable upon viewing one piece after another of his paintings and sculptures that depict broad swatches of American life, African-American specifically.

But there are more influences on the work of Otis than meet the eye. Growing up in a Greek immigrant household, he found himself in a wonderful collision of cultures whose threads are located in the Mediterranean, Africa, and America. Pattern on pattern, symbol on symbol, he has reclaimed much of this cultural amalgamation and has constructed a world that is his own reality. The power of the people he is depicting—the presence of the subjects themselves, forced into our consciousness—is what gives the work its significance.

What pushes the untrained seventy-three-year-old artist to create paintings, sculptures, and cartoons is the same overwhelming inner need to "make" that drives his music. His visual art has an affinity with Outsider Art and the work of other unschooled artists that has increasingly drawn attention from the art establishment over the past ten years. "Let's make no mistake—I'm a musician who happens to throw some paint on a canvas, or draw a cartoon, or make something out of plaster," Otis says. "I'm not a visual artist, but I consider myself very lucky to have other ways to express and interpret what I see in the world. If I told you anything else, it would be a bunch of bullshit."

Otis's interest in painting and sculpture was ignited by one salient event in the early '60s. During a political meeting at a friend's house, Otis pulled a book about Picasso and another on classical African wood sculpture off the shelves and began perusing the pages. "It was like a bombshell exploded in me," Otis recalls. "I'd never seen Picasso's work, and I'd never really seen African sculpture page after page. I saw the connection between the two, and it was overwhelming. I had to beg the guy to let me borrow them." After this revelation, Otis was seldom without the precious books. He later found material on Henri Matisse and Marc Chagall. One can clearly see the influence of Matisse and Picasso—the beneficiaries of the African art that continued to pour into Europe at the turn of the century—in Otis's later paintings. Sometime afterward he discovered and fell in love with a trio of Mexican artists: Jose Orozco, Diego Rivera, and Alfaro Siqueiros.

Although Otis has skipped over Western art training, his rituals are the same. A teller of tales in his art, as in his music, he follows in the footsteps of other great storytellers and becomes a part of the legacy of social commentary. He moves close to Jacob Lawrence, Archibald Motley, Jr., Robert Colescott, Ben Shahn, Siqueiros, and Rivera—artists who paint their environments and the circumstances of the people they know. Sometimes the works are romanticized, sometimes they are inaccurate, and sometimes they are the absolute truth. In his case, Otis speaks of his own life and experience as a musician and a member of the African-American community.

Much of his painting and sculpture is deeply rooted in his world of music; it is one of his prime points of reference, constituting the vocabulary of images used in his work and moving him along in his exploration. When work is not mounted in a musical context, he sometimes uses titles or lyrics of songs to invoke musical content. For Otis, music and art are emotional tandems, and in some basic ways he interchanges the technical structure of music and painting in his process.

"On one level there is the harmonic structure of music," he explains. "For instance, a major chord is made up of the tonic [or key note], the third, and the fifth. This is the basic triad upon which all chords are based. In painting, one looks at the color wheel and sees the triad again. The three primary colors—red, blue, and yellow—are, in my mind at least, the equivalent of the musical triad. As we mix primary colors, we get secondary tints, and further mixing produces subtle and more involved colors. This reminds me of the minor, augmented, diminished, sevenths, ninths, etc. And the fact that both visual and audible sights and sounds are waves—that is, sound waves and light waves—makes the whole thing more and more exciting."

Toni Morrison suggests in *Jazz* (Penguin Books, 1993) that music is the cement of a community. That is, wherever African Americans went, they brought with them their music and creativity. They forged it into iron. They sewed it into petticoats and they embroidered it onto pillow slips and wedding dresses. They built it into mansions of wood and stone and they modeled baby cradles. The music evolved from slave chants that fused into the music of the great black migration from the South to the North in the '20s. It became gospel. It became blues. It became jazz. It became boogie-woogie. It became signifying and rap. It becomes the music that connects a community.

This fusion sparked the music of the 1940s and '50s. B. B. King and James Brown speak eloquently of this time. For those of us who came of age during the '60s, it became a part of the mythology. All of this is seam, an intricate part of the cloth called American culture—and it is seen throughout Otis's work. One can argue about the imagery—it's certainly necessary: He sometimes portrays barely digestible stereotypes. Yet the work has a truth about it—truth found in juke joints, in sassy, big-backed women in scarlet dresses with blond hair, and in places where the music threatens to tear down the house. And somewhere on the musical streets of Oakland and Berkeley during the '30s and '40s, Otis incorporated those sounds and sensibilities into his life, his music, and his art.

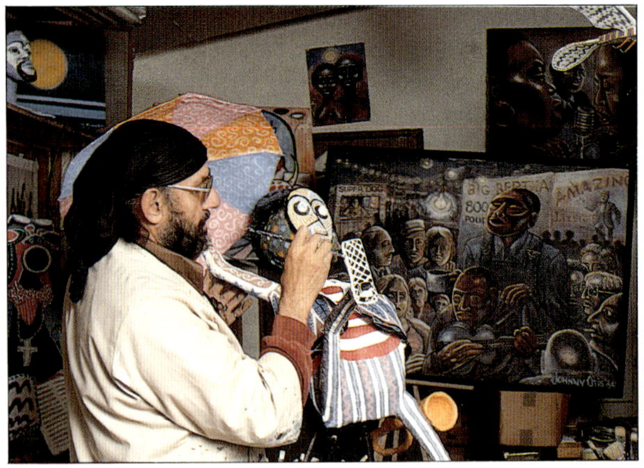

In the studio, 1986. Photograph by Stephan Rockwerk.

Otis makes his art work in sporadic binges that are, more often than not, linked to his productivity in the music and entertainment industry. "My music feeds my art," he explains. "In the '60s the white boys from England took our music and recycled it, to use a polite term. After the British invasion, we were forgotten. In a way, it was the end of our lives—our musical lives, at least. Music and art were so closely interwoven in me that trying to do one without the other was very uninspiring—hell, it was depressing." In the earliest paintings we don't find a great deal that is remarkable. These first efforts—*Nat Turner, Red Seascape,* and portraits of his family—seem to suggest that he is involved in not much more than filling the blanks that occur in a once active and invigorating life. Except for the cartoons he'd been drawing since the late '40s, he pretty much stopped making paintings in the mid-'60s.

But what is extraordinary about Otis is that when he reconnects with oils, acrylic, and canvases he becomes hooked on the making of the visual and the concrete. Like indulging in an exotic drug, the more he does the more he has to do. When queried about why he creates and the images he creates, Otis replies: "Why don't you ask me about the theory of relativity, nuclear science, physics, brain surgery, or trigonometry? I don't know. It is something inside of me. I can't explain it without becoming presumptuous. Maybe I see a voluptuous woman in a bright scarlet dress, or I browsed through a book of Picasso's, see something on the street or television. Suddenly those things move me to throw paint on the canvas or write a song. It's an impulse and it comes to me."

In 1984–1985 we find Otis combining the art of storytelling with rhythm and blues. Created in the subdued colors of the rich forbidden pleasures of night life—dark greens and blues and reds—this work covers the spiritual and the secular, rural and urban life that includes tent shows, juke joints, and night clubs. He focuses on both the audience and the performers; they invite the viewer to take the plunge as a participant in the front row. The work from this period tends toward the illustrative—the naturalistic—as he struggles to tell us about the nature of his life in music. Paintings like *Silas Green, Little Esther,* and *Doo Wop* are the first examples of a stylistically cohesive collection. Done in 1985, Otis's nocturnal parade is reminiscent of his days as an impresario. As in his earlier portraits and landscapes, he takes a straightforward approach to the subject matter. It was an emotional and stylistic struggle, and he vowed never to paint in this style again.

One of his more popular images produced during this period is *Coors.* There is very little allusion to deep space here, and almost all the action is squeezed into a single plane. The rounded bodies of performers and customers—even a cat—are placed squarely at the viewer. The masklike oval faces are treatments dependent on deeply reworked elements. We see traces of this formula repeated throughout his work, especially in the naturalistic narratives executed in the early '60s and in the most individual of his work, the sculptures of the '80s. Otis changed the title to *Jazz* and produced a sixteen-color lithograph that is used on the cover of his book, *Upside Your Head!* (Wesleyan/New England, 1994). A political activist in the African-American community since the '50s, Otis changed the name when the beer company became controversial in the community.

In 1986, he introduced pastels and bright colors to his palette and became a self-directed student of art, exploring and experimenting with different styles and approaches. He hopscotched his way through the artists that were his first influences. It seems that, at this point, he said good-bye to an era that had long since passed. Big silver-plated microphones of the early dance bands, Stetson hats, close dancing, and bellying up to the bar were all but romantic memories. He came to deal with the changing times, the bitterness and unhappiness resulting from the invasion of "the white boys from England," strobe lights, miniskirts, free love, and the post-modern tide of events. He set out on his visual artistic journey anew. He dipped back into the earlier imagery a few times, but his decision had been made—he was out to break new ground. We see a growing strength and straightforwardness coming from Otis's hand in such still-life examples as *Three Women, Three Children and Cat,* and *Grandmother and Granddaughter.*

In *Three Women* there is a sophisticated sweetness. He clearly owes much to Matisse at this time, but is finding his own voice. The oval faces, like masks, are hauntingly expressive. He has found pattern and some shallow space, and is using it in a new way to talk about—a brothel, perhaps? This work has a wholeness and unbroken stillness—a pause for the viewer's narration. *Three Children and Cat* is swathed in silence and does not wander around in the articulation of the figures or the space they occupy; everything has a place and everything is in its place—who are they waiting for? In *Grandmother and Granddaughter* we see the honesty of Otis's cultural interest staring us dead in the face; the youthful oval grown into the elderly oval echoed in what is perhaps the death mask. In each example the figures are frozen.

Otis has developed an eloquent commentary on patriotism and the American dream that is embodied in the flag. Like Jasper Johns, his use of the flag is at once patriotic and iconoclastic. Emerging from a postwar experience that was filled with pride of country, Johns demystified the flag. He manipulated its appearance by using a broad spectrum of materials and color combinations, dismantled its traditional meaning, and served it up as a pop American icon—just another familiar object. In doing so, Johns ironically infused the flag with the power of expression and creative availability for a generation of artists and baby boomers to come.

Otis uses this approach to provoke the viewer into revisiting the dichotomy of American culture and the sociopolitical climate, and suggests that a sacred covenant has been broken. "America has let our people down," he says. "When I had my church in the late '70s and '80s, our parishioners were always going to downtown L.A. to give away food to the homeless and the hungry. You could see that things were getting worse; it felt like the bread lines during the Depression. It wasn't just black folks down there—it was some of everybody being represented. It really upset me, because we could do much better than that."

American Scenic Express and *Inner City Nocturne #1* and *#2* are paintings that deal with sociopolitical matter that is as relevant today as it was in 1988 when he created the work. *American Scenic Express* is of great interest. In this work Otis strikes an ironic note by infusing a pristine red-white-and-blue erect flag into a sterile black-white-and-blue environment, producing a dramatic burst of color in the void. The Stars and Stripes in *Inner City Nocturne #1* appears on an elongated, faceless figure. Stepping almost out of the picture, he leads his slumbering partner in a dance over the tracing of a murder scene. A pure

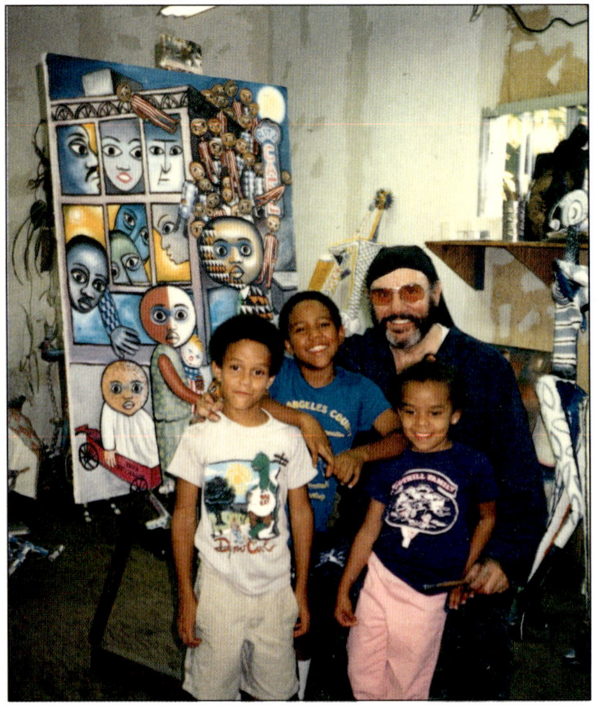

Otis with his grandchildren, 1988. Photograph by Stephan Rockwerk.

Chagall figure floats over the crowd in this nocturnal cityscape. "America is in demise," Otis says about the form floating from east to west. "Drugs are all over the place, and the people in this painting are so anesthetized they can't even see what's going on around them." *In Inner City Nocturne #2* we again see Otis's particular take on the American flag. Here he continues to confound us. What is to be made of Otis's symbolic treatment of the flag? The obvious is the Raggedy Ann doll draped in the Stars and Stripes. But in the background, he fragments the flag into prison garments—red-and-white-striped body-suits and star-studded blue-and-white dresses for a somnambulistic group of figures floating en masse over the edge of the pawn shop. Their sheer numbers counterbalance the colorless faces that are reminiscent of *American Scenic Express.*

Arriving at Otis's home in Sebastopol, California, one is met by a fleet of old cars, buses, and boats. Three full-figured women, their naked bodies brightly painted, guard the entrance to his house. Visitors are enthusiastically greeted inside by a crowd of people, including teenagers, toddlers, and babies in mothers' arms. A large saloon holds dozens and dozens of others, variously arranged throughout the room. At first glance, they all seem very small and quiet, yet animated and involved with each other. It takes a few minutes to realize that these are not people at all—but rather the sculptures of Johnny Otis. Tens and tens of them. For a time, one is quite stunned and unsure of just what to do next. The etiquette of the situation is in question. Where shall we sit? Next to two children eating watermelon is an old man with seemingly all of his worldly possessions surrounding him, a harmonica in his mouth and various musical instruments attached to his body, and next to him an old woman bent over her shopping cart. Does one ask a little man perched on a little stool enjoying his cigar to move over? You decide to laugh nervously, as chairs are being pulled from a long dining table, others brought from scattered parts of the interior, and offered along with invitations for a cup of coffee or tea—or, perhaps, a glass of Johnny Otis Organic Apple Juice. After quieting down one's heart, it's appropriate to try to become acquainted with these little folk, many of whom are seated quite comfortably on little chairs. Finally, once having adjusted to the abnormal and magical ambiance of the space, it all seems quite normal for the living room gathering.

Otis acquired children's chairs from a fellow minister while living in Altadena, California. Sunday school pupils at Otis's Landmark Community Church hated those chairs so much that he pressed them into the service of his art to fashion *The Chair Series,* done from 1985 to 1988. As in the paintings of this period, he uses bold colors and steps away—but not too far—from musical themes to create his observations of everyday life. What he has dematerialized in his paintings comes full force into a three-dimensional construct. The sculptures are organic and were his first experience in working in mixed media: plaster of paris, wood, found objects, and paints.

A dedicated collector of discards, Otis considers nothing rubbish, nothing useless, nothing without some salvation and grace. He searches through dumpsters and lots filled with bundled rags, broken glass, bottle tops, soap cans, sticks, broken tree branches and trunks, and instruments and utensils once used to beautify—plastic curlers, mirrors, lip-

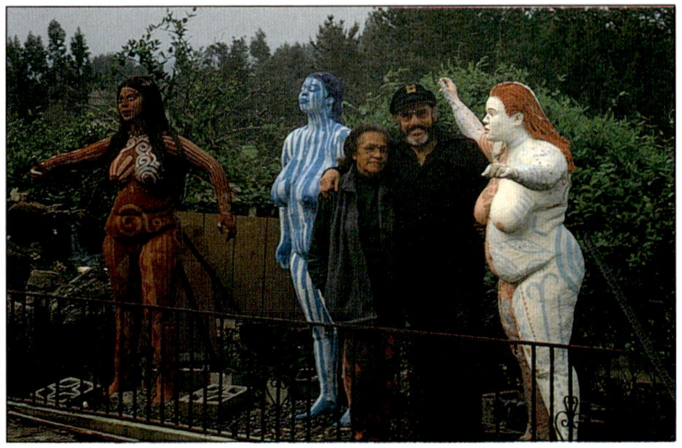

Phyllis and Johnny Otis and the Three Muses, *1992. Photograph by Joe Angle.*

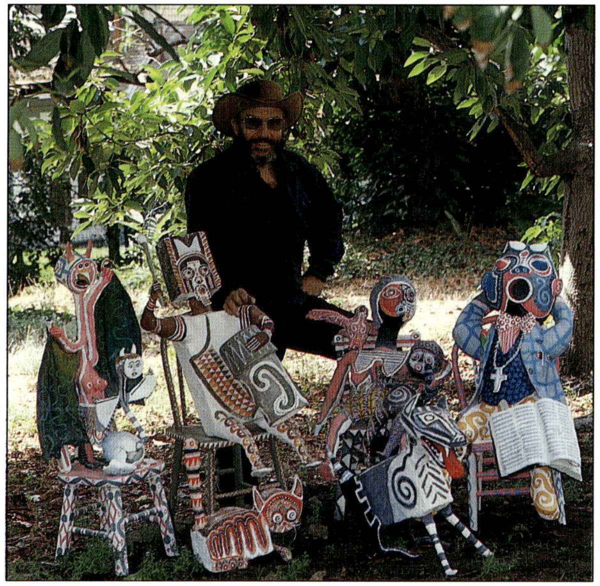

1986. Photograph by Stephan Rockwerk.

stick, unmatched shoes—but forsaken by those without his vision.

In many African cultures, chairs are symbols of power. Otis delves into this spirituality and unwittingly calls upon the *ancestors.* Contemporary African-American artist Martin Puryear deals with the power of the chair in his work, stripping bare the Western concept of chair and igniting it with spiritual authority. Otis's approach is to embellish it, taking away the abstraction and infusing it with human possibilities. In broad, heavy strokes, he uses yellow, pink, battleship gray, electric white, and glossy black to adorn the sculptured characters with signs and symbols reminiscent of mystical body painting and tattoos.

After completing *The Chair Series* and other sculptures of this period, he hid them away in a workroom at his home in Altadena. Few eyes, other than those of family members, saw them. "What is this shit?" he asked his wife. "When I was just having a ball with it and nobody had seen it," he recalls, "I didn't have any reason to laugh or to chuckle or really be puzzled about it. But once people I respect began to rhapsodize about it, I said, 'I think it's jerkin' off, but it's great fun.'"

This is a very telling statement, for unlike Otis's music, which he creates to be performed in front of an audience or to be captured on phonograph records that people, he hopes, will listen to; unlike his early cartoons, which were drawn to be passed around the band bus, looked and laughed at; unlike his paintings, which (unless kept in storage) were hung on walls in plain view; these sculptures were, like masturbation, a most private act inspired by his deepest fantasies.

It is often said that artists are only concerned with sex and death. These concerns are repeated throughout the Otis's sculptures. In *You Gotta Die of Somethin'* we see a tiny figure playing out his hand against widely reported killers: pork, alcohol, and tobacco. The figure is at once comic and tragic as he perches precariously on a stool that is supported by the back of a small chair. Blowing imaginary smoke rings, he ponders his risky lifestyle. His body is tattooed; an ominous snake design suggests the digestive system. Totemic in nature, the work is a vertical structure—top to bottom and bottom to top. The issue, as always, is the difficulty in getting things to flow because the structure itself is static and linear. The piece acquires rhythm, however, by relying on color pattern and shape and on being broken by some small, although dramatic naturalistic gesture, i.e., the rounded plate with rib bones, cup, cigar, and circular mouth. These elements are very risky, yet Otis, the visual juggler, has balanced them to achieve spontaneity and rhythm.

In *Red Beans and Rice* we find Otis involved in the concept of universal maternity. A mother seated on the small chair spoons red beans and rice into the rounded mouth of her child. This work—another small totem of box, chair, and figures—is nonetheless in constant, rounded motion. Great attention has been given to detail. The intricately patterned garment harks back to the seamless weaving of design as seen in Matisse and in Otis's painting *Three Women.* Most of the color in this work is mediated by a milky patina which keeps the electric colors in check. He rounds and molds the posterior of the mother to repeat the roundness of the chair back. He finds a way to soften the sculpture with the feeding spoon and the roundness of the baby's head. This sculpture, as with almost all of his three-dimensional work, has a strong sense of drawing in space—it operates in and creates its own reality.

At the Crossroads is composed of three elements: two mother figures and a railroad crossing sign. Otis uses the sign as a metaphor to express the two sides of a dramatic tale. The cradle on one side and the coffin on the other side could be mistaken for one another. Because both figures are essentially the same in color—a neutral blue-gray impression is given—one has to look closely to discover that the mother of the living child is dressed in a garment slightly more gay than the mother of the still child. The face of the mother has a kind of blankness; her gesture forms a loose attachment to the coffin of her child; long arms allow her hands to lightly touch the container, suggesting a willingness to let the child be taken away.

This sculpture in its entirety suggests that there is neither rhyme nor reason to explain what happens in life. The gods are neutral in meting out the pain and joy to those that pray to them. The crossing sign is the third and largest element. The cross bars are painted black and white, signaling caution. The vertical post is humanoid, with a suggestion of stick feet, topped by another cross form with two round eyes. Blues, pinks, grays, and white are of equal value; the painting and drawing on the structure are key. The pieces are held together by gesture and composition.

Throughout the work of Otis, one is consistently aware of his intuitive composition. This sculpture is surely the most riveting of this entire body of work. It is completely without sentimentality, while telling the most frightening and dreadful tale.

Owl Killing the Snake is a sculpture that is quite straightforward. Without chair, bench, or any encumbrances, this is death in flight. Furious and funny faced, the owl is at once fierce and frivolous with its slightly crossed eyes and lipstick mouth. The true furiousness occurs when the owl grabs the snake with its talons as it takes off on its deadly flight. The markings are sober, and ripples suggest flight over water to the owl's cavern for feasting. The snake remains elegant in its death throes, flashing all of its bright colors and signaling its deadly venom. Otis over the years has been a bird man of sorts, raising chickens, pigeons, and exotic parrots. He now maintains a number of aviaries for his pigeons, macaws, and cockatoos.

While the paintings and sculptures are tributes to Otis's experience, the cartoons are running commen-

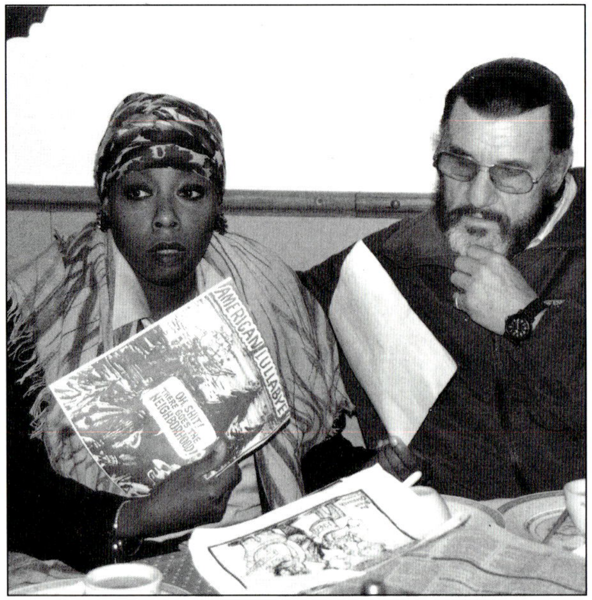

Veronica Aiken and Johnny Otis, 1995
Photograph by Heath R. E. Fennell

taries on American culture, society, and Otis's everyday life. It is here that he breaks through the confines of paint, canvas, plaster, and found objects and taps into humor in a prolific outpouring of satirical pictorial recordings. The results are thousands of comic strips and cartoons that are a mix of George Herriman's *Krazy Kat,* R. Crumb, and Otis's own brand of wisdom and wit. Otis, however, credits the slapstick humor of Elzie Segar, the creator of Thimble Theater, as having great influence on his work. "Segar was such an inspiration and wonderful cartoonist," he says. "The way he drew cartoons of large crowds in fight arenas used to fascinate me." Among Otis's favorite characters in the funny pages were Alice the Goon, Whimpy, Lil Sweetpea, Olive Oyl and Popeye—all creations of Segar.

Otis sketches most of his cartoons at night. This ritual began in 1950 when band vocalist Little Esther drew a derogatory sketch of roadie and fellow performer Little Arthur Matthews. "Esther and Arthur got into a really bitter argument on the bus," Otis recalls. "He insulted her, and she pitched a bitch. She plopped down next to me and said, 'Okay, draw a picture of him and make it ugly. Do a little ugly, bug-eyed motherfucker just like him.' I said, 'No, Esther,' so she grabbed the pencil and paper and drew it herself." Under the title Li'l Booger, Otis improved on the illustration, and other members of the band began placing orders for comic antidotes. Filled with in-jokes and what was known then as blue humor, the series consisted of situation comedies in pencil, pen, and ink that collectively went under the title *Black Dispatch.* Performers like Redd Foxx, Etta James, LaWanda Page, Sammy Davis Jr., Jackie Wilson, and Little Willie John were a part of the procession that traveled through the panels of Otis's *Dispatch* between 1950 and 1960. Unlike Otis and most of the band members, the majority of the work created during the years the band toured didn't survive the trip.

Otis remembers his first cartoon—a sketch of Otto Messmer's Felix the Cat—done in the eighth grade to amuse his classmates. Impressed by his ability to draw, the teacher asked Otis if he would like to have an art scholarship. "I wasn't actually moving toward music yet, but I didn't know what scholarship meant," he says. "I think my teacher mistook my confused reaction for disinterest."

When Otis dismantled his band in the mid-'60s, the antics chronicled in the *Black Dispatch* came to an end. He stopped painting and sculpturing in wood, but he never stopped drawing cartoons. "I guess it was laughin' to keep from crying," he explains. During the early '70s his cartoons were a series of random subjects, but in 1976, Otis began creating cartoons and strips in response to letters from childhood friend Hal Kronick and from long-time buddy, saxophonist Preston Love. With the ushering in of the Reagan era, politicians and political issues became favorite topics. Otis's panels currently appear in the *Sebastopol Times and News.* "The illustrations speak for themselves," he says.

Like his music of the '40s, '50s, and '60s, Otis's cartoon characters have voices filled with streetwise attitude—and very few of them are immune to words like "bullshit" and "motherfucker." "These words are not used for shock value," he explains. "It's the way I talk. We bandied these words about on the bus, in a loving way, in an insulting way. Everybody knows what they mean, and the context that I use them in makes it real rather than forced."

Over the years, friends like Kronick, Love, Ron Rothstein, booking agent Rob Heller, and former congressman Mervin Dymally have appeared in and received such letters, but it is Kronick who has a continuous role. He emerges throughout Otis's work as Hal, Hal the K, Moishe, Moishe Kronick, Moishe Pipick, Pip, and The Pip—all names Kronick has signed in his letters to Otis. Kronick has received hundreds of these cartoon-letters over the past twenty years.

Otis often includes himself in the human follies. In the early years we see him as the functioning bandleader who has to keep his performers in line and on time. In the mid '80s, however, he makes his first appearance as the easygoing and sometimes per-

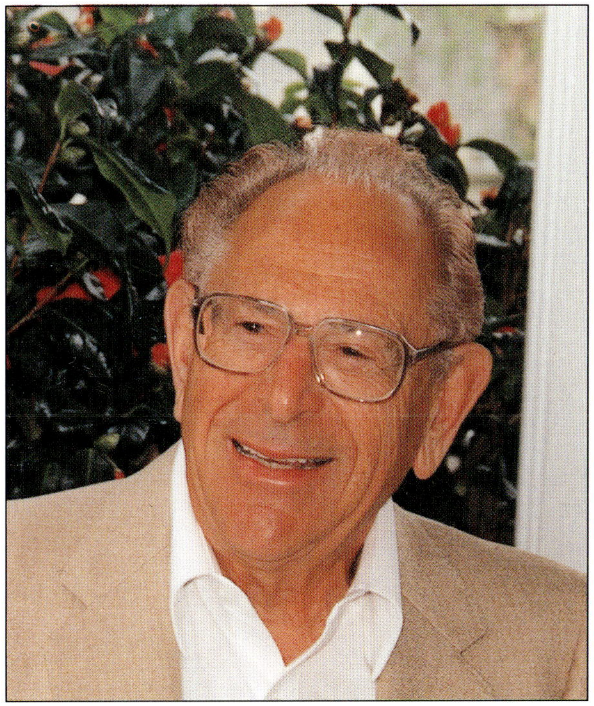

Hal Kronick, 1995. Photograph by Heath R. E. Finnell.

plexed Ol' Geezer. Otis admits that this character is a self-portrait: like himself, Geezer takes life as it comes, and enjoys life whenever he can. "With the emergence of my alter-ego, Ol' Geezer, I'm able to come up with a lot of nonsense that contains more than a grain of truth," he says. "Hal's reactions to these midnight meanderings are great fun." Strips like *Ol' Geezer* and *Down on the Farm* feature son Nicky Otis (a vegetarian and organic farmer) as Tofu Man. Their storylines reflect the everyday activities of a serene life-style surrounded by family and friends.

While *Ol' Geezer* is a collection of single-panel, one-page illustrations intertwined with text, *Sid* is an ongoing series that is more often than not two to three pages of panels and wonderful storytelling. Here Otis reaches into his role as pastor to comment on human frailties, and proclaims Sid is God. In a nine-page explanation, which begins with the birth of his friend Hal the K, we discover that Sid—who, like Hal, is Jewish—is really the father of God, who is a black woman. "Sid was married to a black blues singer he met in Galilee, thousands of years ago," Otis explains. Sid's daughter relinquishes her duties to him, however ("Who needs this headache!"), and Sid visits Earth to check things out. Eventually he goes off to live with Schnookie, a woman he meets in church during one of his earthly commutes. Typically, in the opening frame, Sid begins with a monologue directed to Kronick. The cast of characters includes jazz trumpeter Gabriel (the Archangel), the scheming Big Red (the Devil), and the impatient Dr. Bye Bye (Death).

And then, of course, there are the spin-offs: *My, Oh My!* by the Ol' Geezer; *Geezer* by Yors Trooly, and *From the Desk of Dr. Bye Bye.* Segmented into myriad situations, topics covered in the panels can be put into three categories: the struggle for immortality, the "goings on" in heaven and on Earth, and what you do with your life while waiting for impending death.

It is only leaving Otis's space that you realize he is a genuine cultural anomaly—and that he does not live on the fringes. Nor has he skimmed his experience from the top. Otis has lived it. Other questions can certainly be raised, given the state of race relations in America over the past two centuries and the images that he makes, but after spending time with him, the answers are not that pat. "I am always intrigued by people who want to pigeonhole me,"

Otis says. "But at my age I've given up on questioning every nuance of my life. I just live and enjoy it." The orchestration of his work is like his family life: vigorous, full of rich color and texture and clear blue notes. You can get close to him or not. You can like his art or not. From his music to his political activism, he has made himself a part of the African-American cultural tradition—which is uniquely American. And in the end, the viewer is left to ponder this most interesting man who has chosen to reposition himself and express himself in the American landscape, and who derives his inspiration from one abstraction to another abstraction: life . . . to music . . . to art . . . to life again.

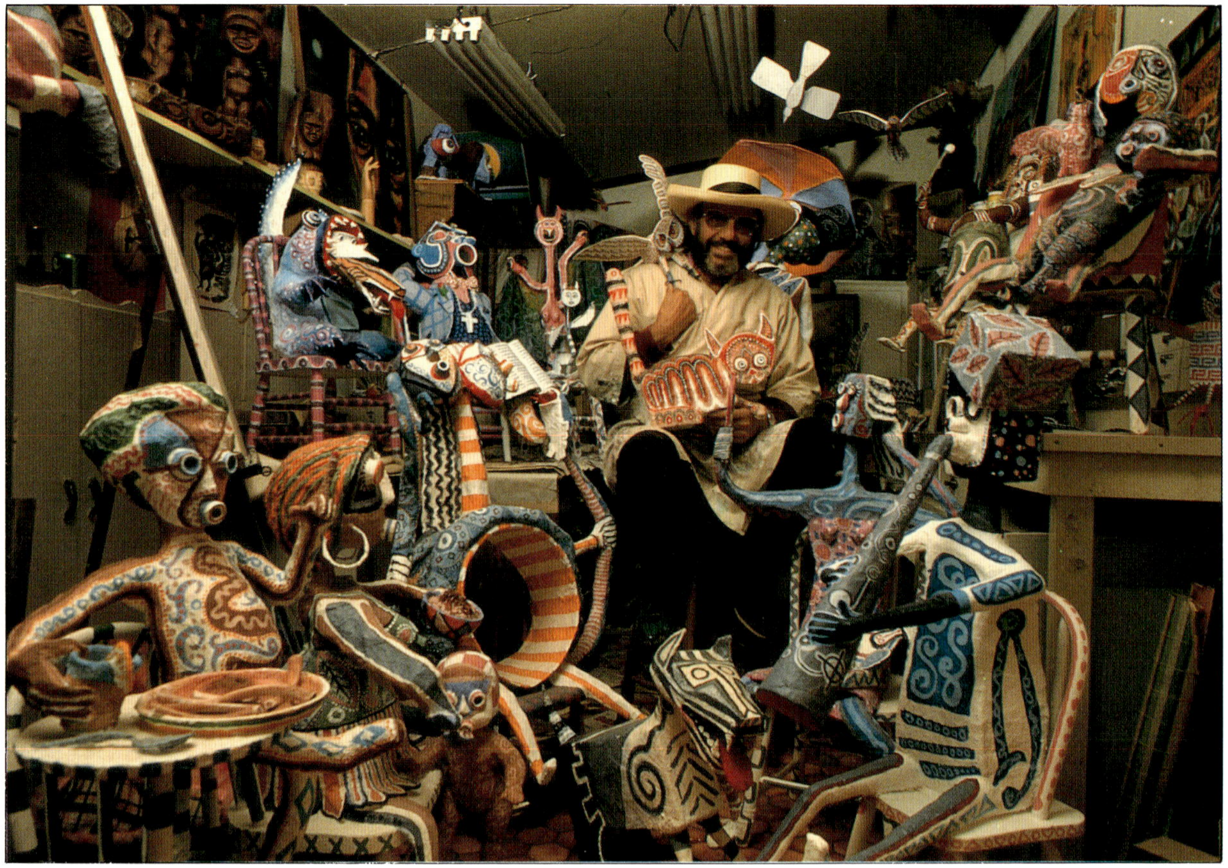

Photograph by Stephan Rockwerk, 1986

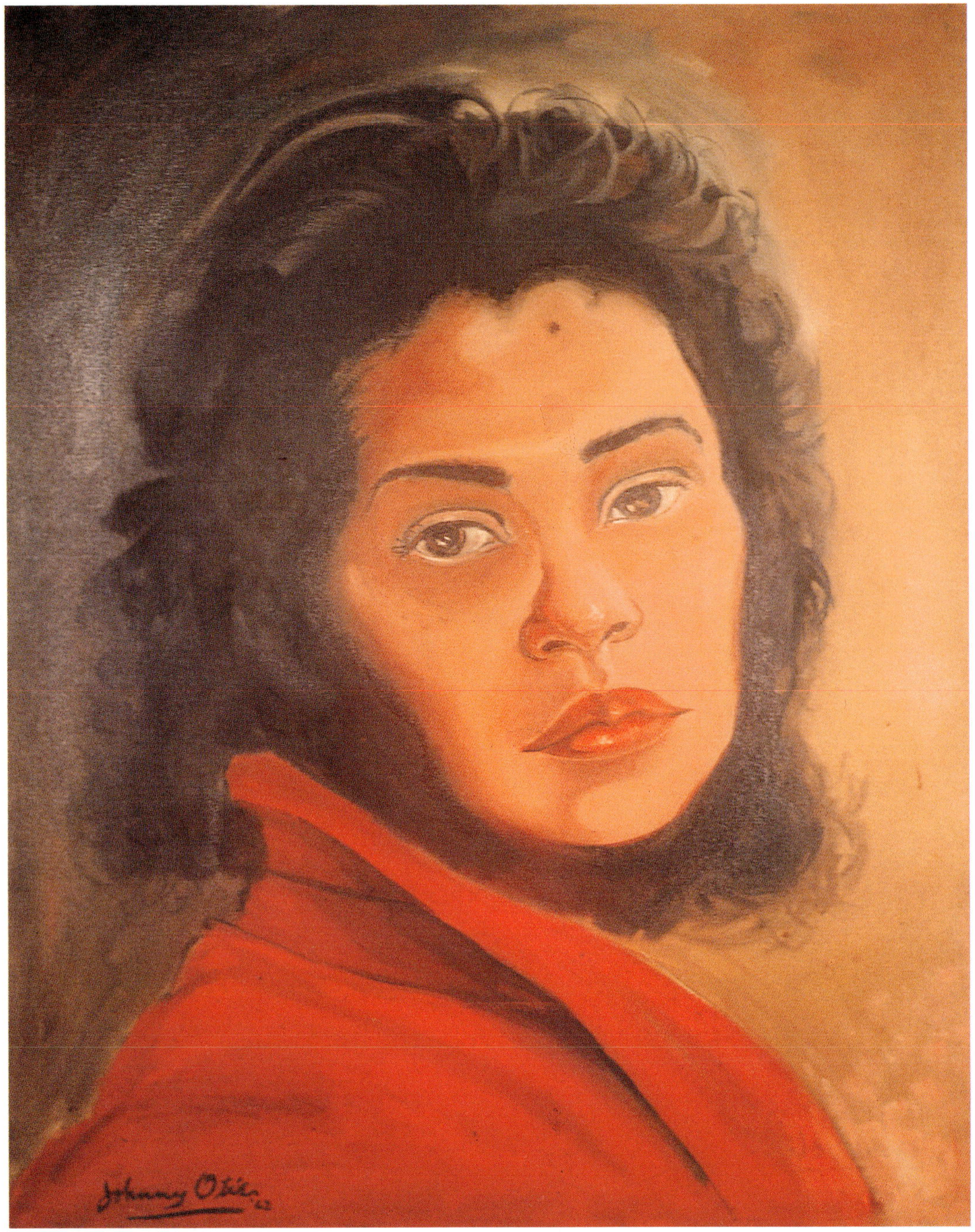

PHYLLIS 1962. Oil on canvas. Photograph by Johnny Otis.

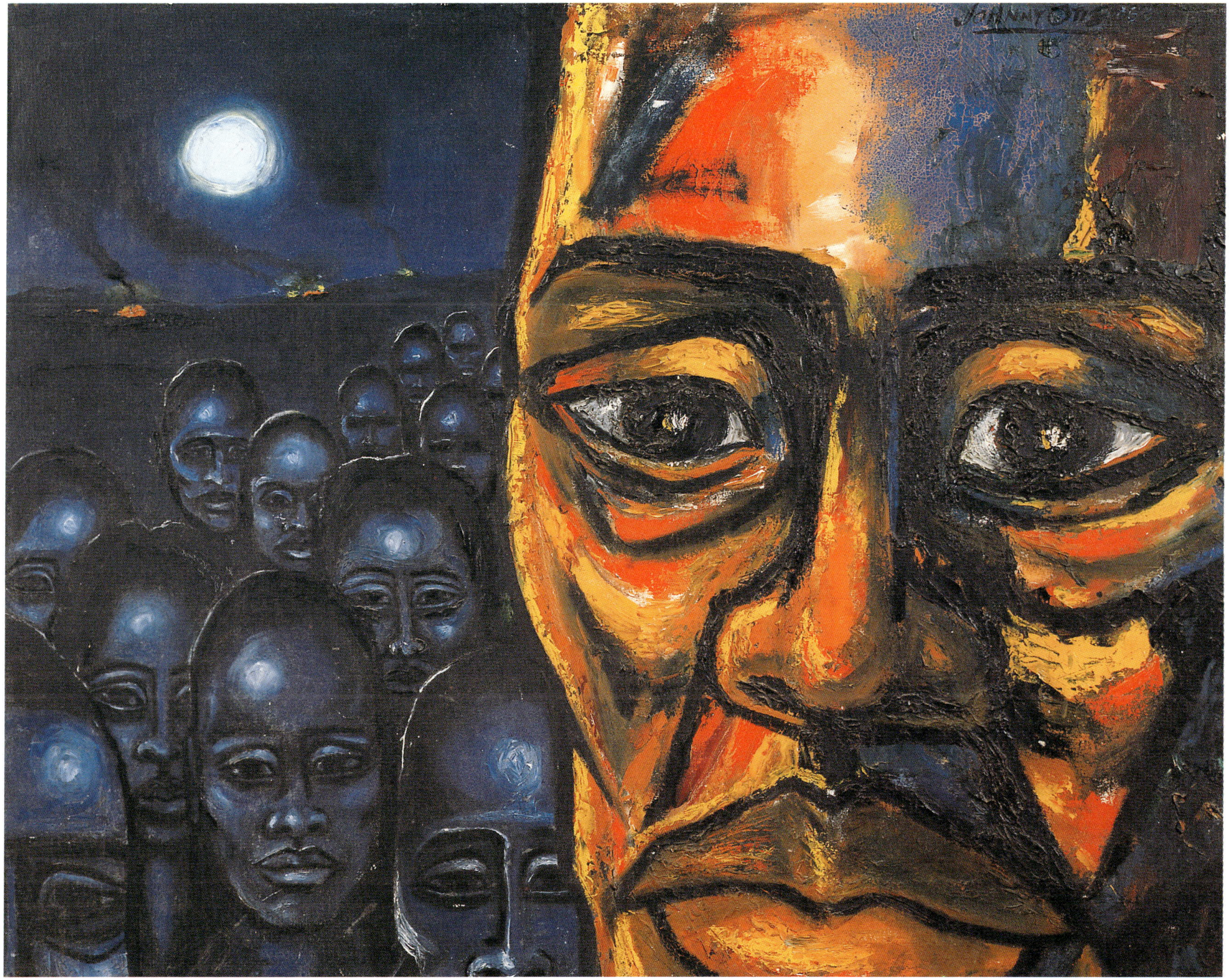

NAT TURNER 1962. Oil on composition board, 32 x 40 in. Photograph by Stephan Rockwerk.

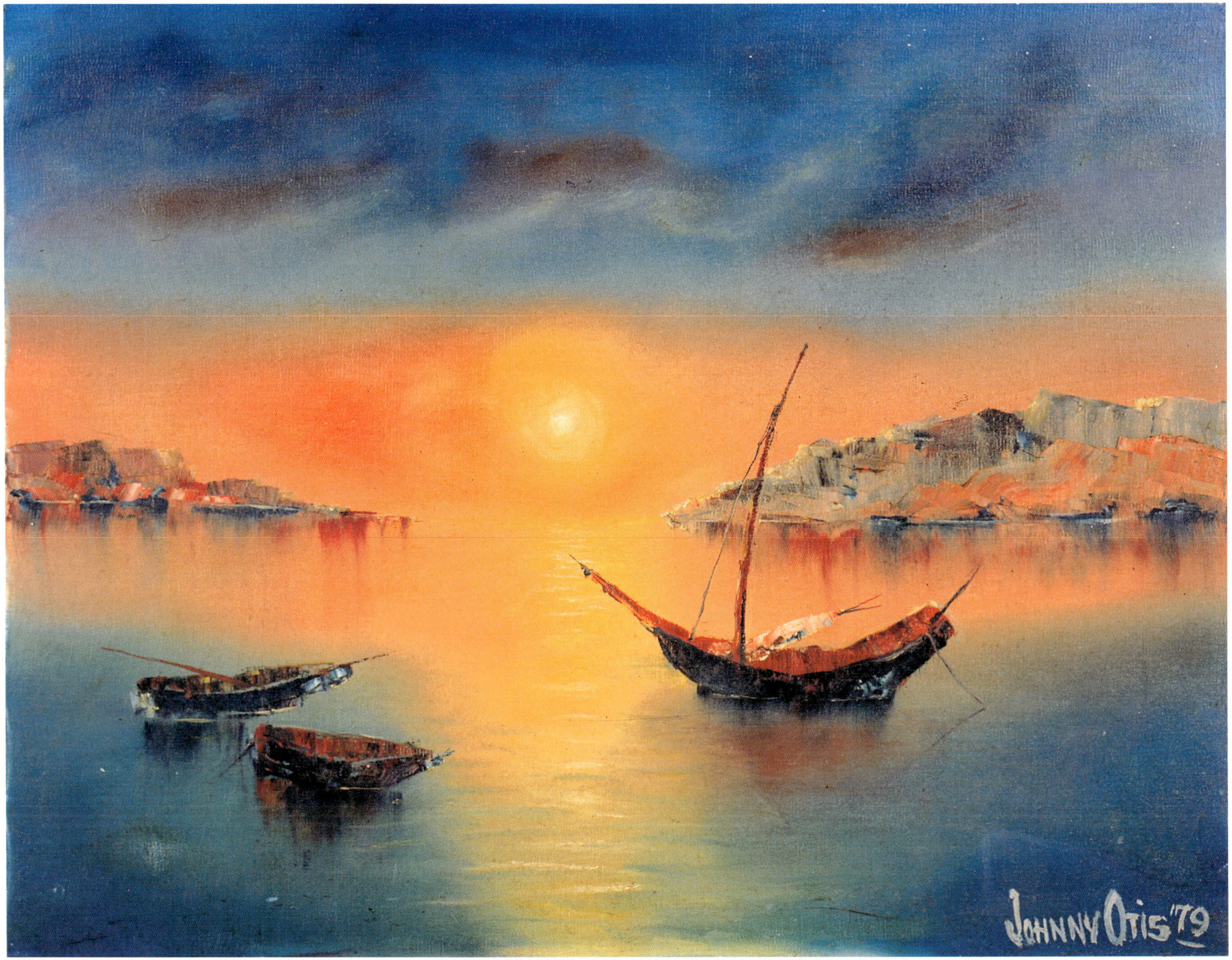

RED SEASCAPE 1979. Oil on canvas, 22 x 28 in. Photograph by Stephan Rockwerk.

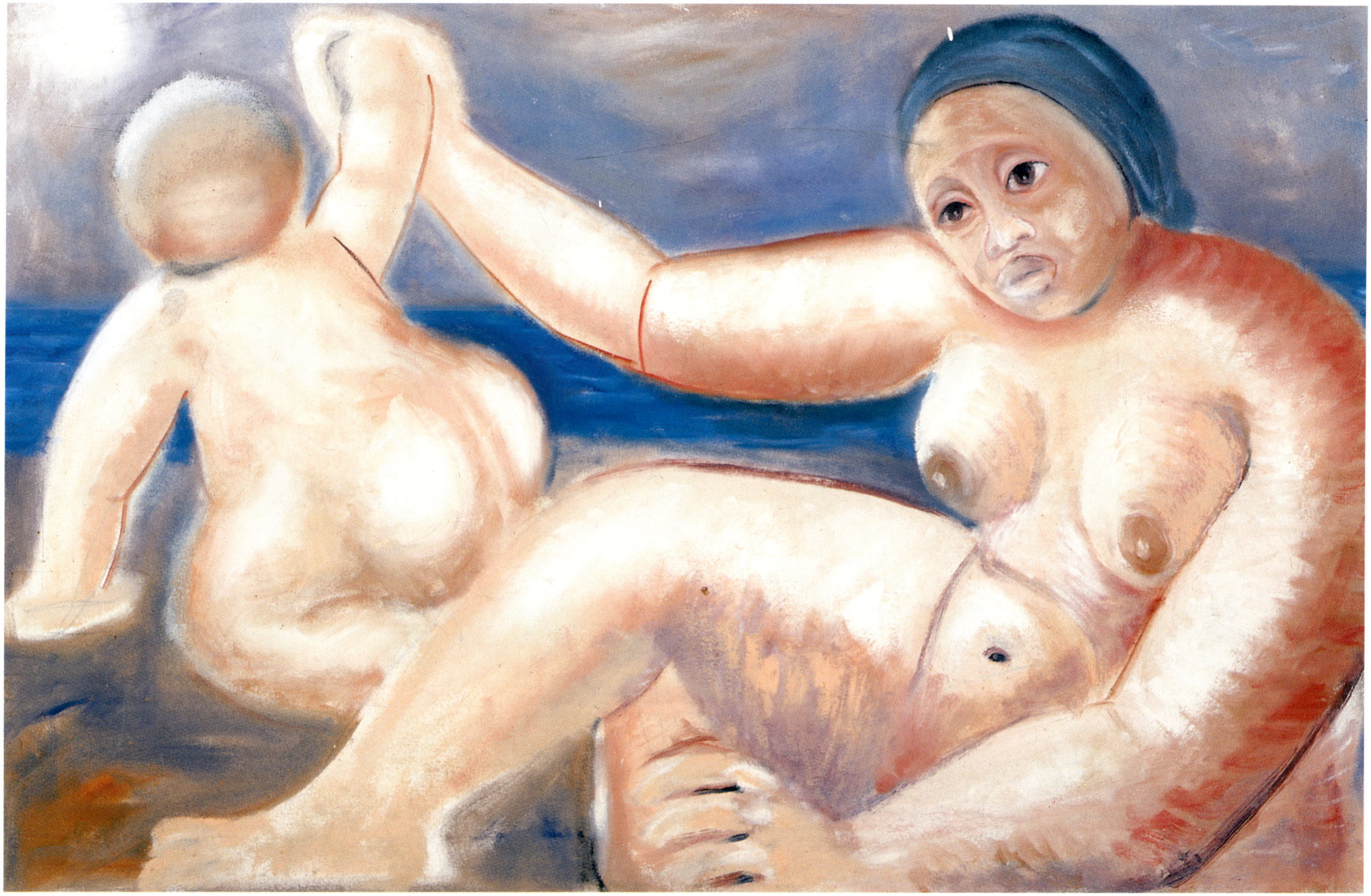

Mother and Child on Beach 1982. Oil on canvas, 24 x 36 in. Photograph by Stephan Rockwerk.

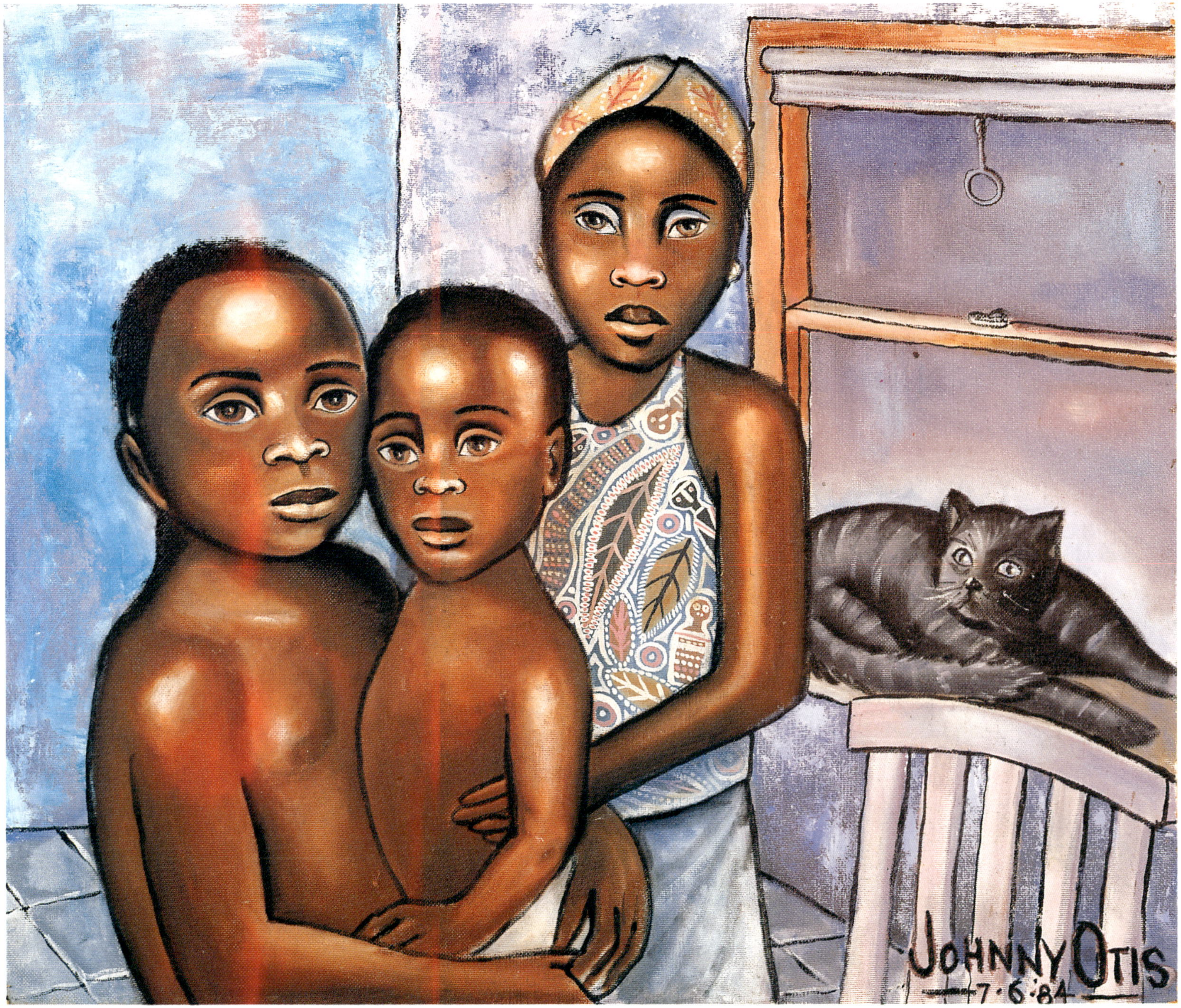

Three Children and Cat 1984. Oil on masonite, 36 x 41½ in. Photograph by Stephan Rockwerk.

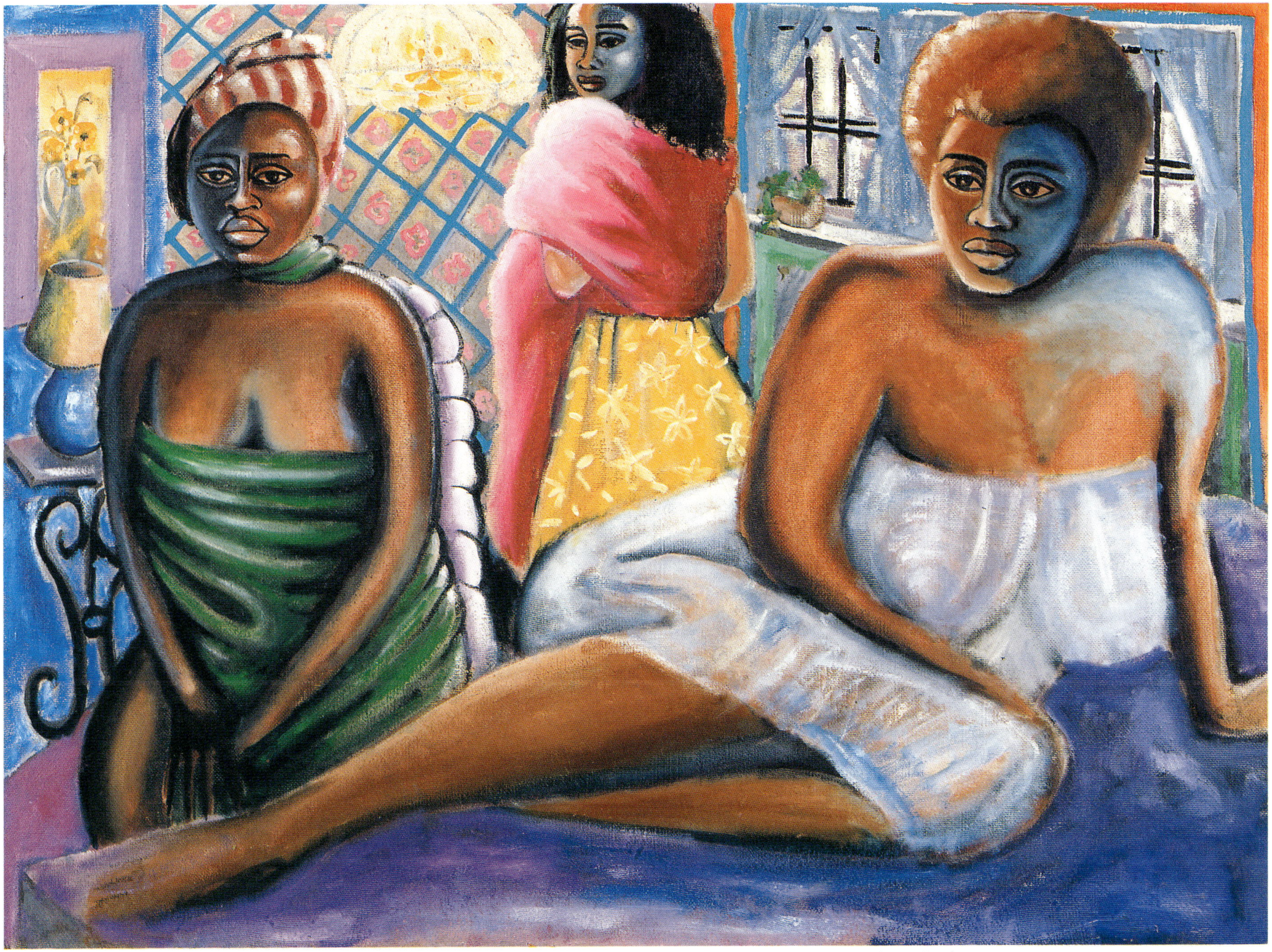

THREE WOMEN 1984. Oil on masonite, 36 x 48 in. Collection of Bob Dylan. Photograph by Stephan Rockwerk.

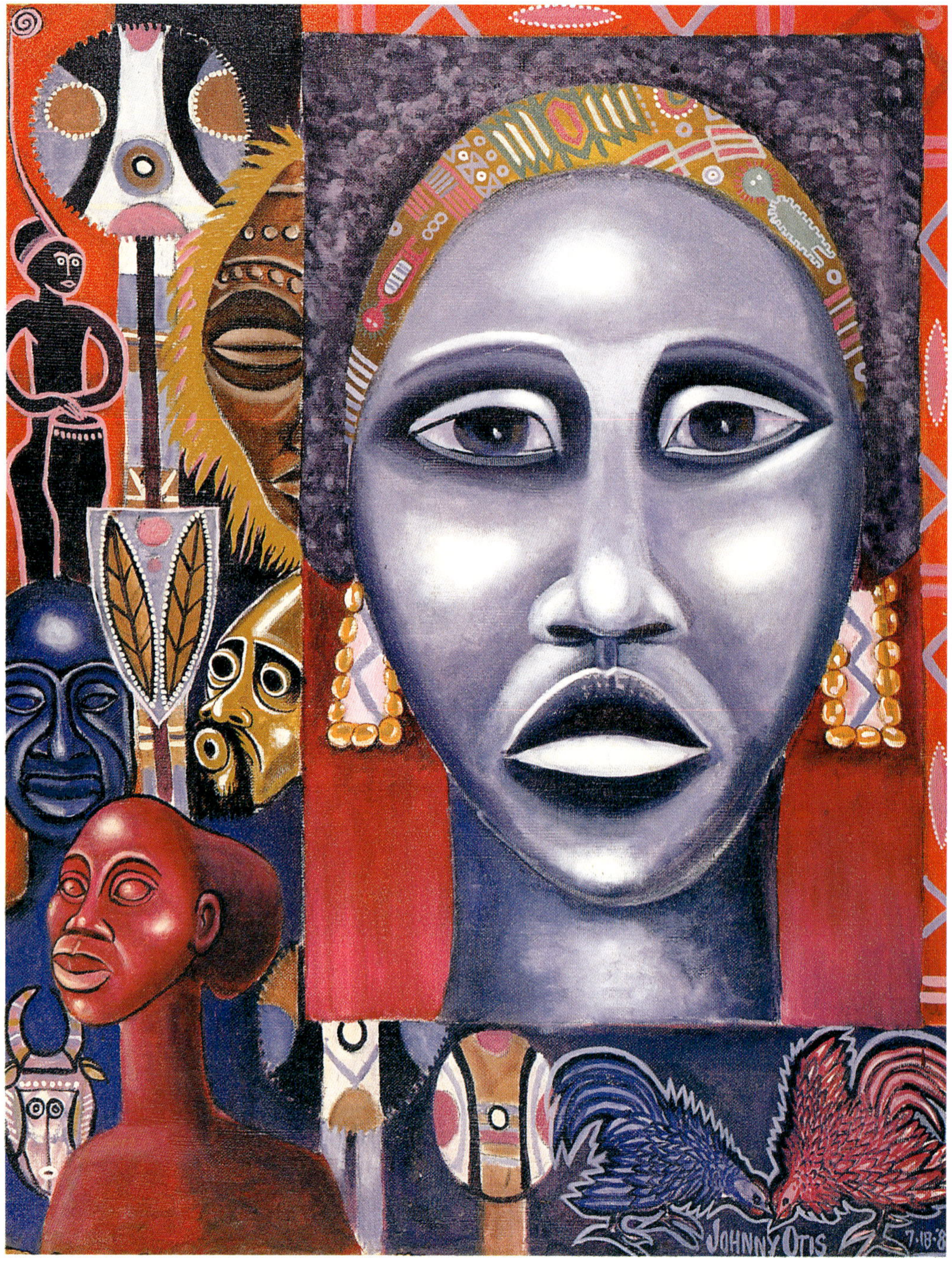

WOMAN FACE WITH MASKS 1984. Oil on masonite, 48 x 36 in. Photograph by Stephan Rockwerk.

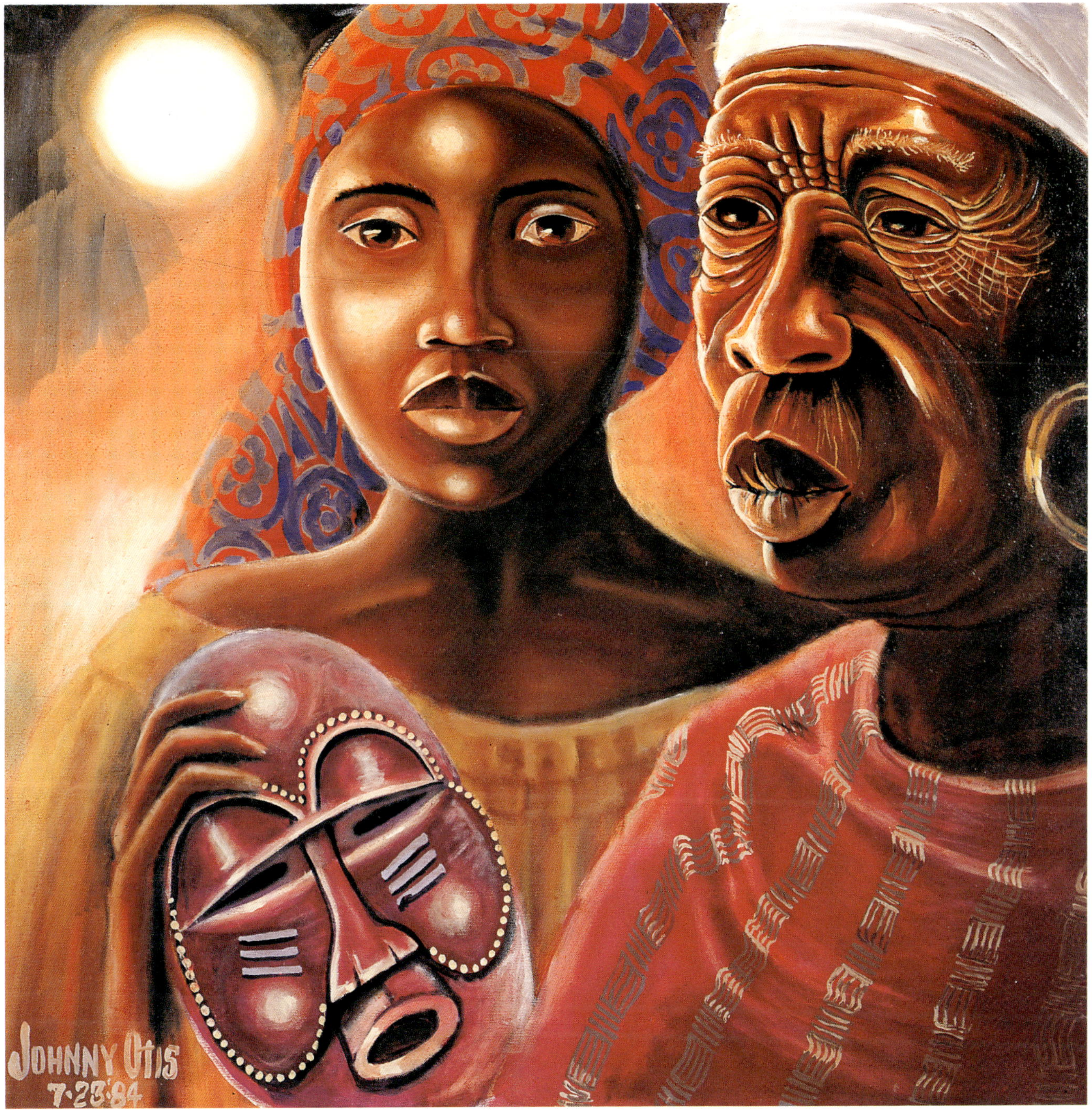

Grandmother and Granddaughter 1984. Oil on canvas, 30 x 30 in. Photograph by Stephan Rockwerk

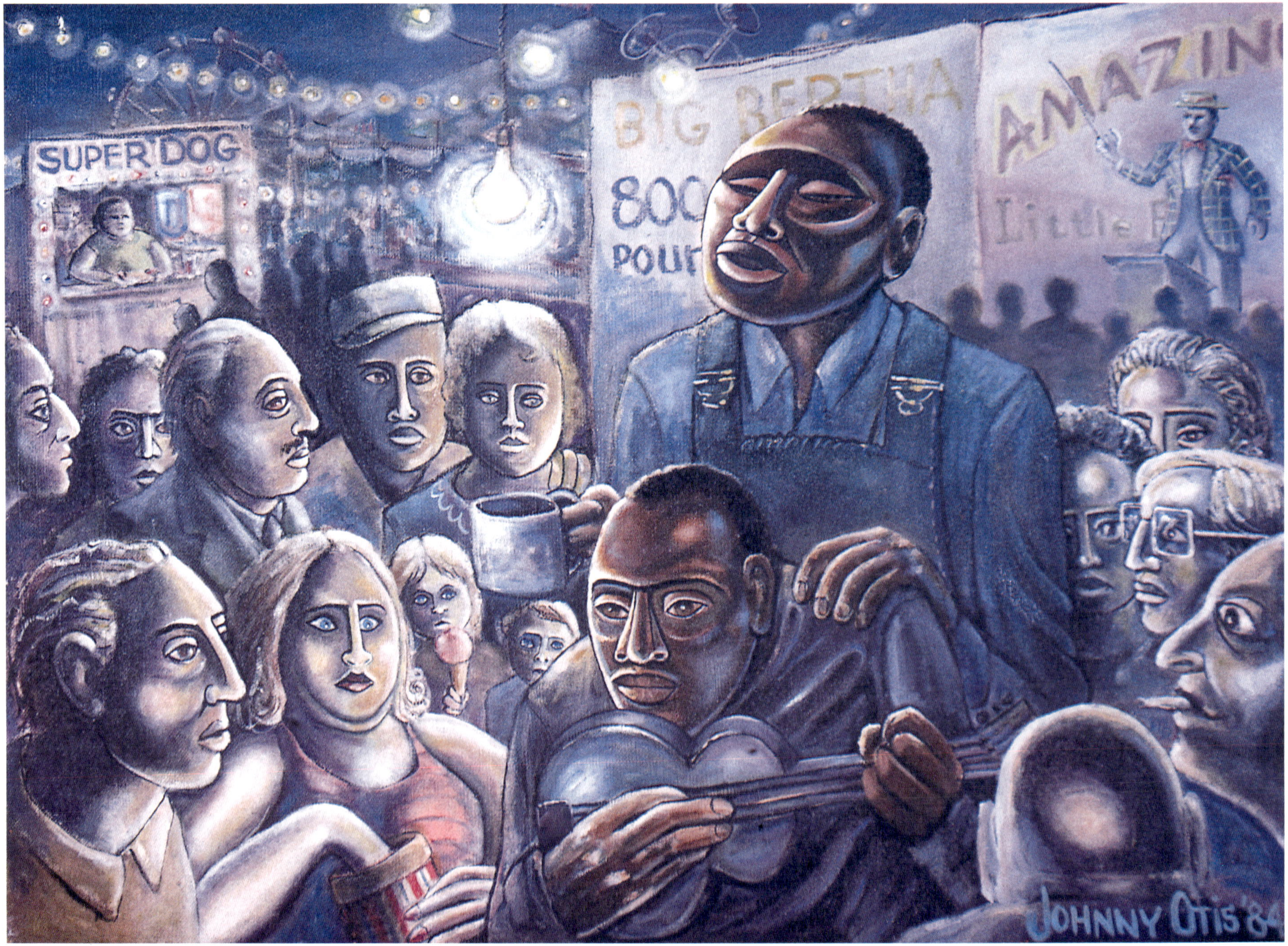

THE BLUES 1984. Oil on masonite, 48 x 36 in. Photograph by Stephan Rockwerk.

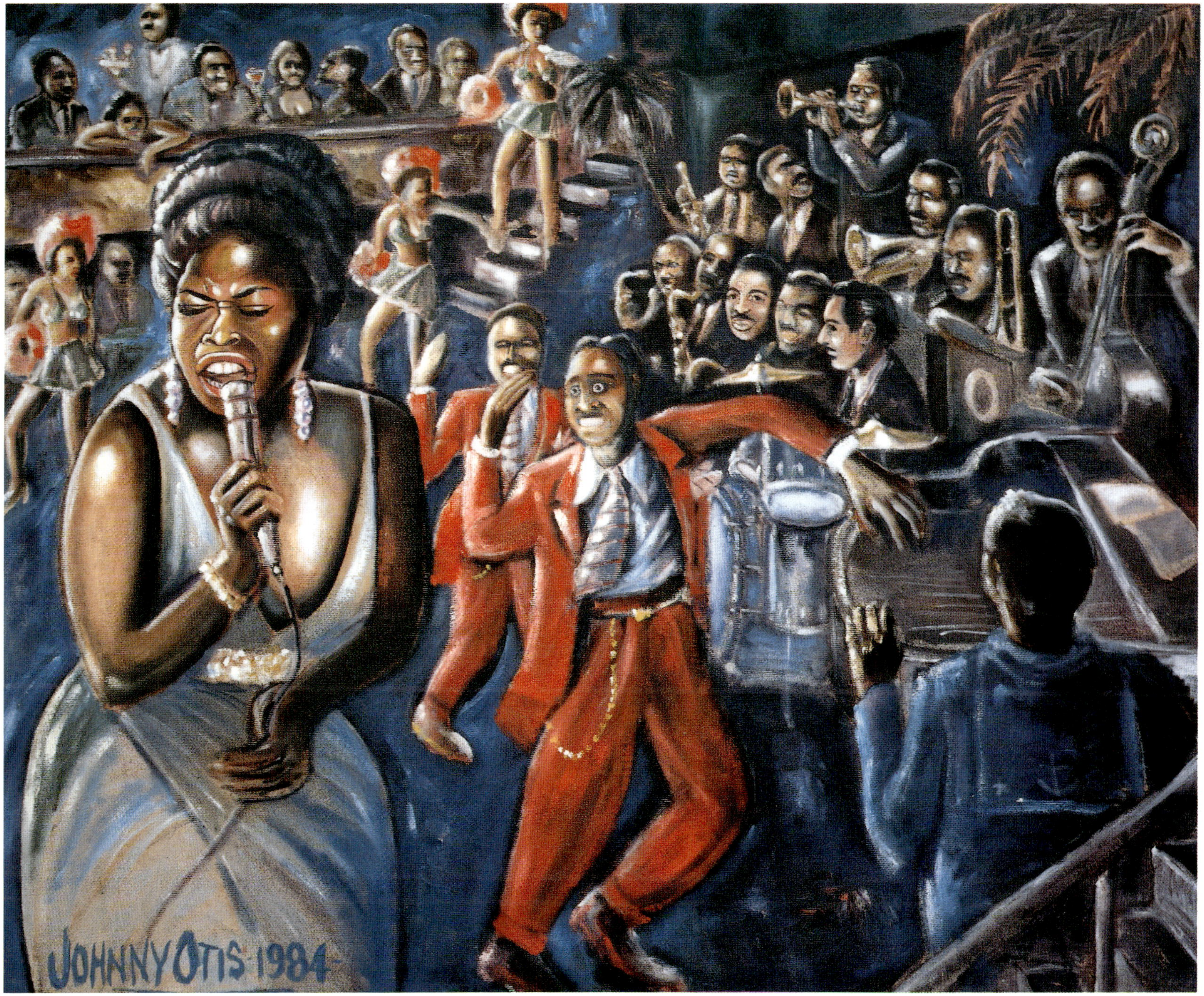

Little Esther 1984. Oil on masonite. Collection of John Goddard. Photograph by Stephan Rockwerk.

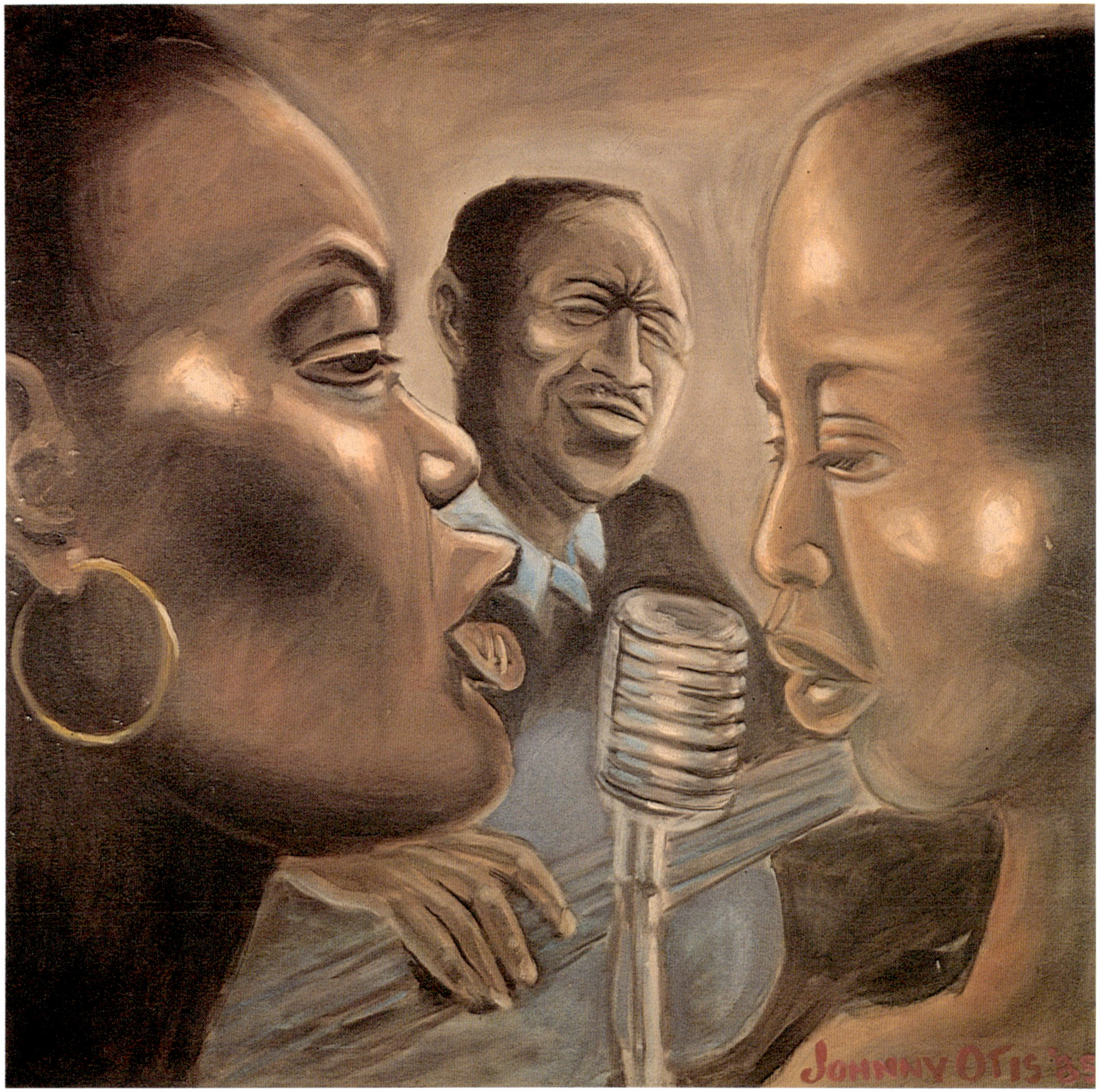

Gospel Singers 1985. Oil on canvas, 30 x 32 in. Photograph by Stephan Rockwerk.

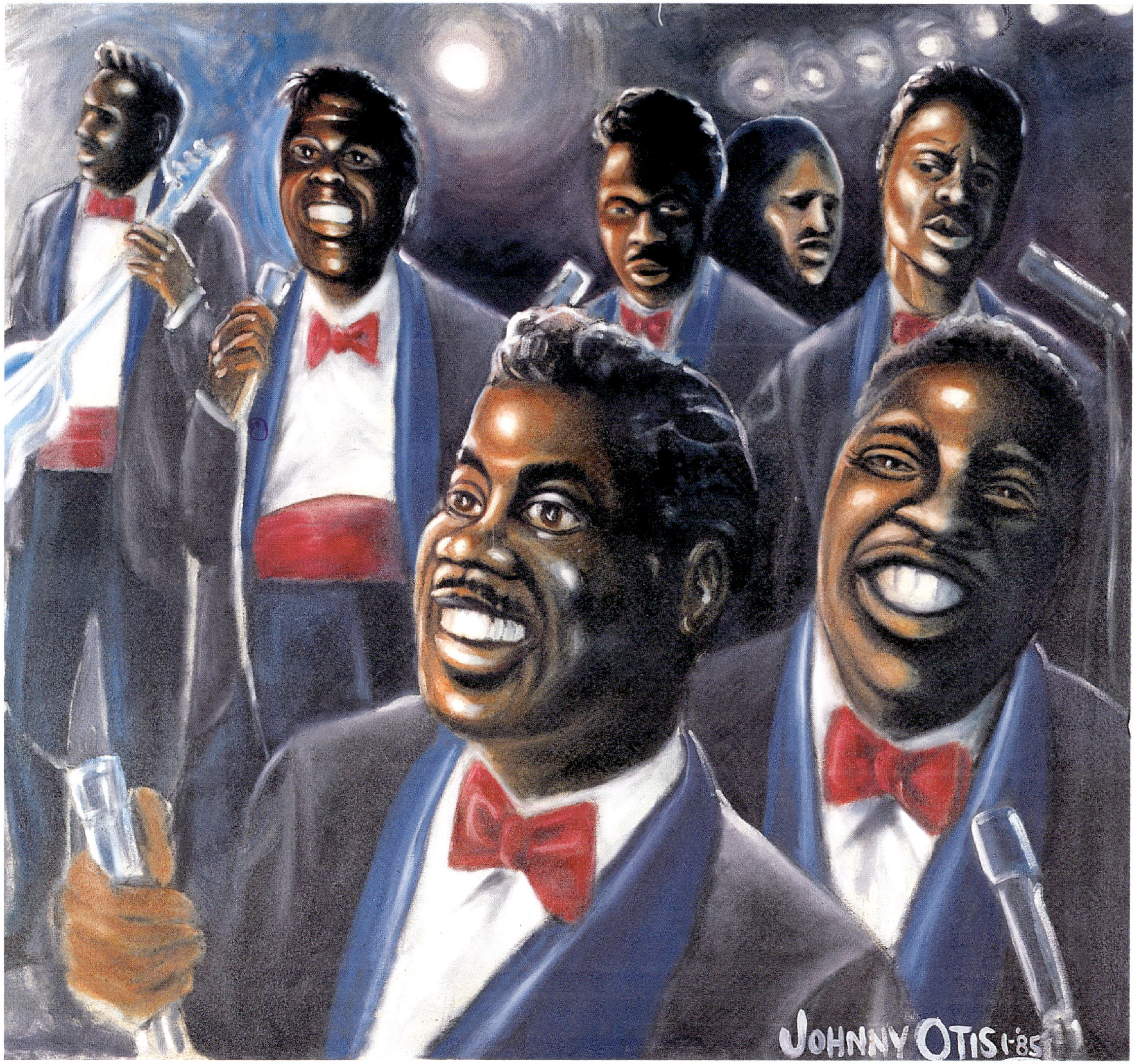

DOO WOP 1985. Oil on canvas, 36 x 40 in. Photograph by Stephan Rockwerk.

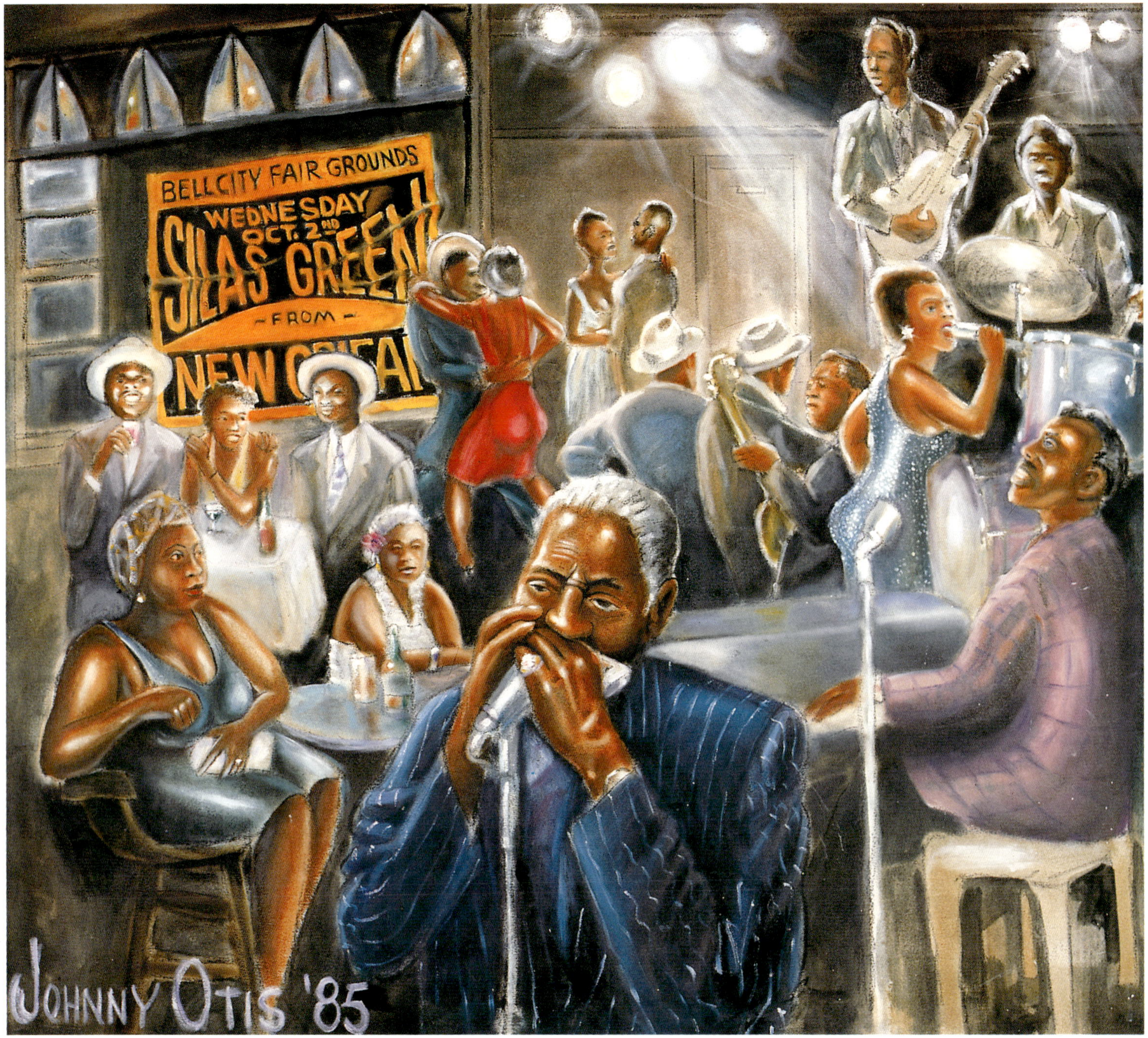

SILAS GREEN 1985. Oil on canvas, 36 x 40 in. Photograph by Stephan Rockwerk.

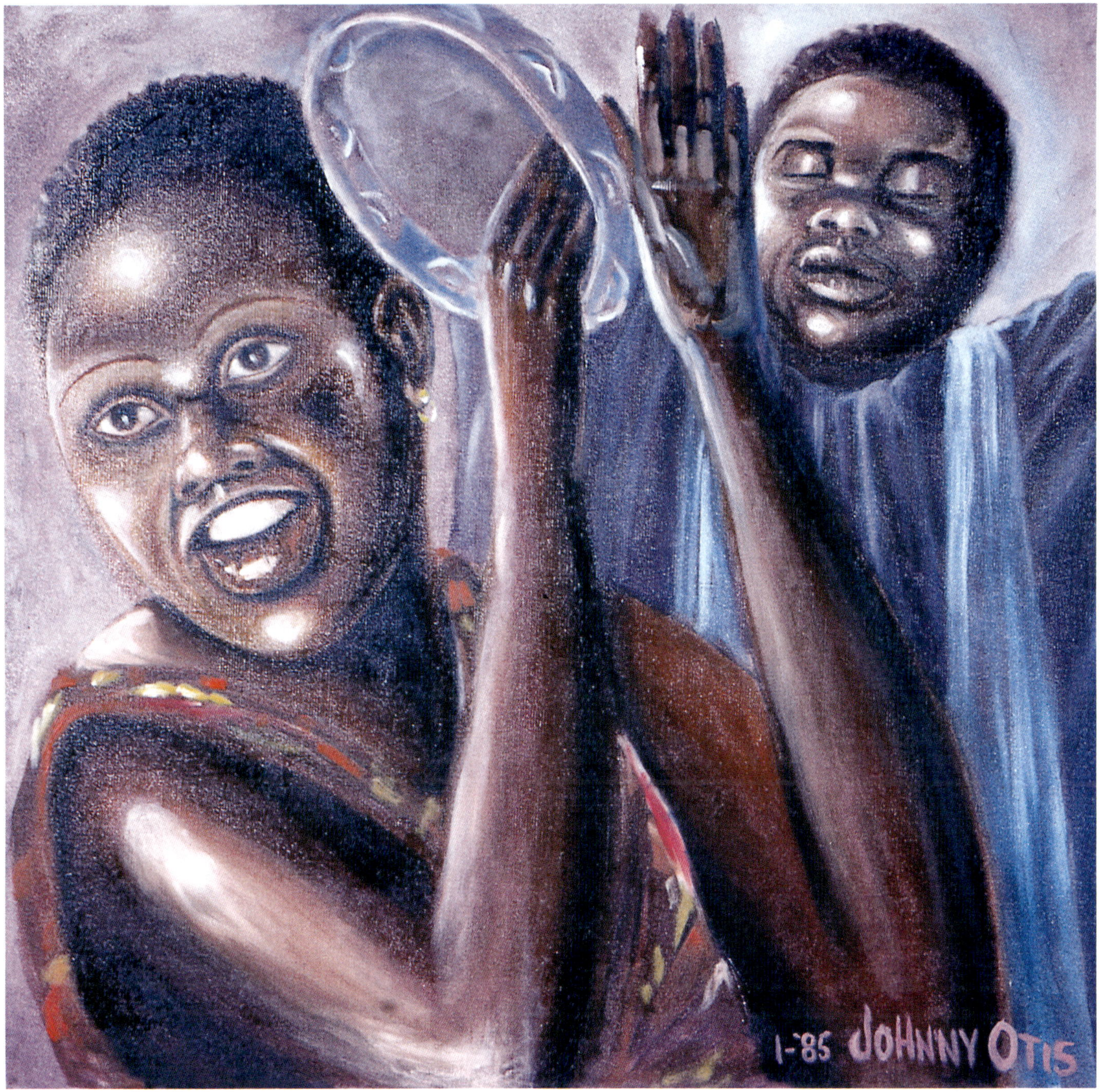

SHOUT 1985. Oil on canvas. Photograph by Stephan Rockwerk.

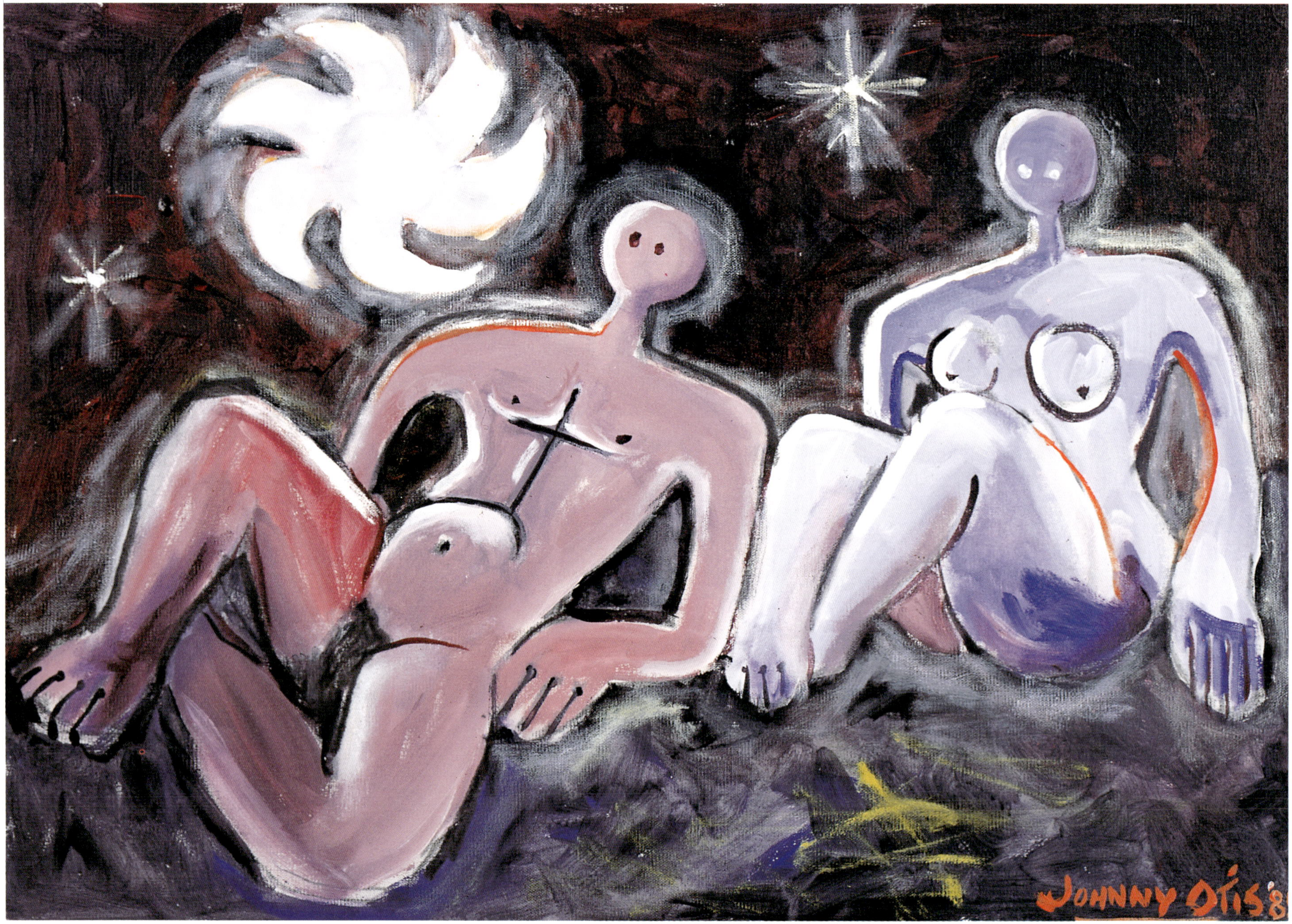

Man, Woman, and Star 1985. Acrylic on canvas, 22 x 28 in. Photograph by Stephan Rockwerk.

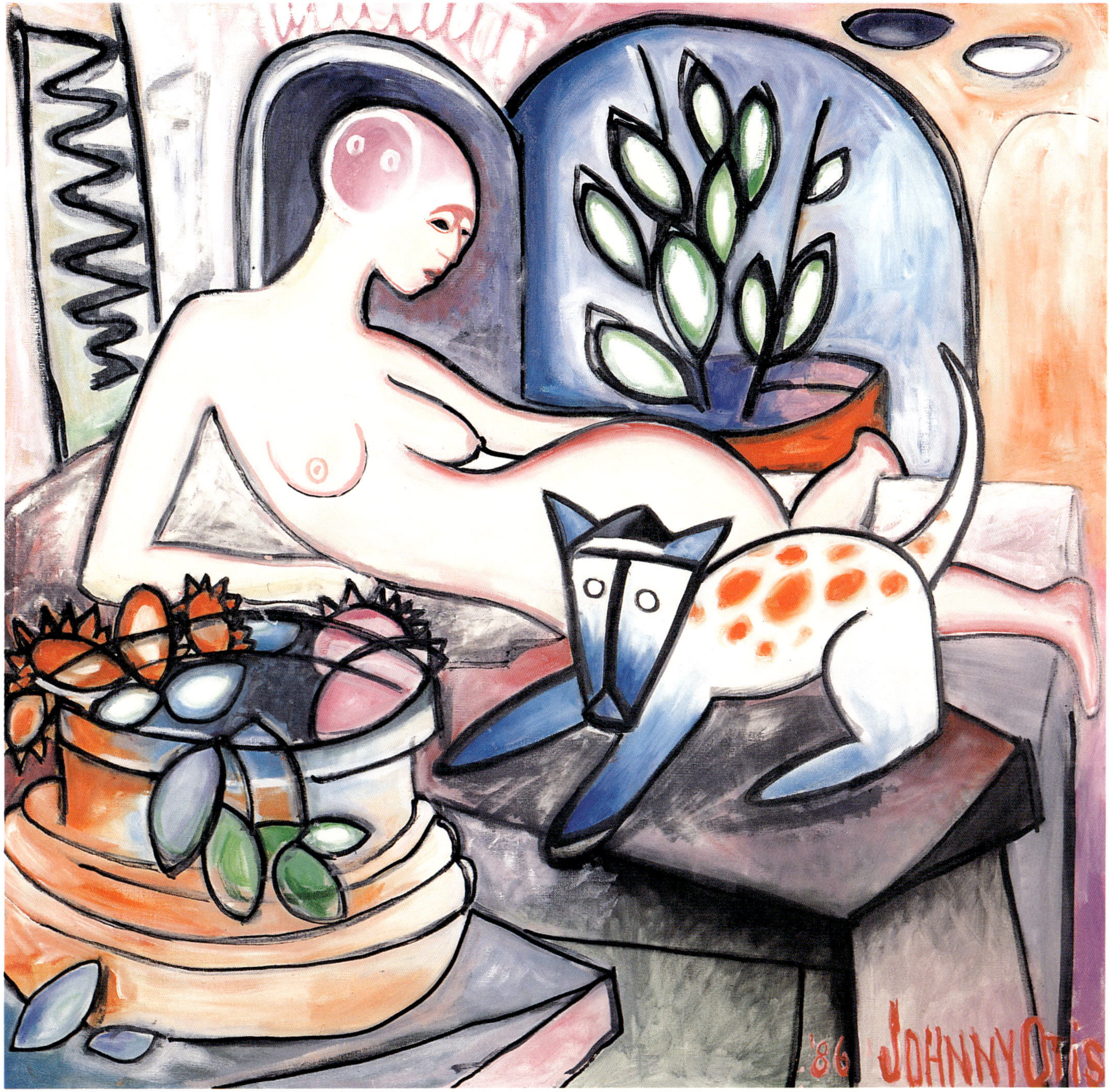

Woman with Dog 1986. Oil on canvas, 32 x 32 in. Photograph by Stephan Rockwerk.

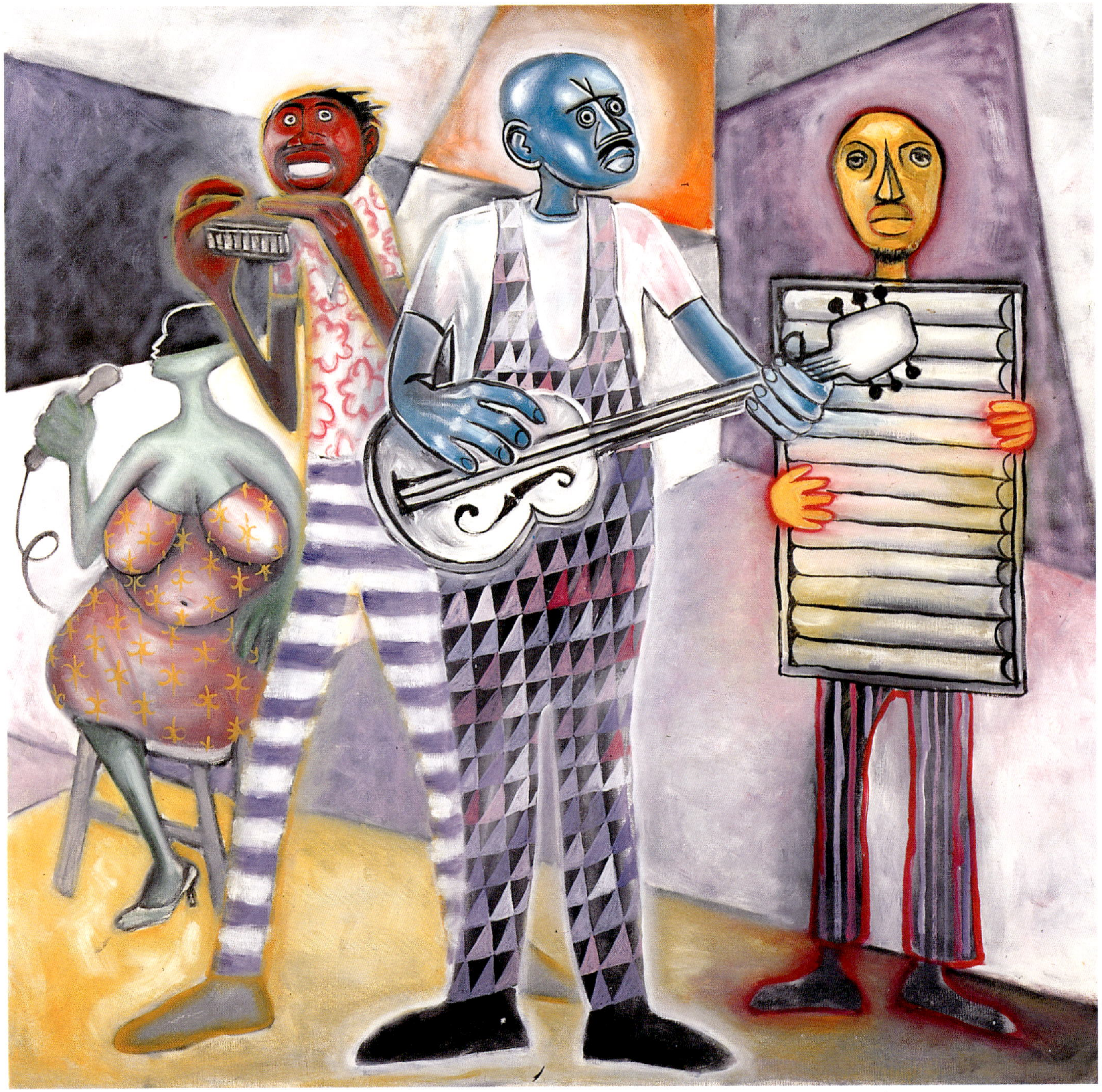

Olive and the Primaries 1986. Oil on canvas, 32 x 32 in. Photograph by Stephan Rockwerk.

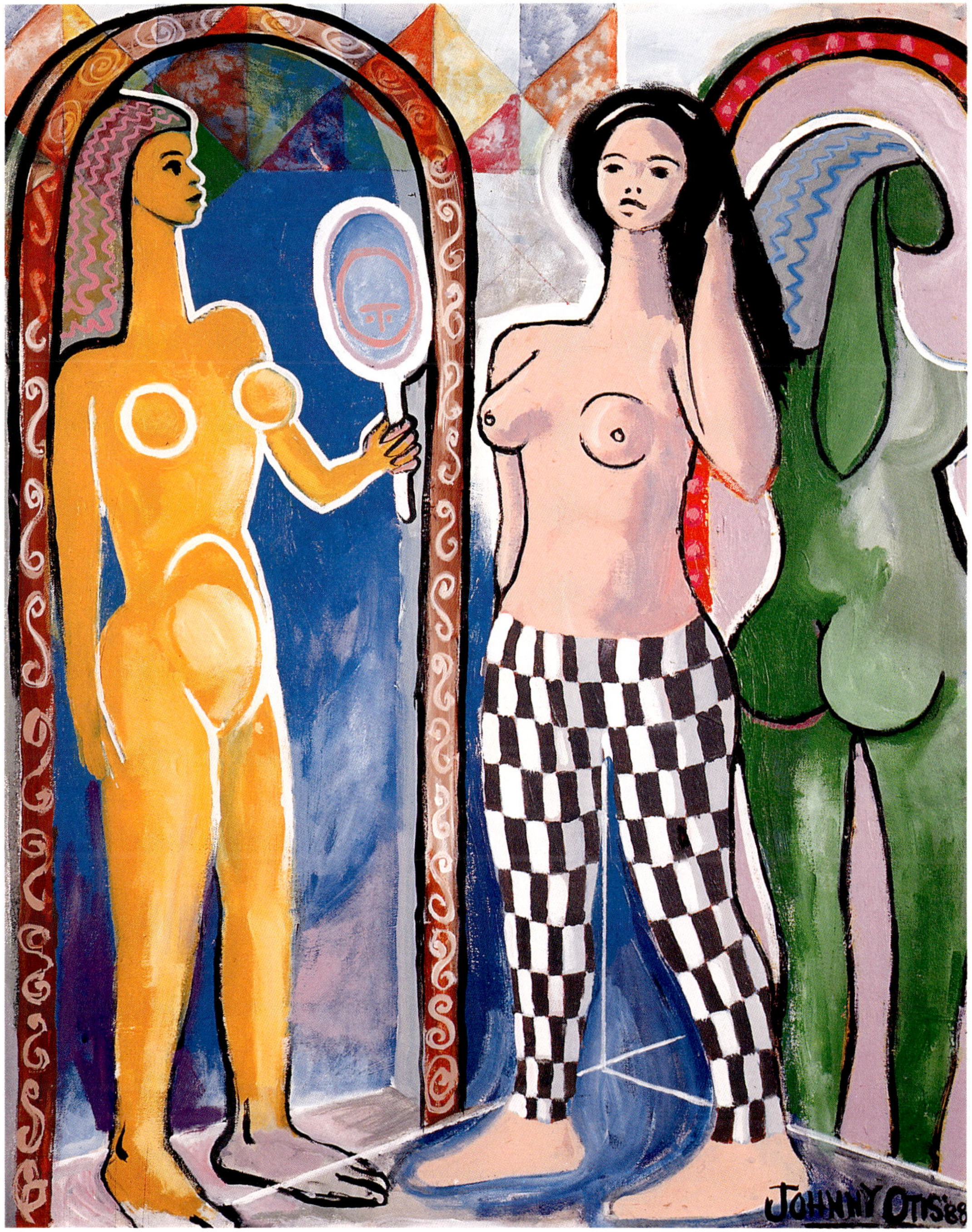

REFLECTIONS 1988. Acrylic on canvas, 22 x 28 in. Photograph by Stephan Rockwerk.

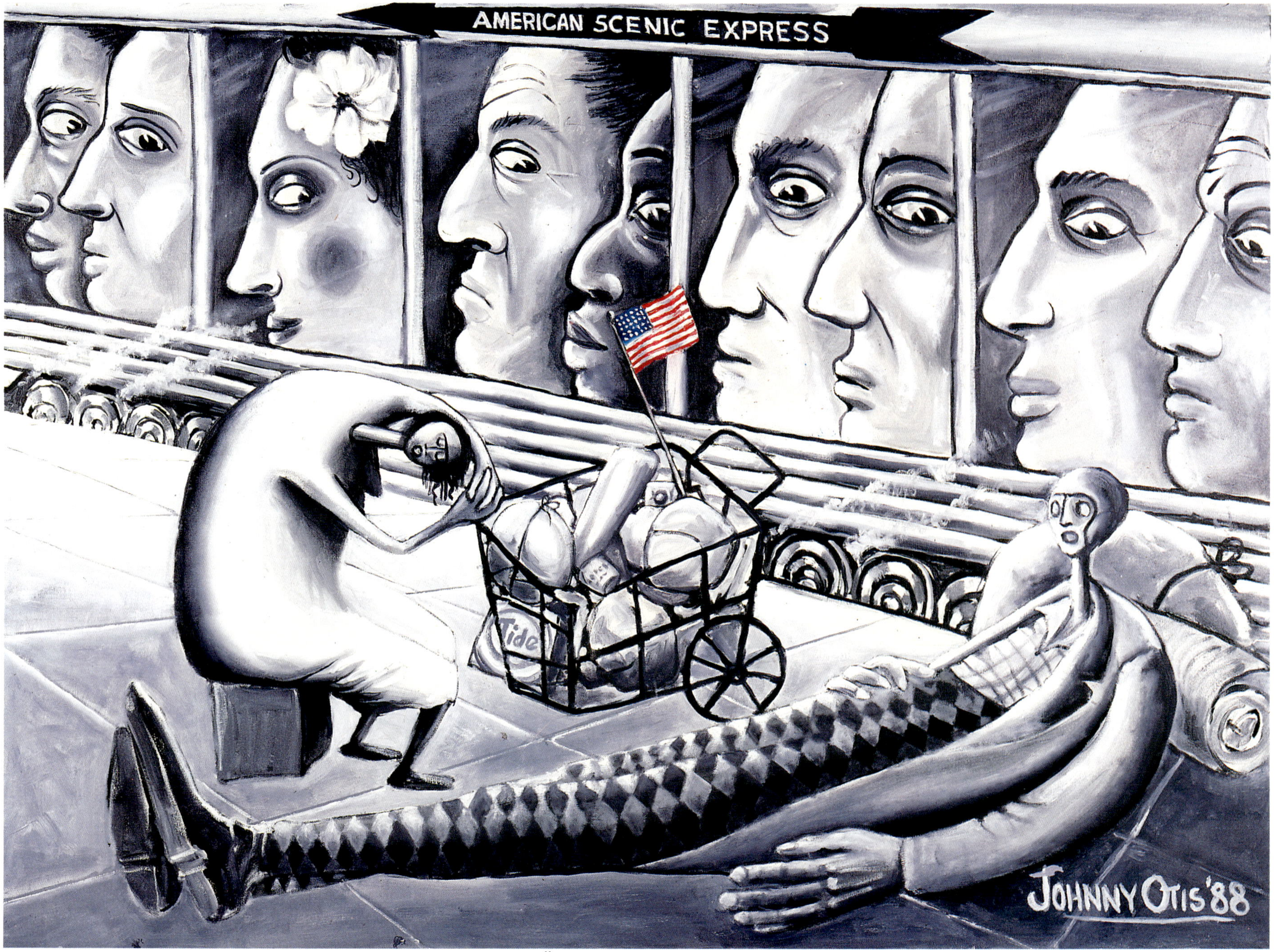

Inner City Nocturne #1 1988. Oil on canvas, 36 x 48 in. Photograph by Stephan Rockwerk.

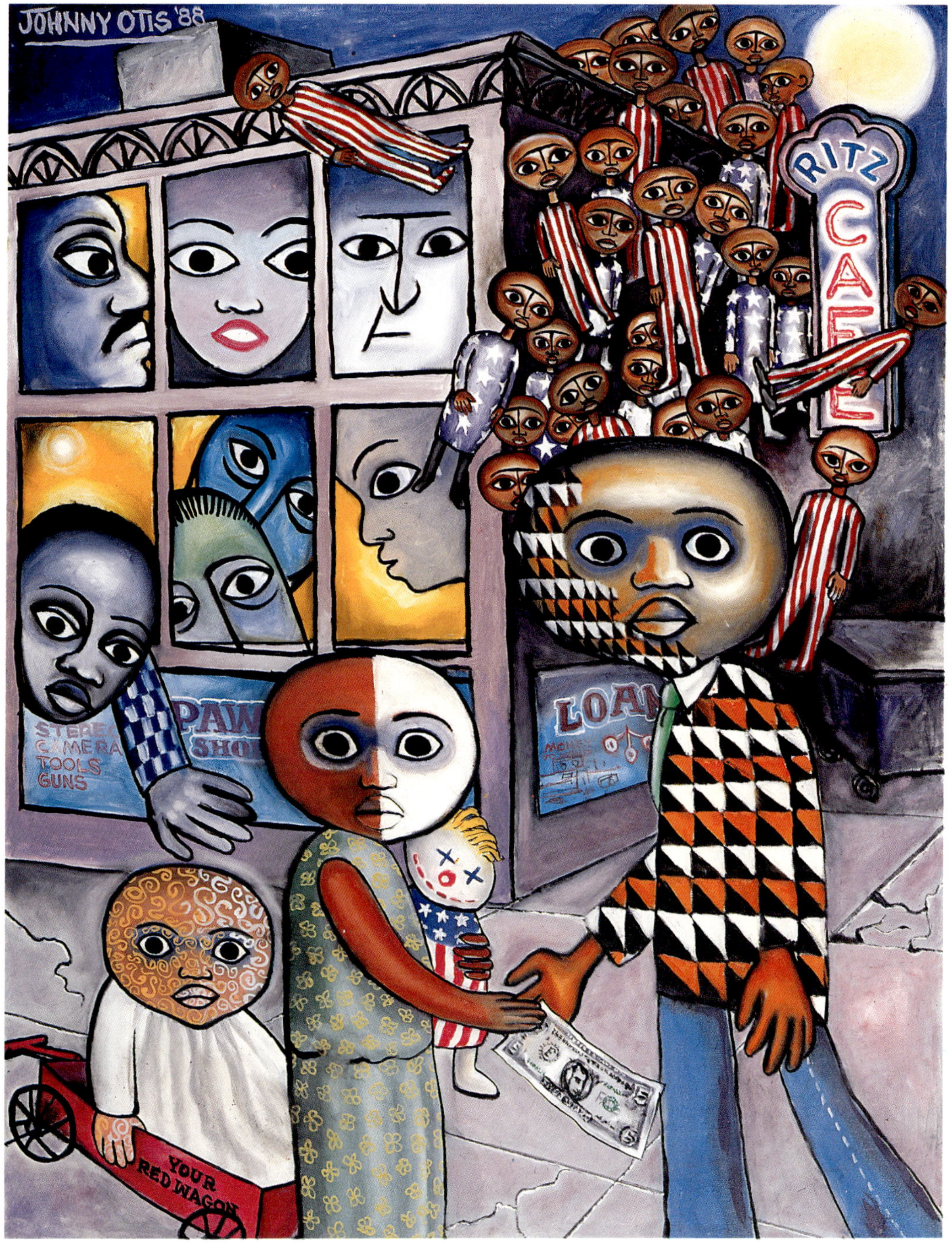

Inner City Nocturne #2 1988. Oil on canvas, 48 x 36 in. Photograph by Stephan Rockwerk.

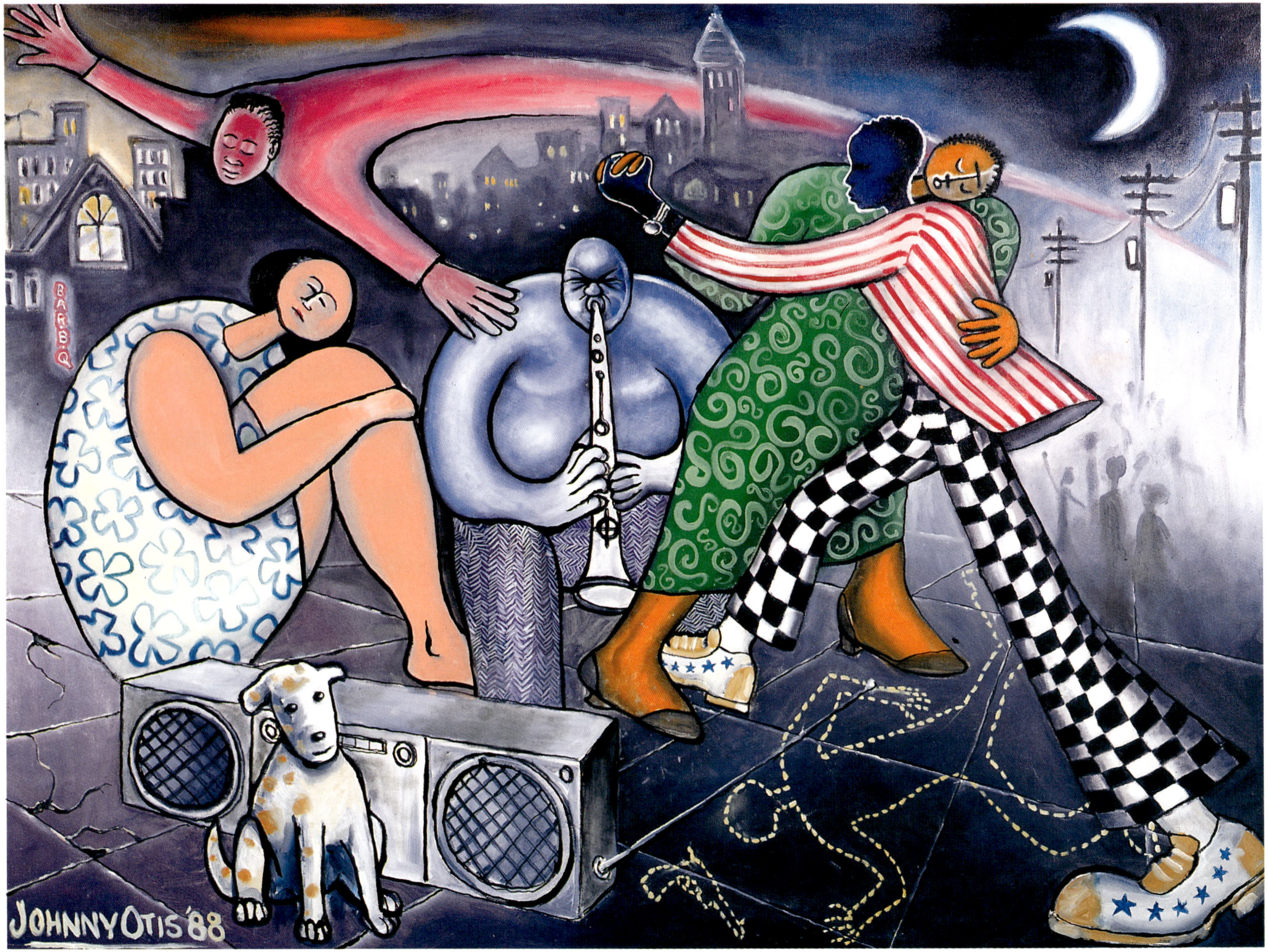

American Scenic Express 1988. Oil on canvas, 36 x 48 in.

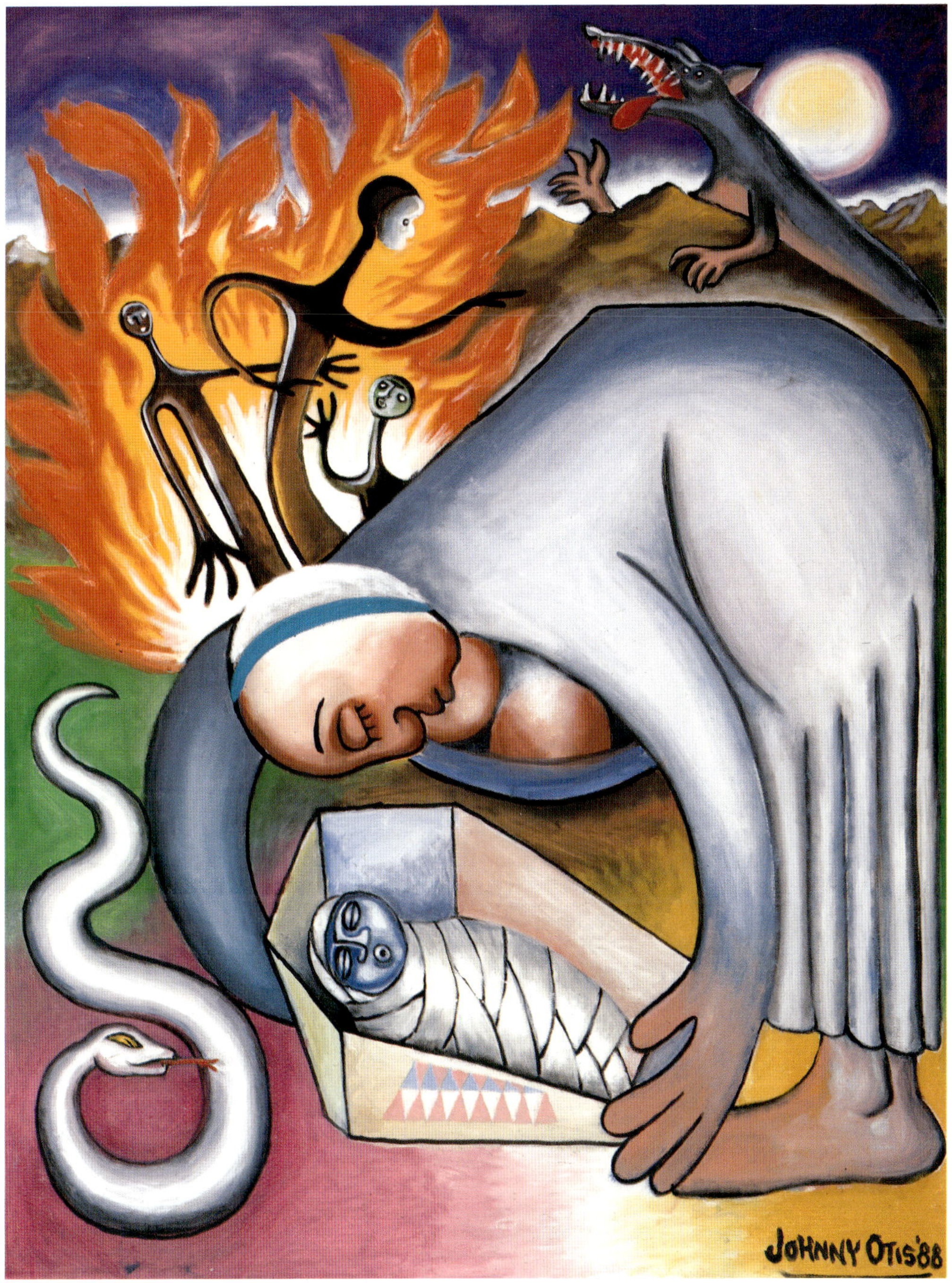

MOURNING 1988. Oil on canvas. Photograph by Stephan Rockwerk.

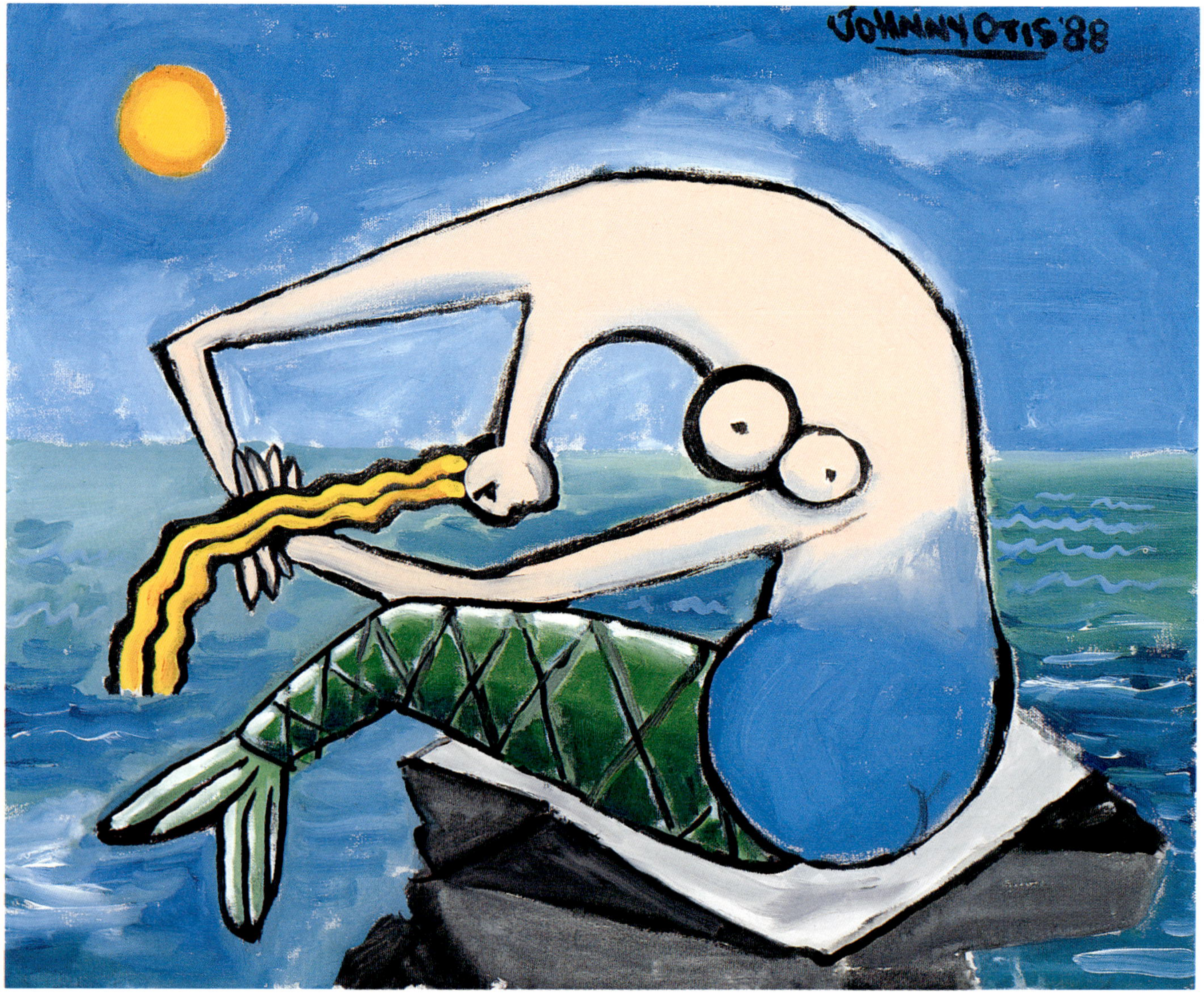

MERMAID 1988. Acrylic on canvas, 20 x 24 in. Photograph by Stephan Rockwerk.

"I'M PREOCCUPIED WITH OWLS and mermaids. I don't know why. I've watched owls swoop down on rodents that don't even know they're there. The owls have silent wings, not like hawks. People who live on islands and coasts have all sorts of legends about sea creatures. My family is from Greece, so I heard all that stuff when I was a kid. You can't see a mermaid unless you are in trouble."

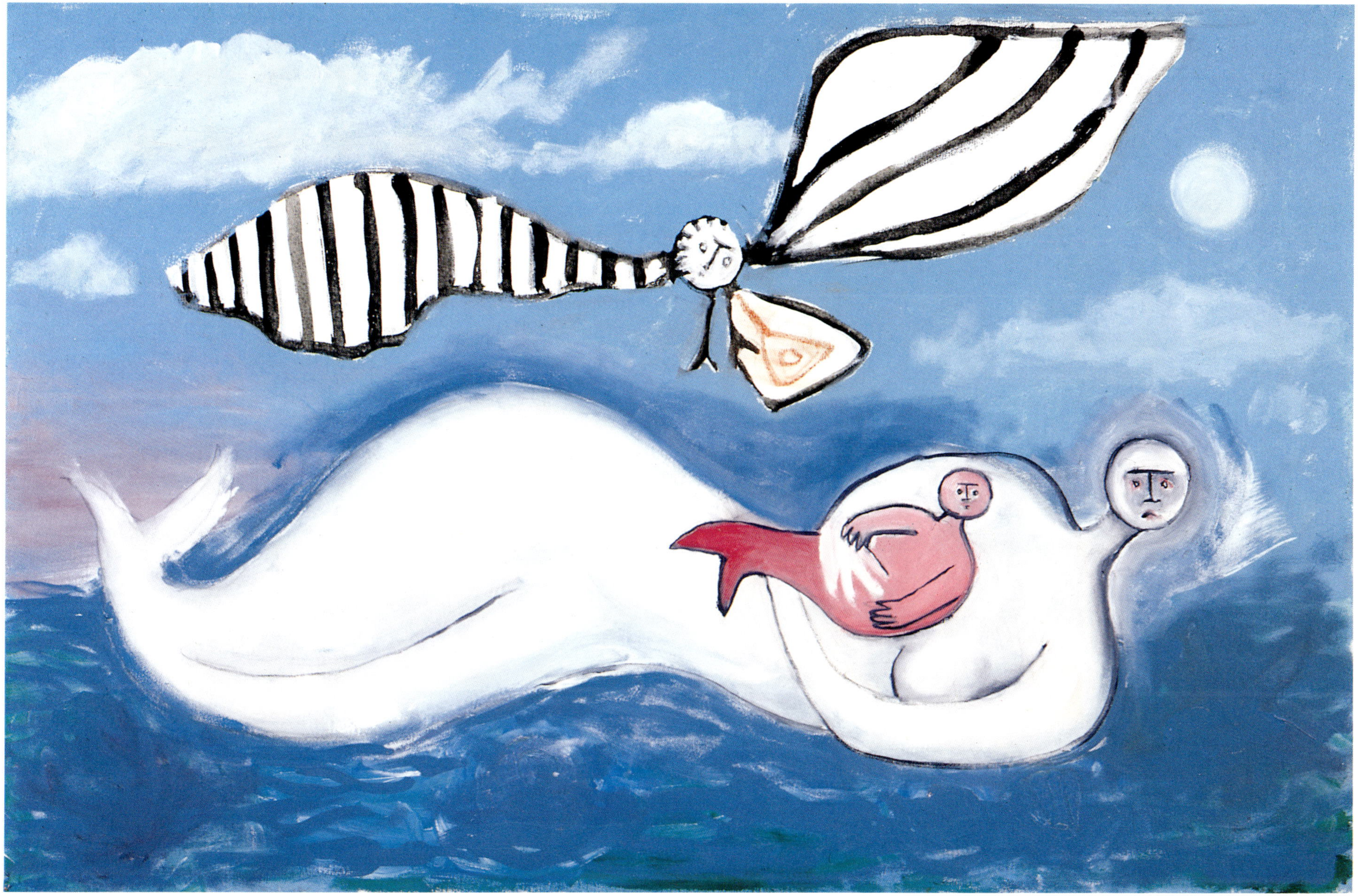

MERMAID, BABY, AND OWL 1988. Acrylic on canvas, 24 x 36 in. Photograph by Stephan Rockwerk.

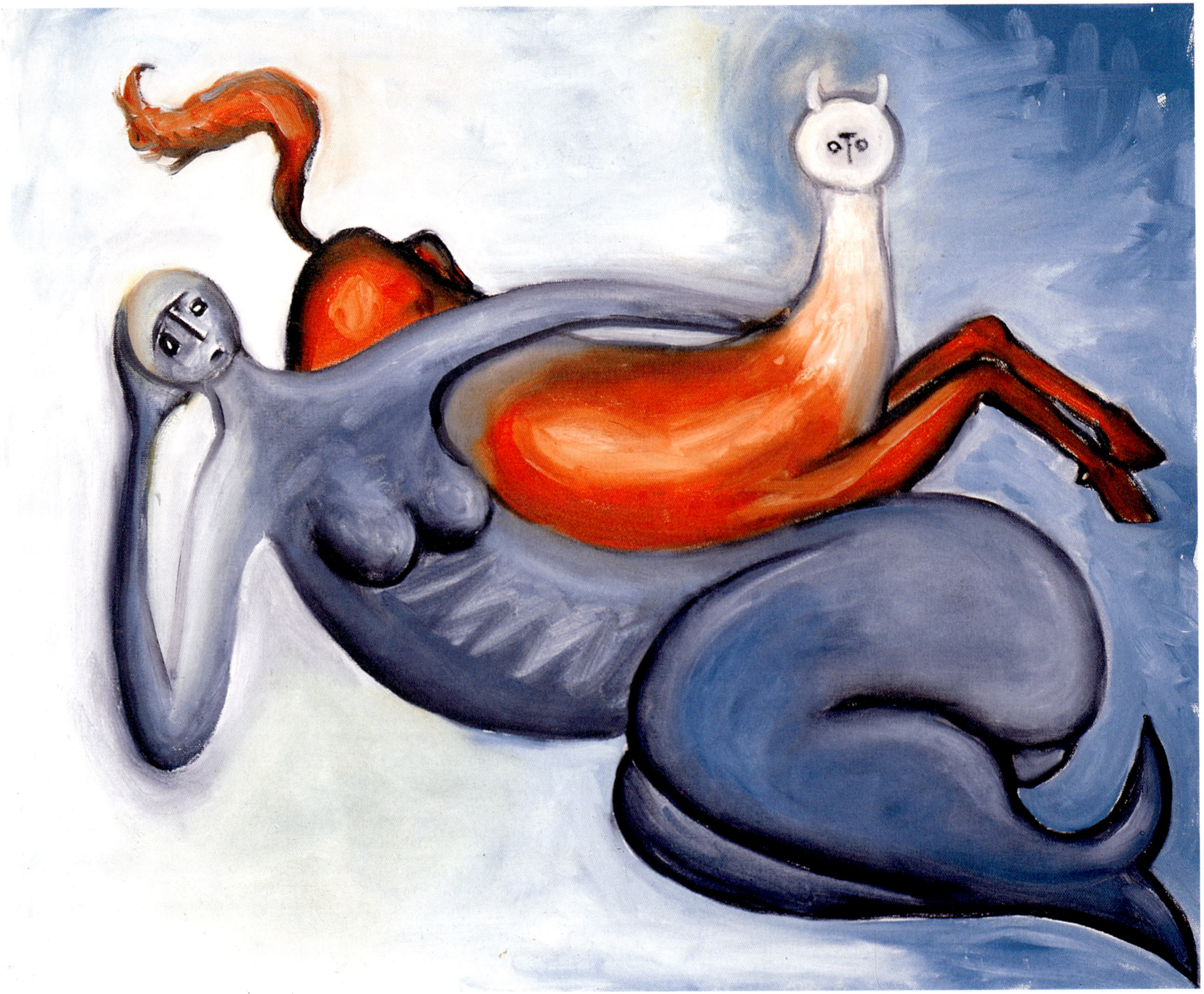

Mermaid and Horned Beast 1988. Acrylic on canvas. Photograph by Stephan Rockwerk.

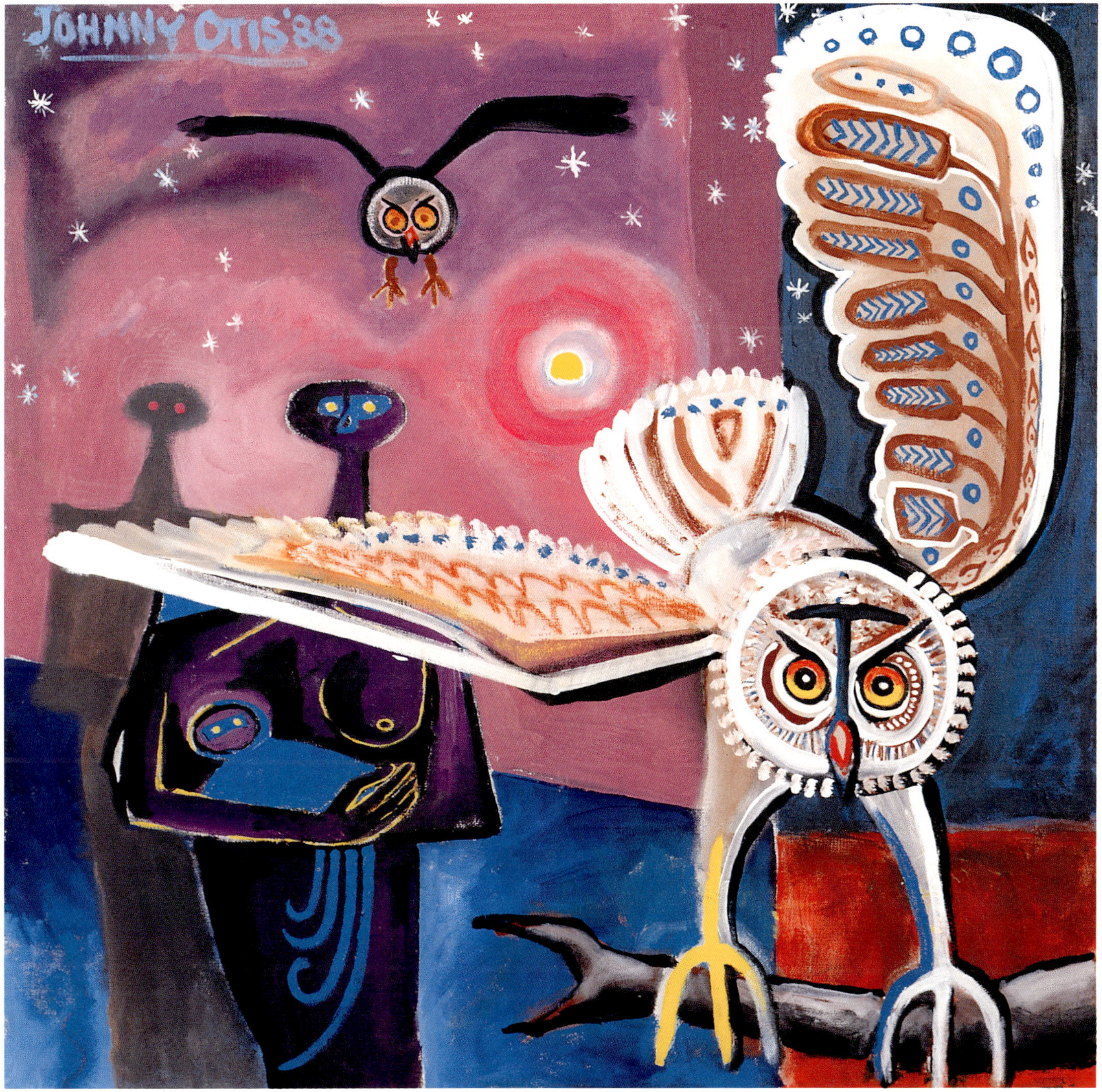

Night Owl 1988. Acrylic on canvas, 24 x 24 in. Photograph by Stephan Rockwerk.

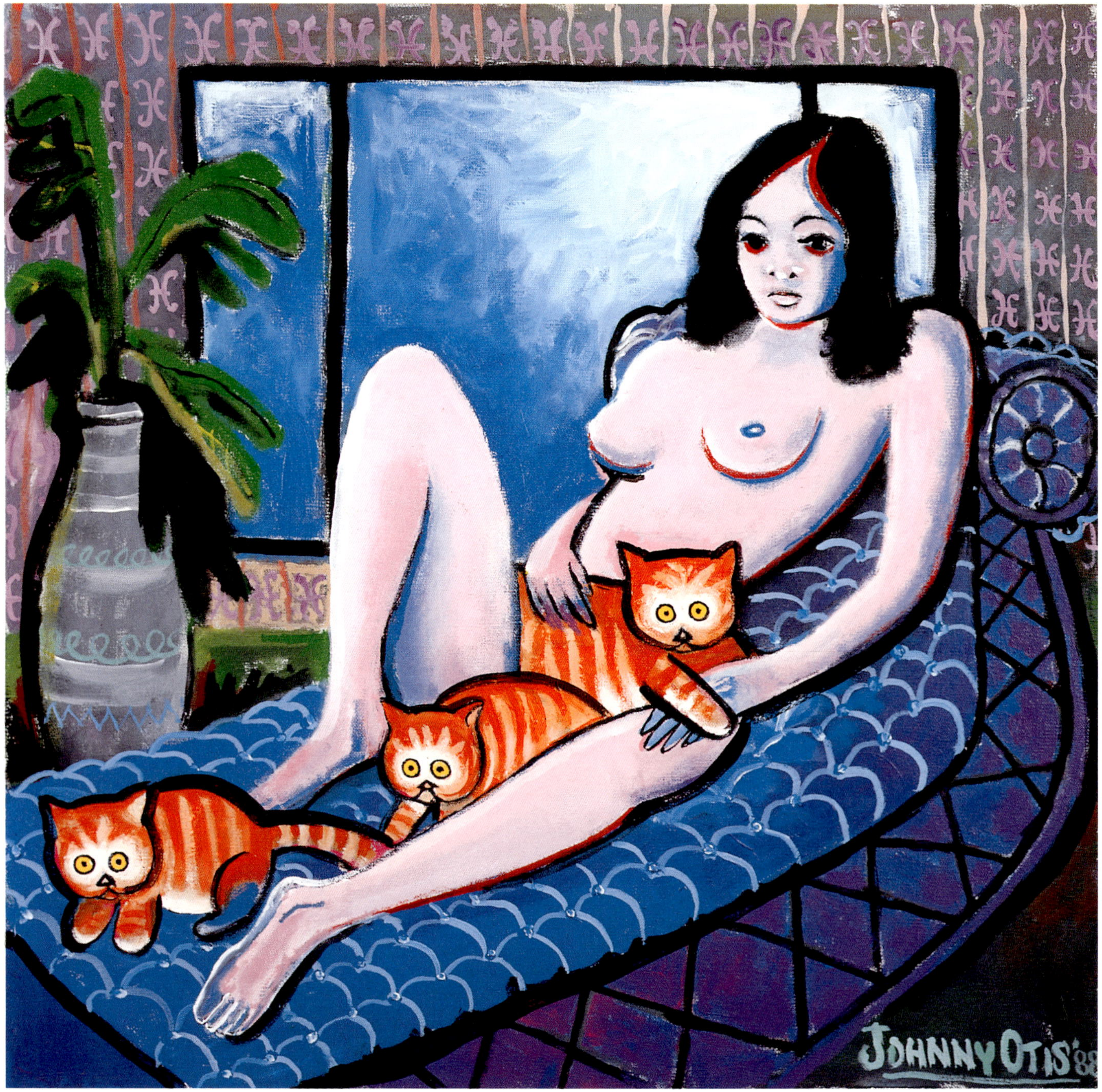

Kittens 1988. Acrylic on canvas, 24 x 24 in. Photograph by Stephan Rockwerk.

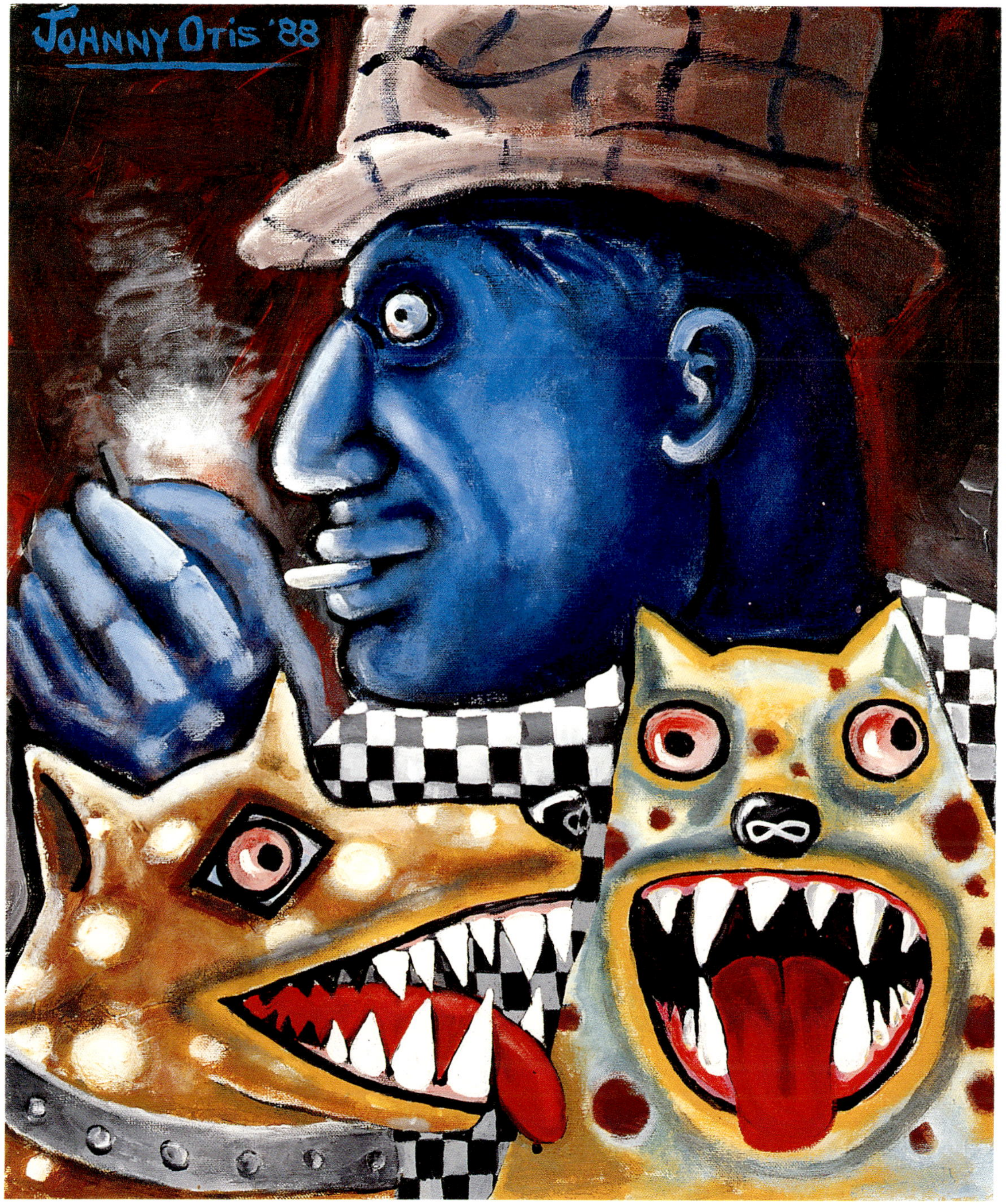

MR. CHARLIE'S DOGS 1988. Acrylic on canvas, 24 x 20 in. Photograph by Stephan Rockwerk.

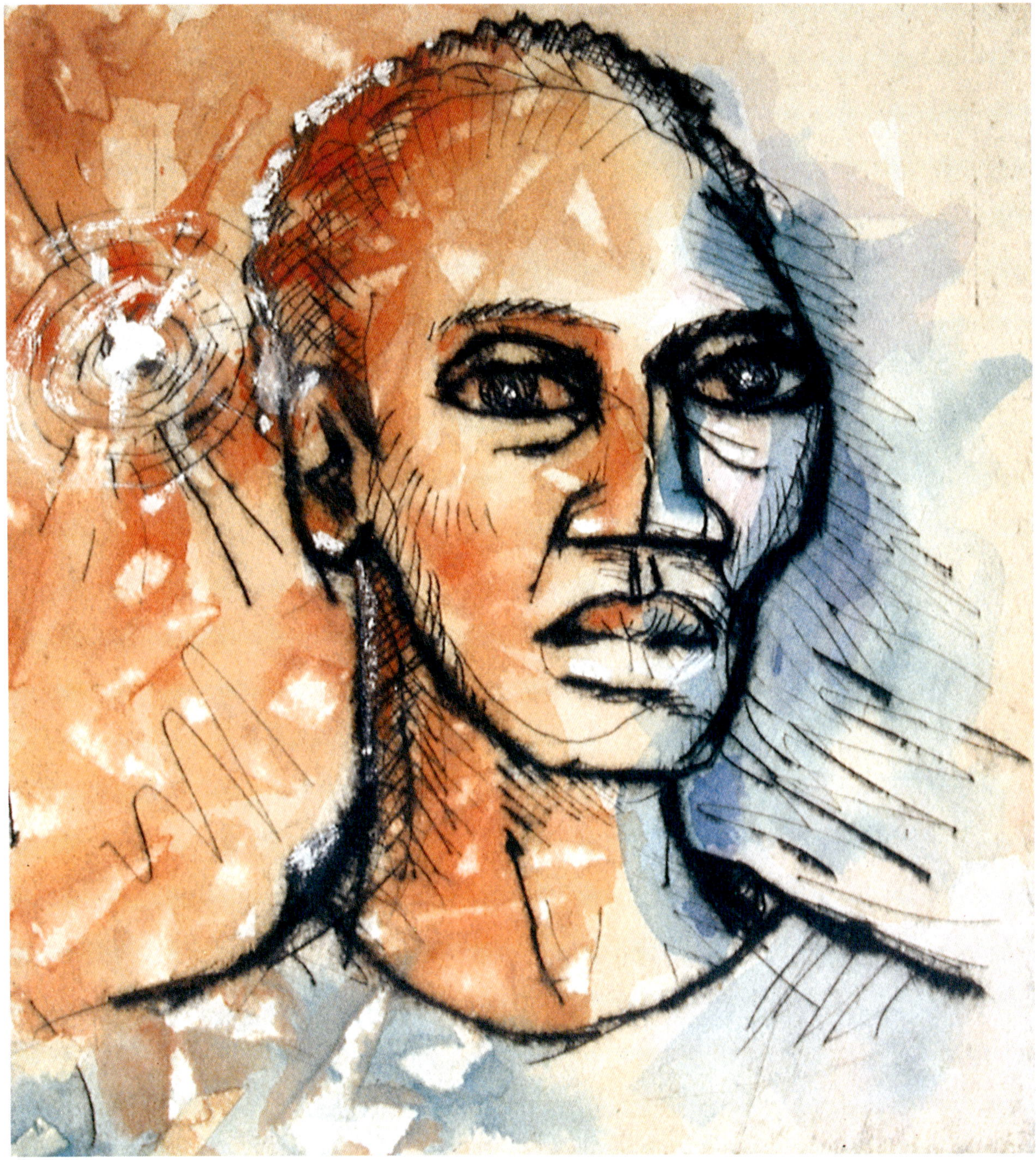

PORTRAIT (MAN'S HEAD) 1988. Hand-painted drypoint. Photograph by Johnny Otis.

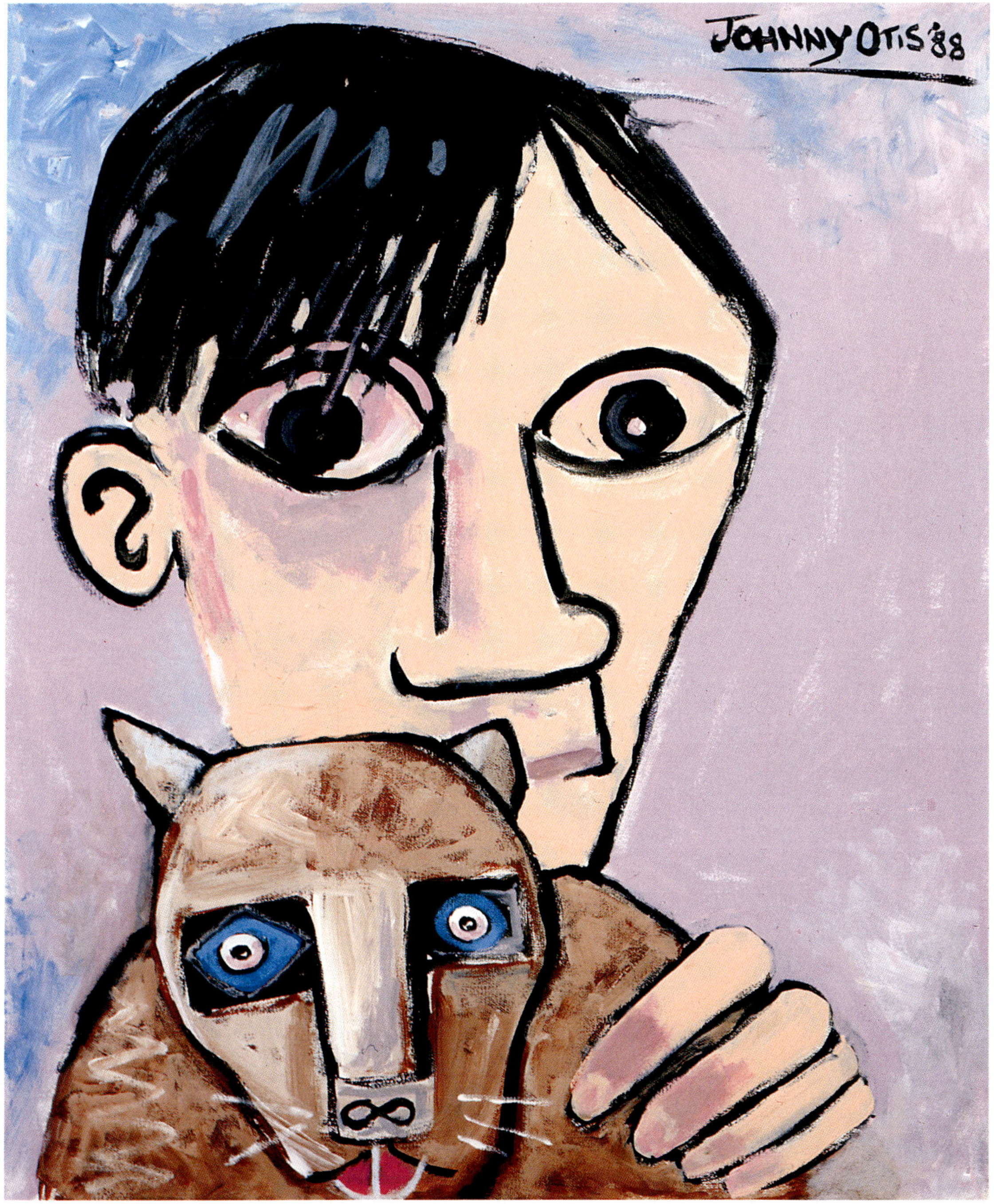

Young Picasso with Dog 1988. Acrylic on canvas, 24 x 20 in. Photograph by Stephan Rockwerk.

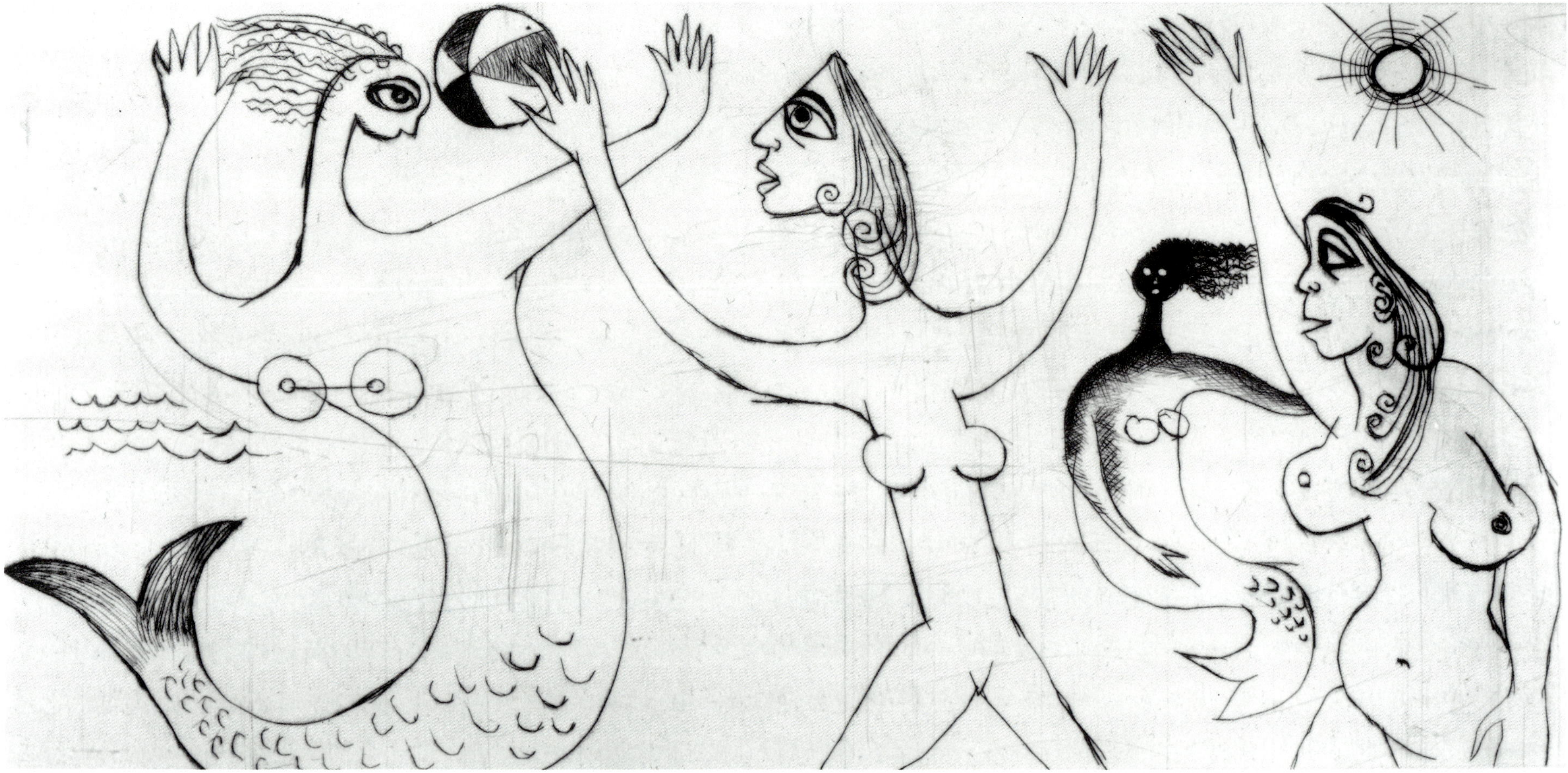

Sirens and Mermaids 1988. Drypoint.

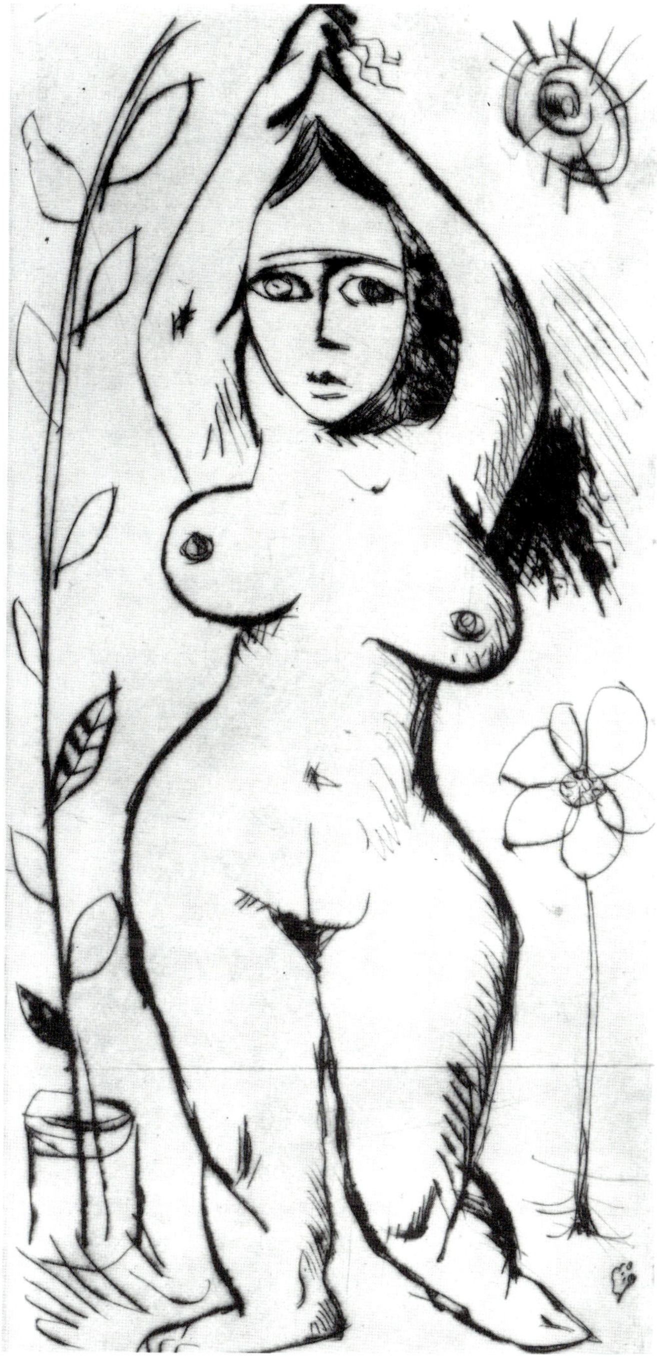

Sunflower Girl 1988. Drypoint.

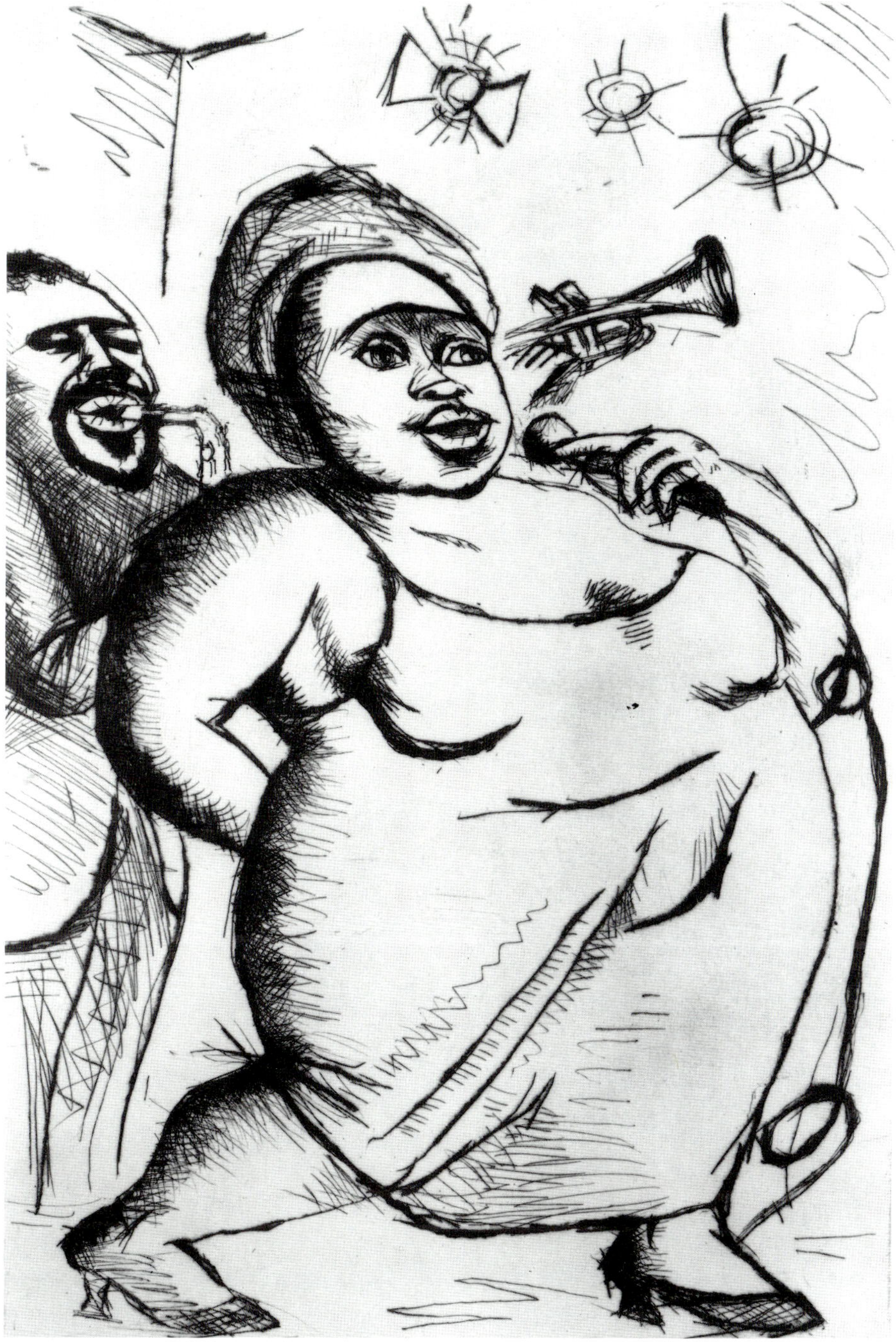

Big Mama 1988. Drypoint.

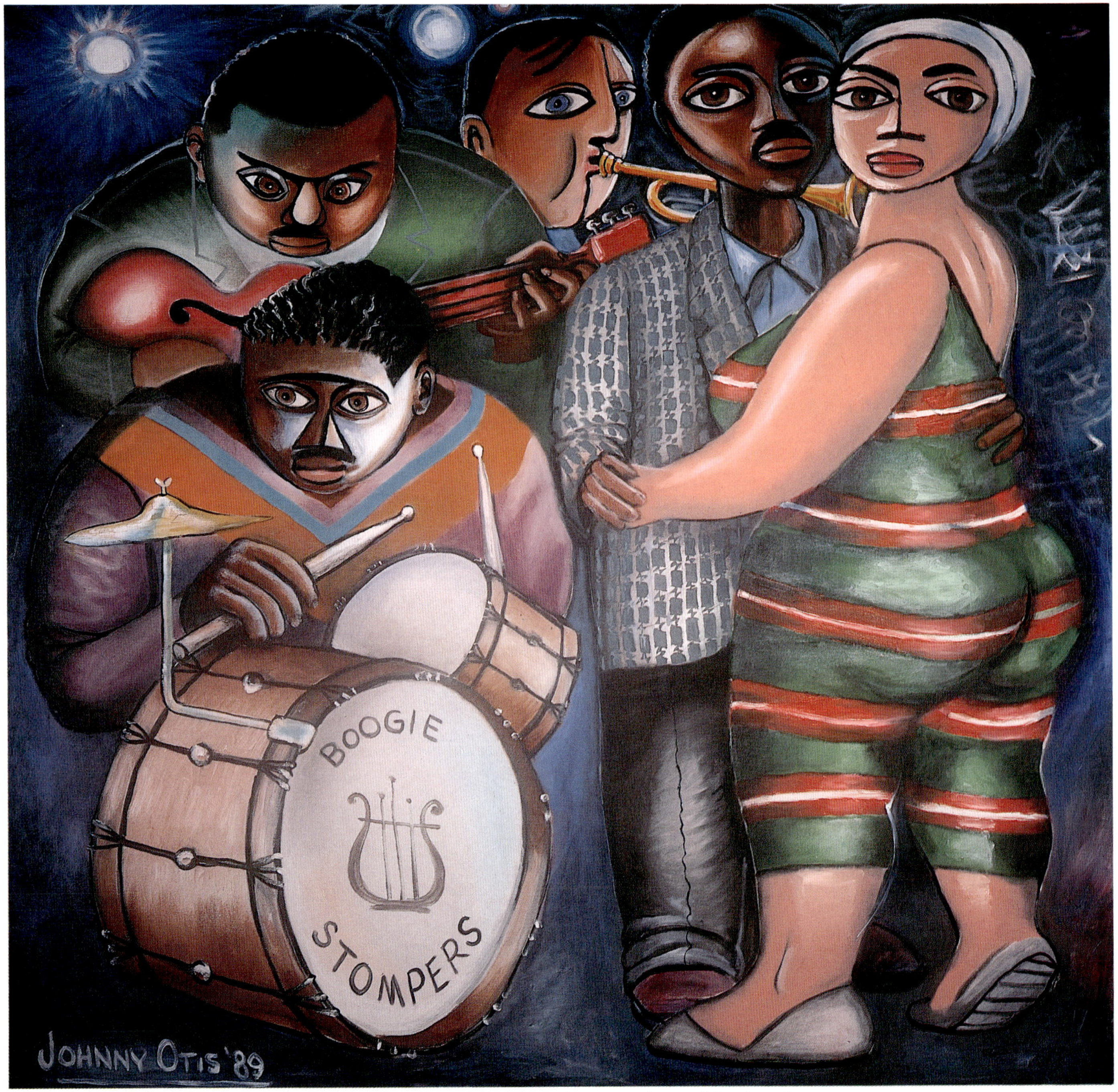

Boogie Stompers 1988. Oil on canvas. Photograph by Johnny Otis.

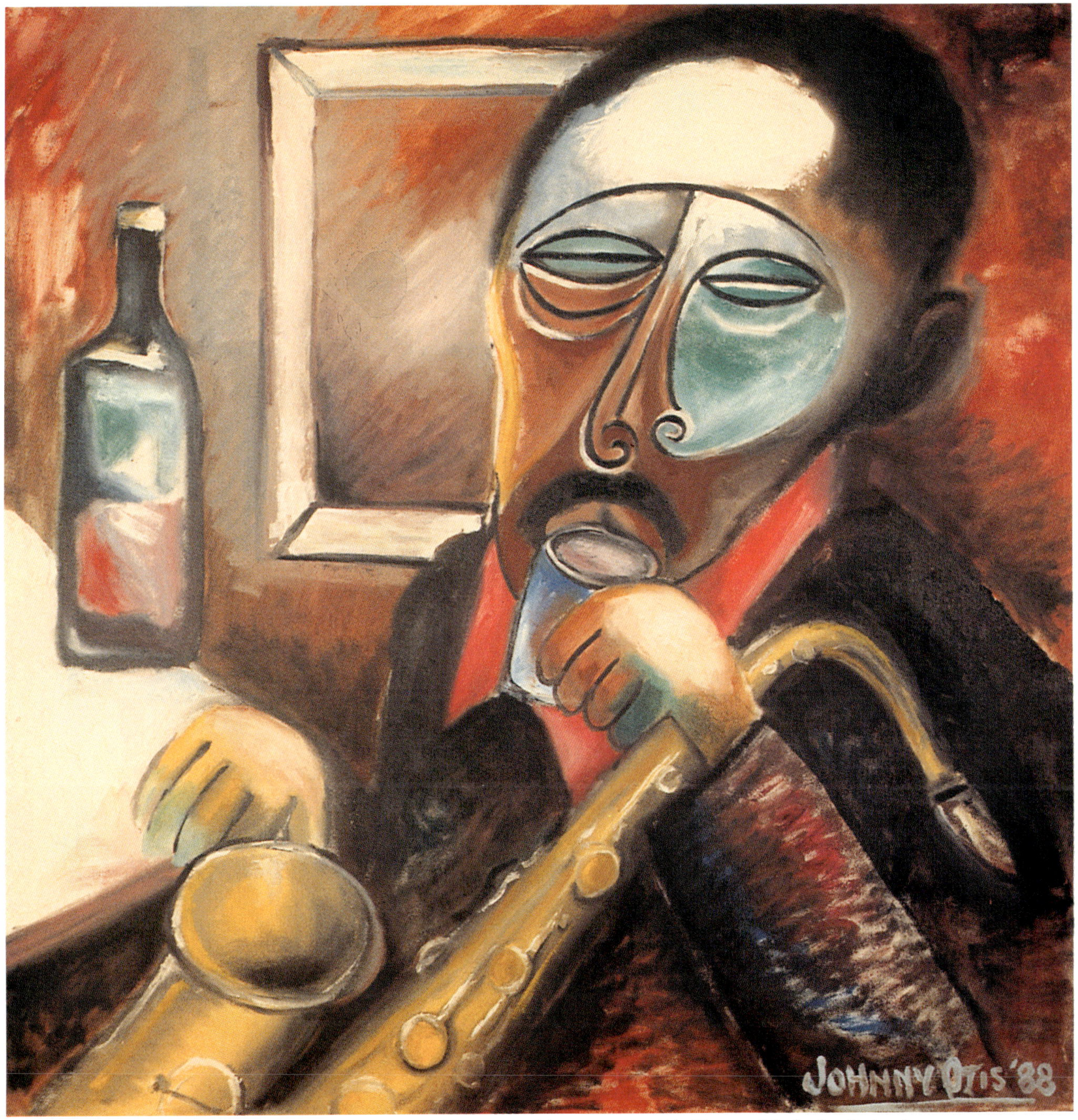

Drinkin' Wine Spo-Tee-O-Tee 1988. Oil on canvas, 30 x 30 in. Photograph by Stephan Rockwerk.

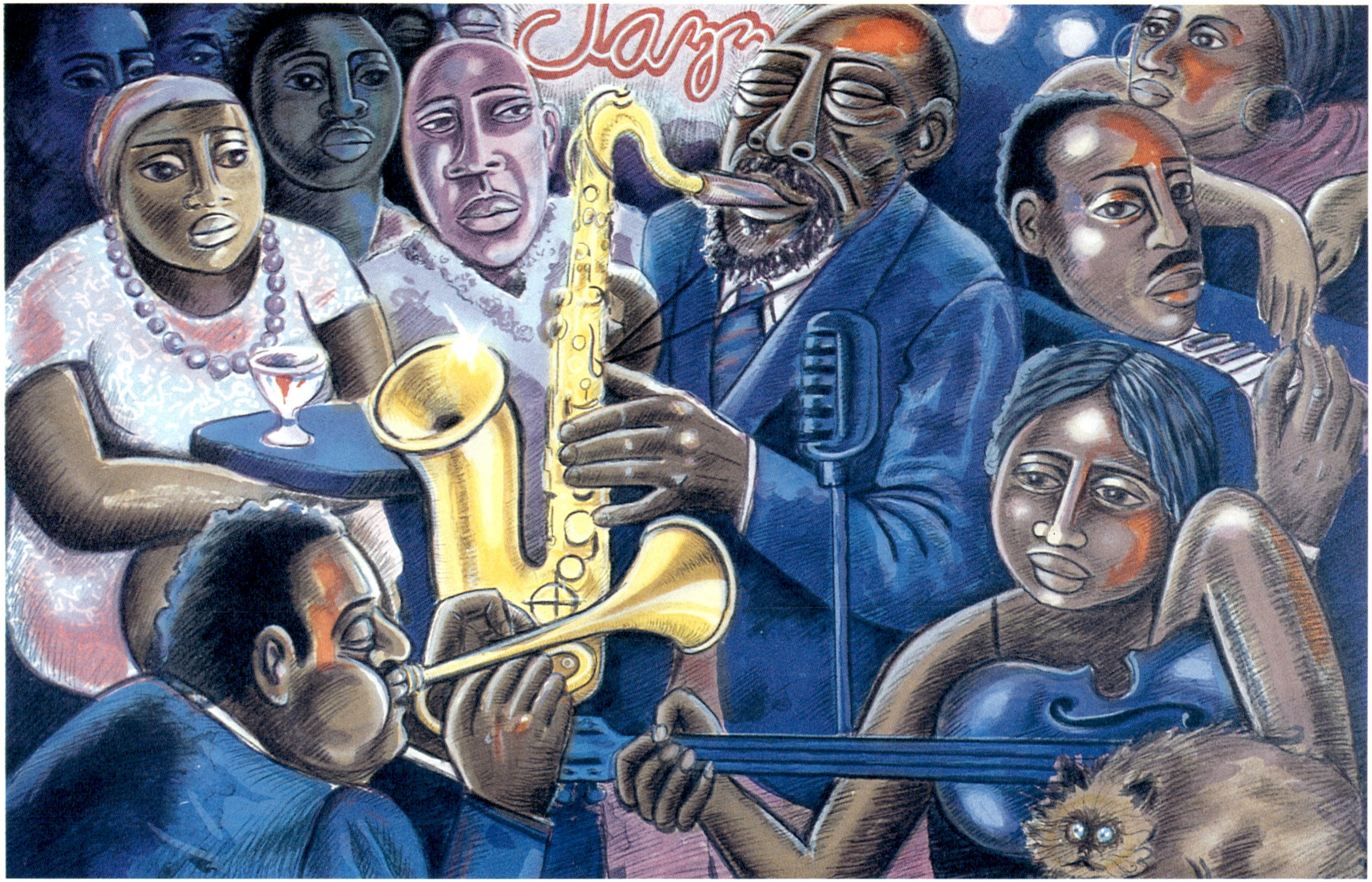

JAZZ 1988. Lithograph, 23½ x 35½ in. Photograph by Donald Farnsworth.

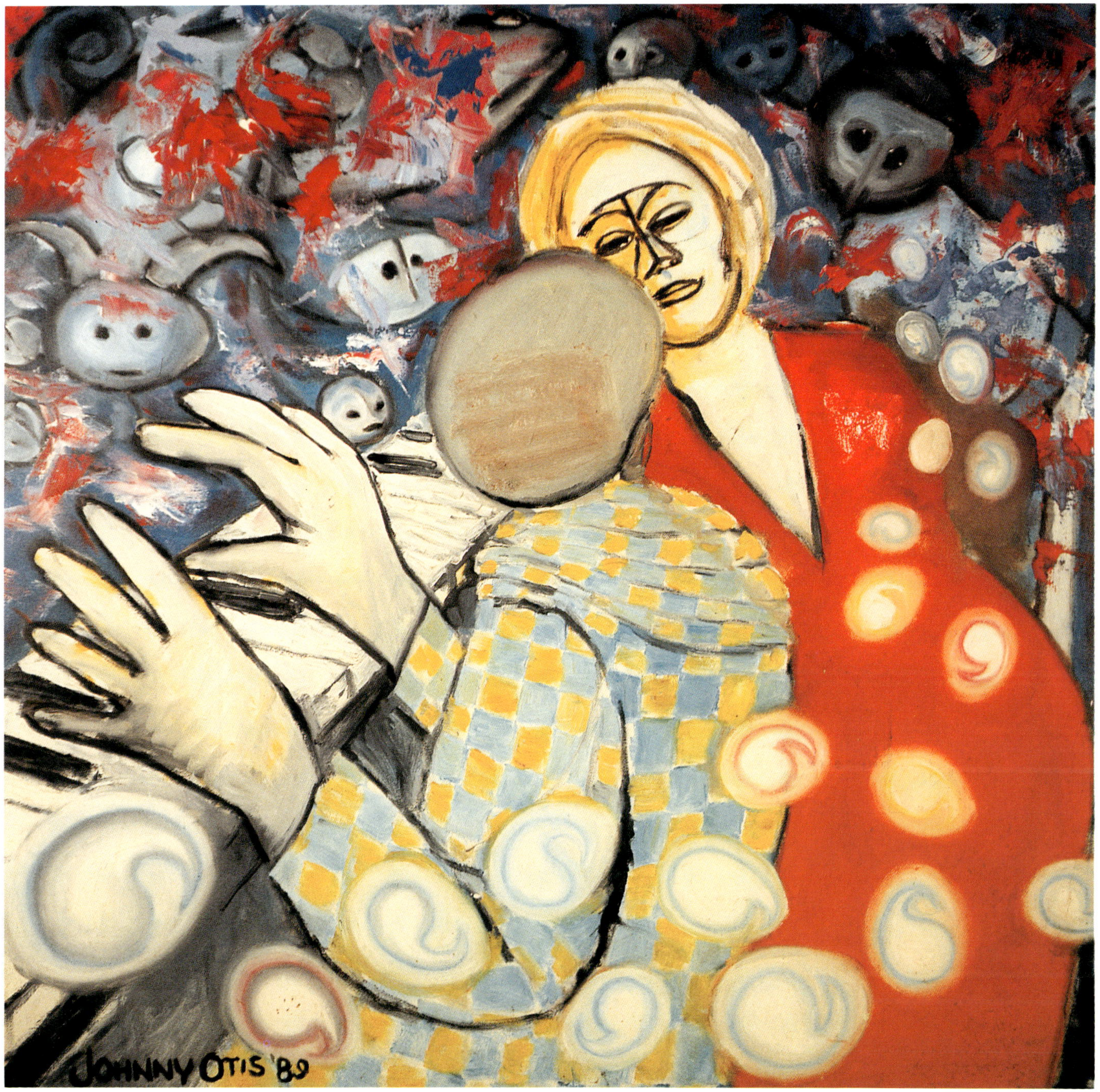

PIANO MAN AND WOMAN 1989. Oil on canvas, 30 x 30 in. Photograph by Johnny Otis.

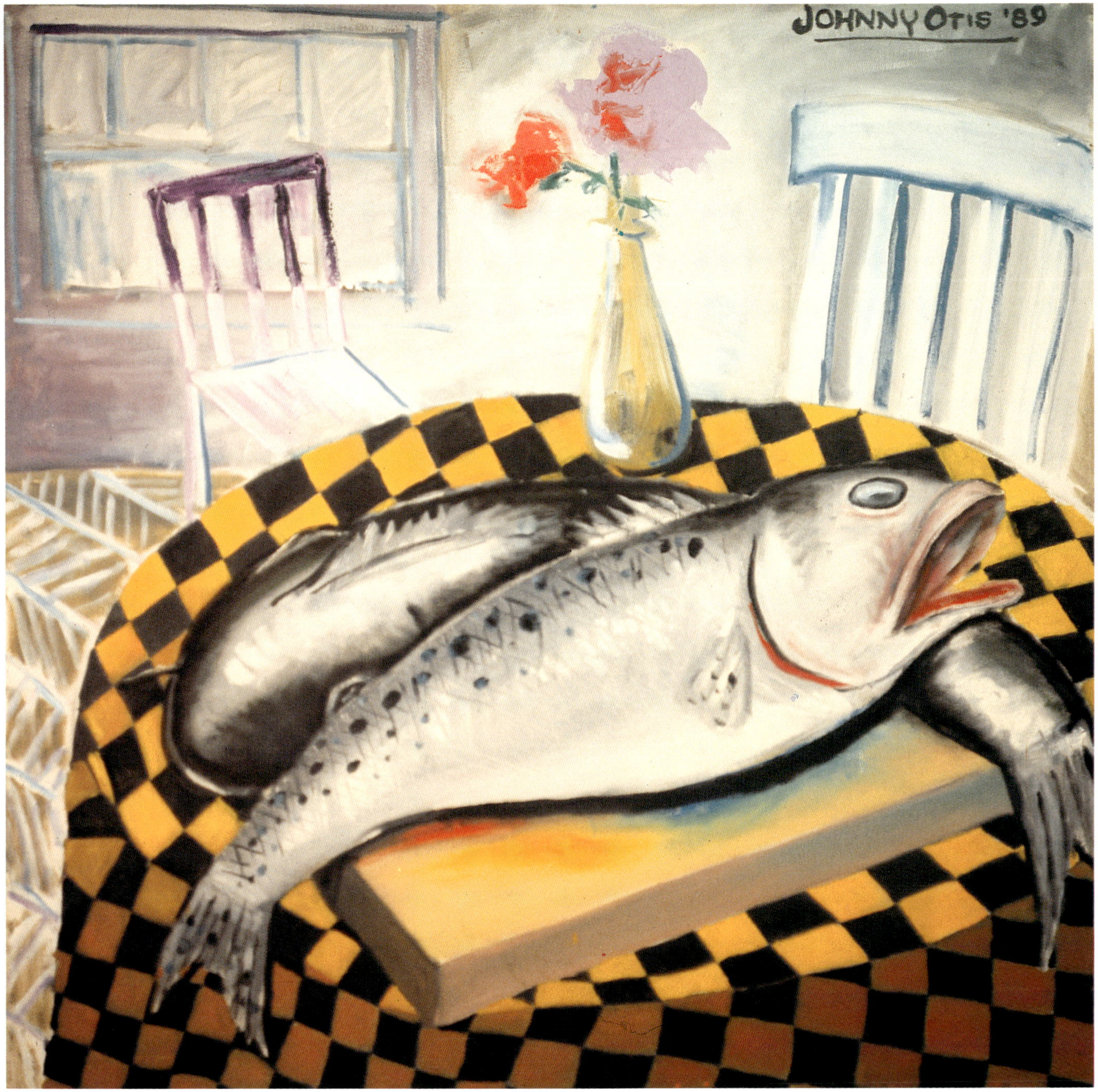

FISH AND FLOWERS 1989. Oil on canvas, 36 x 36 in. Photograph by Johnny Otis.

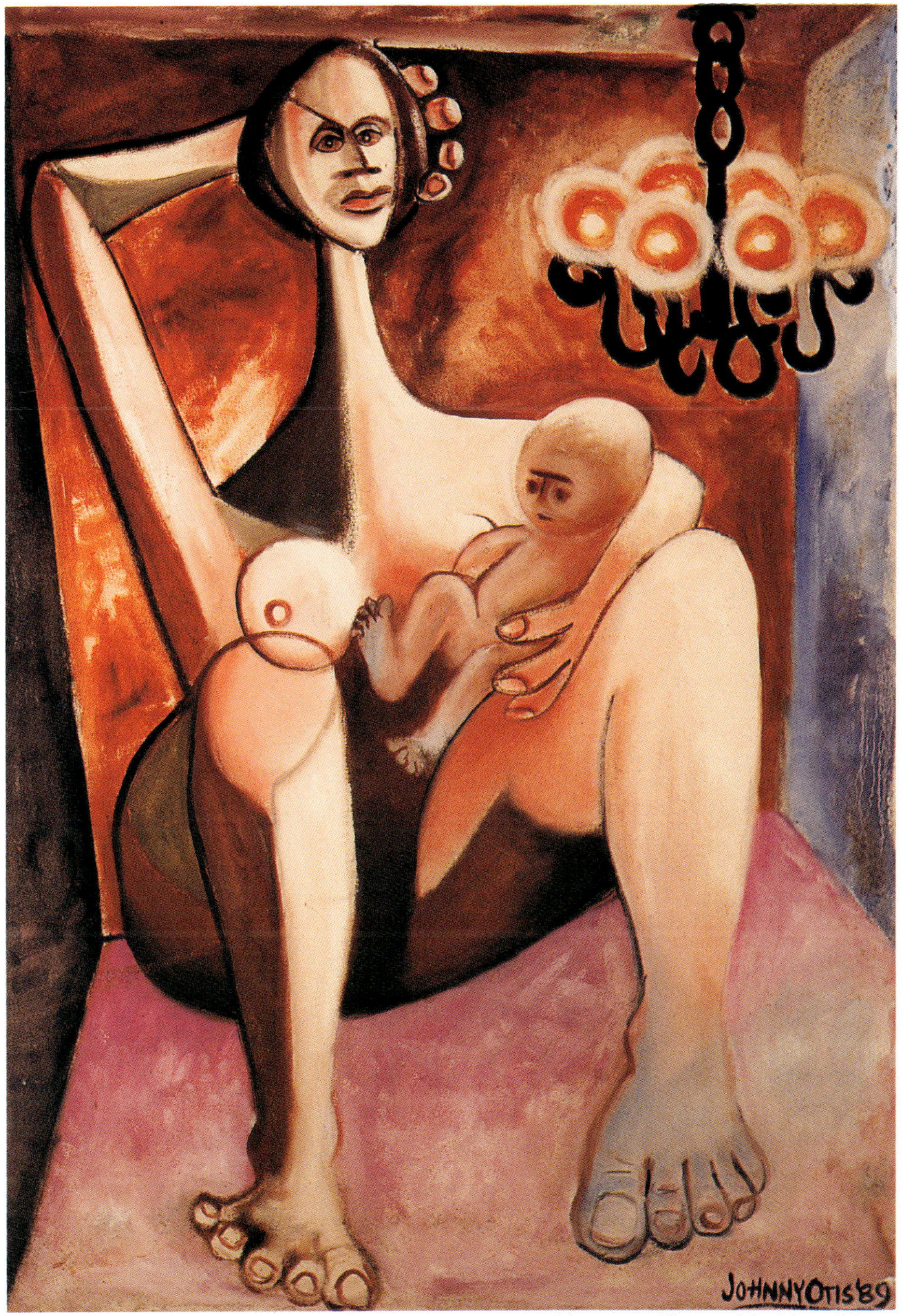

Mother and Child and Chandelier 1989. Oil on canvas. Photograph by Johnny Otis.

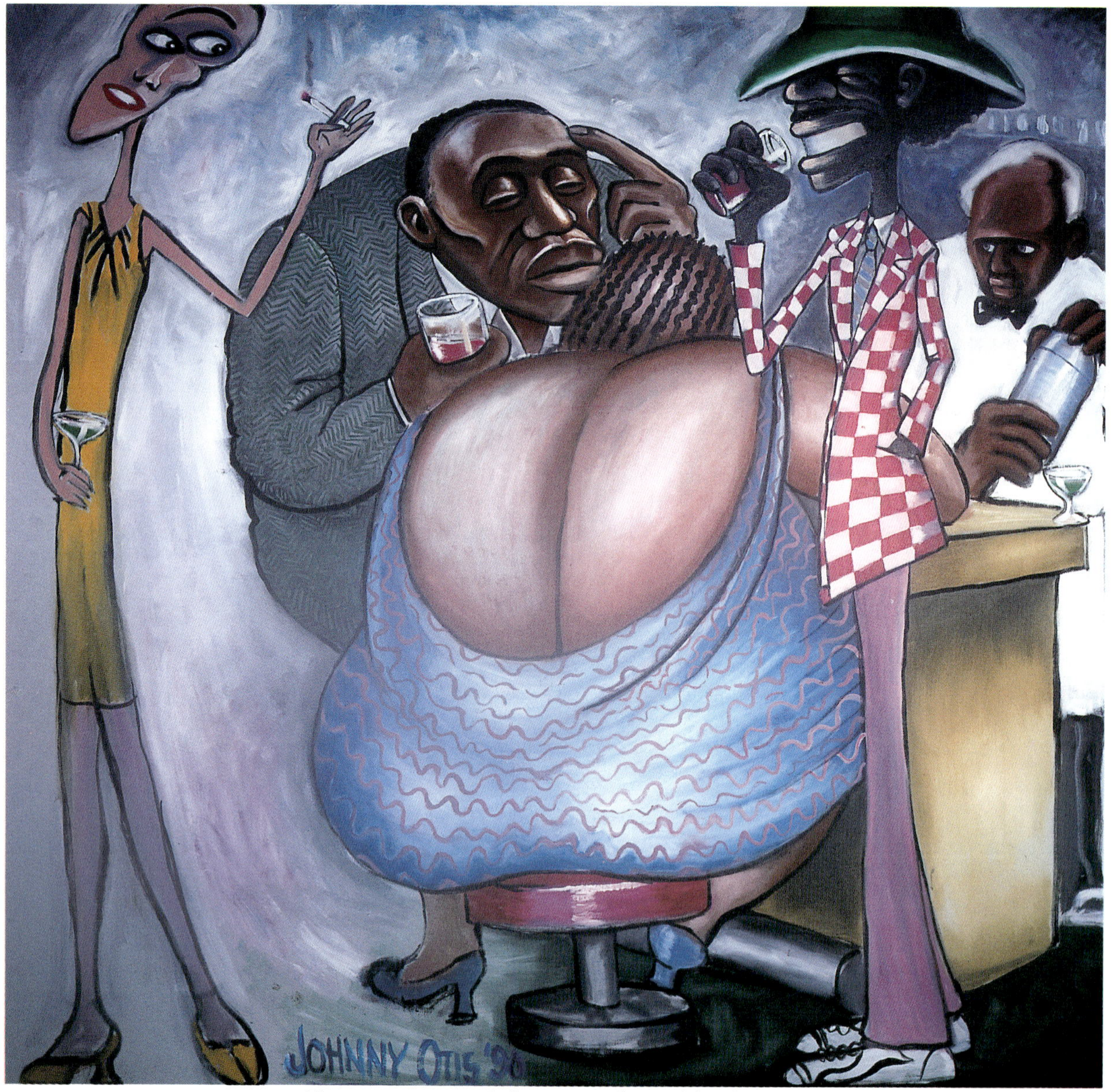

HANGOVER 1990. Acylic on canvas. Photograph by Johnny Otis.

OTIS LANDED ON HIS OWN STYLE when he rediscovered sculpture in 1985. During this period his paintings continued to concentrate on musical themes, but he no longer appeared to be concerned with the performer as his point of reference. For example, in *Boogie Stompers* (see page 64) we see the dancers share center stage with musicians, and in *Hangover* the focus is strictly on the interaction between the bar patrons. "A musician's personal style grows out of the music he or she was exposed to early in life," Otis says. "The instrumentalists who capture our fancy come together to form our own personal musical language. Years ago, I was surprised to hear Lester Young tell me Frankie Trumbauer was one of his saxophone influences. Early life-style and environment surely contribute to the mix as well.

"I think the same holds true in painting and sculpture. If I hadn't happened to see some reproductions of Picasso's work and some African sculpture I doubt that I would be trying to do art as I do—or if I would be doing art at all."

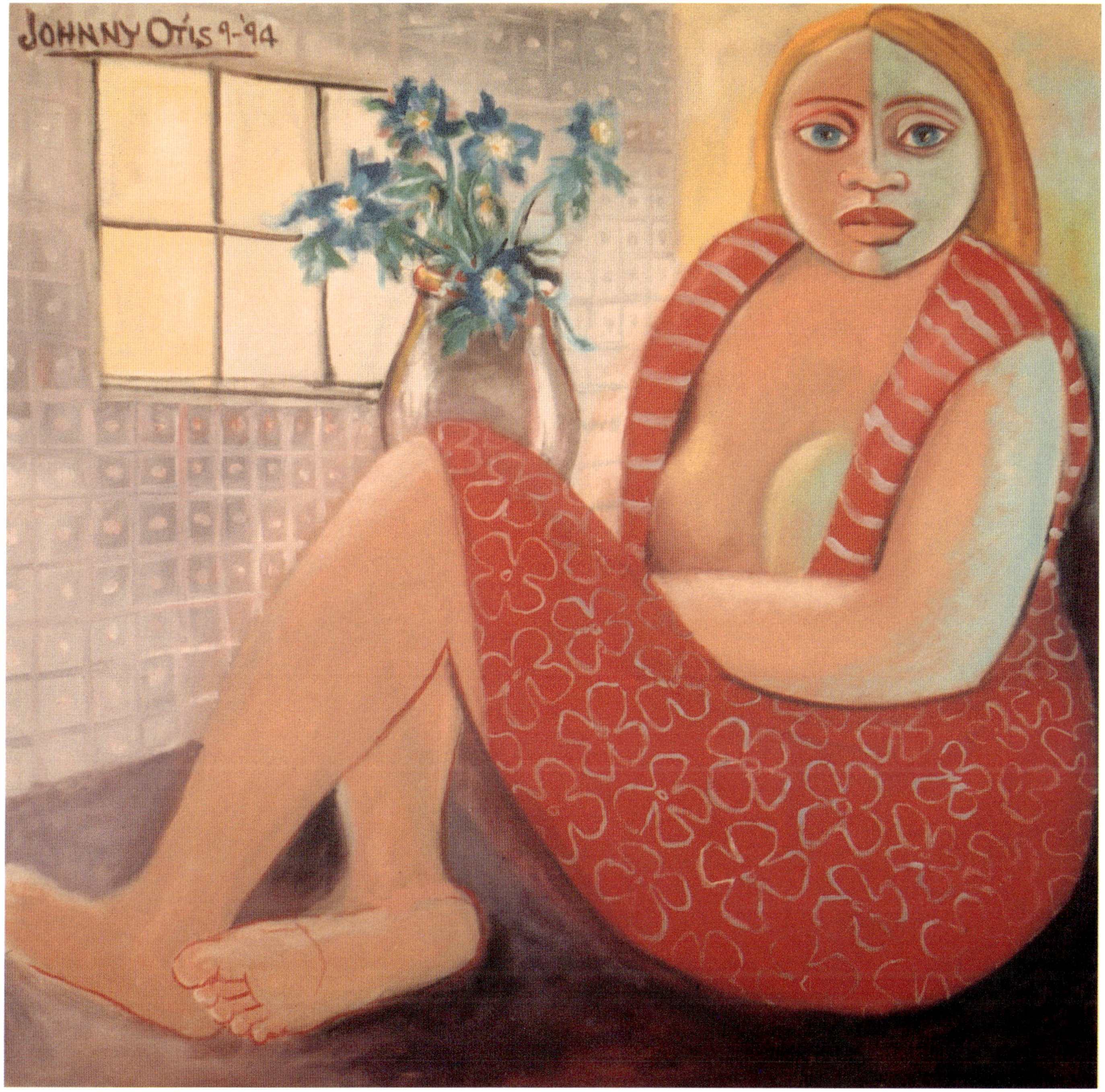

GOLDIE 1994. Oil on canvas. Photograph by Johnny Otis.

"BACK IN THE 1950S, TROMBONIST Gene 'The Mighty Flea' Conners and I were returning from a day's fishing on one of the old San Pedro barges in the L.A. harbor. As we were walking down the beach, a cute little girl ran up and said, 'Hi, Johnny Otis, I see you on T.V. and my mama says she can sing good enough to be on your show.' Her mother turned out to be a young, buxom three hundred pounder. Not a bit bashful, she sang for me but, unfortunately, sounded like shit. She kept adjusting her bathing suit and turning around so we couldn't miss her big, round, dimpled bootie. I couldn't resist calling her 'Dimples,' and her buddy, another bikinied, big-hipped sexy mama, cracked-up and said, 'Girl, that's your new name—Dimples! Ha, ha!'

"A year later, I spotted her at a bar in L.A. A man stood up and called out, 'Come on, Dimples, let's go!' The nickname had stuck! I made my way through the crowd but when I got to the bar, she was gone."

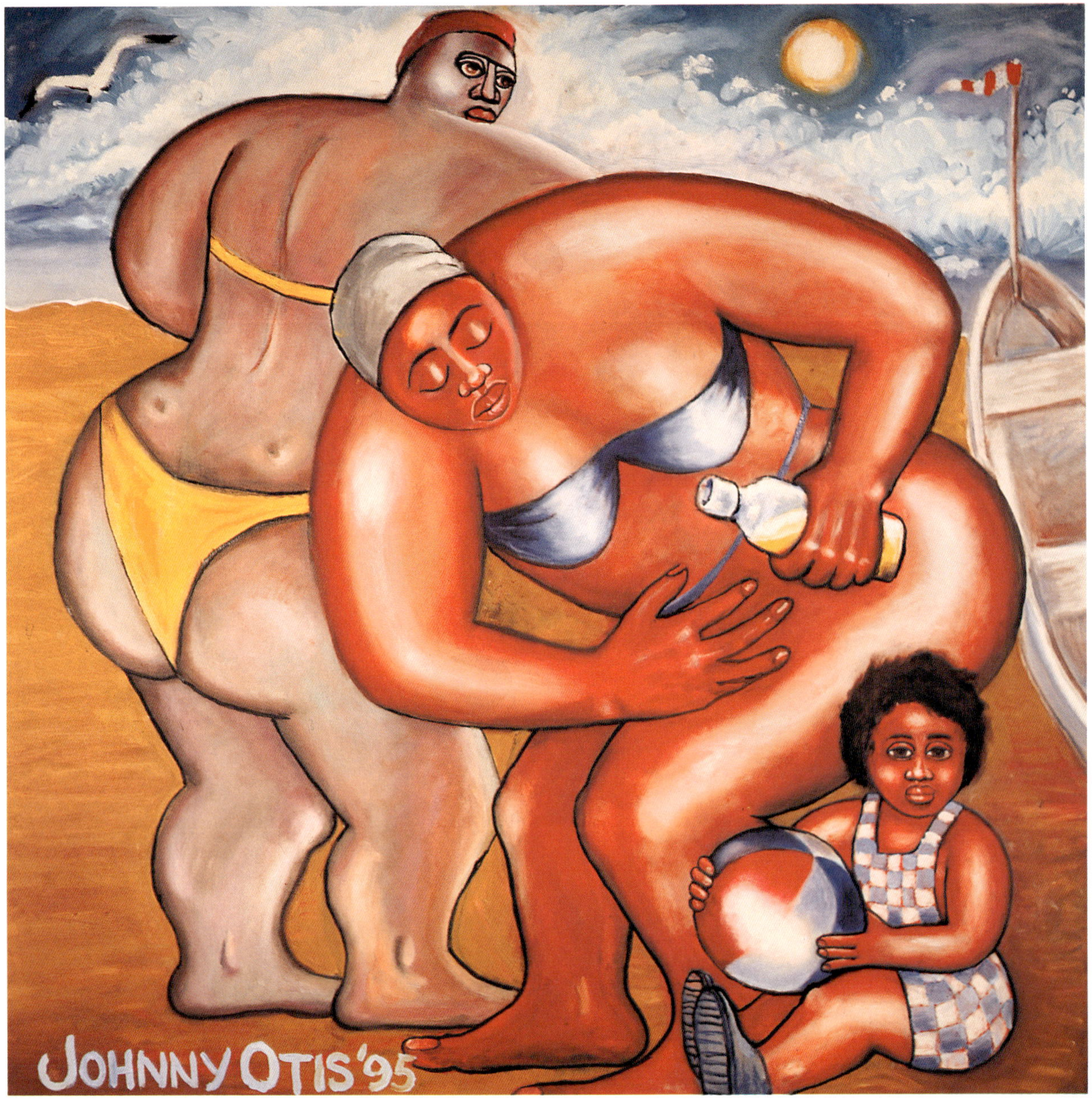

DIMPLES 1995. Oil on canvas. Photograph by Johnny Otis.

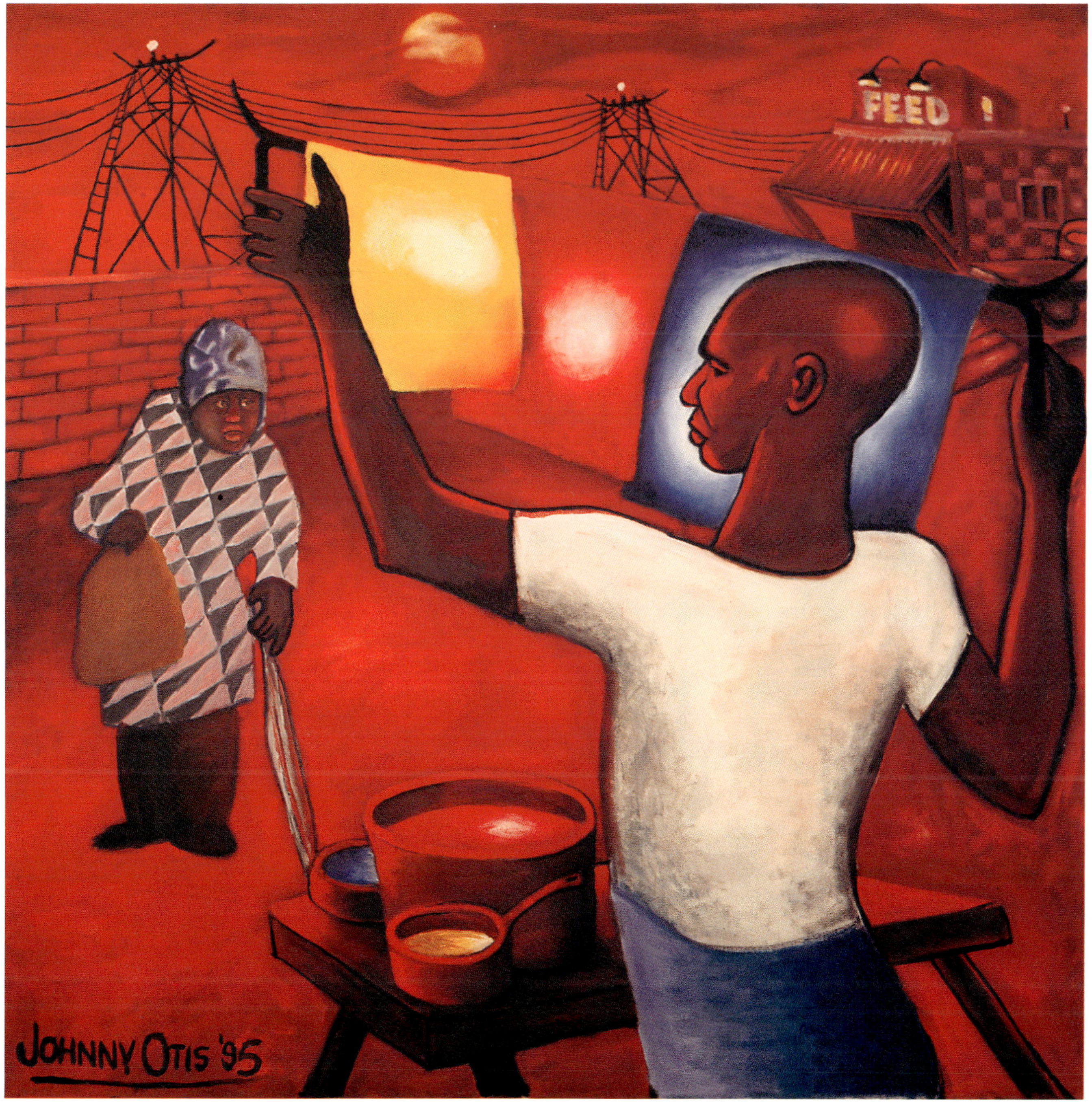

WATTS NOCTURNE 1995. Oil on canvas. Photograph by Johnny Otis.

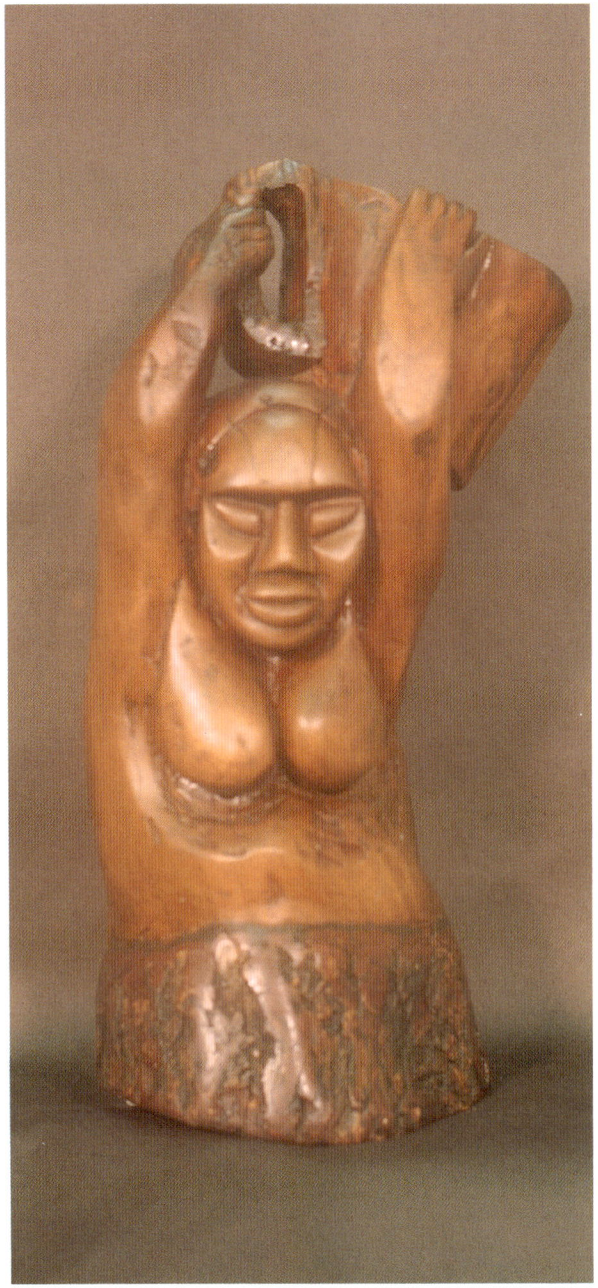

Woman with Pail 1975. Wood. Photograph by Johnny Otis.

"Redd Foxx and Slappy White were comedians with my show in the 1950s. Redd was a riot on stage, but offstage he was often morose and grumpy. Slappy, on the other hand, was the life of the party, always ad-libbing quips and keeping us in stitches on the bus. Redd could be generous and genial, but more often than not, he was mean spirited and even cruel. After serving as his manager for almost a year back in the '70s, I watched him reduce one of his employees—an old comedian crony—to tears in the presence of a group of show people. I left that day and never went back. I figured , if he'd treat his old friend Billy like that, maybe one day, zonked on coke, he would decide to come on to me that way and one of us would get hurt. That brooding characteristic was always there, but when he became a big star the Mr. Hyde inside became more dominant.

"One day he told me his mother and stepfather were coming to L.A. from Chicago and, since his house was crowded, could I put them up for a few days. I said, 'Sure.' Mary and Harry Carson stayed with us for years. I said, 'Goddamn, Redd. Mary and Harry are swell folks, but they've been with us for five fuckin' years! Whatcha gonna do about your mother and father?' He answered, 'Harry's okay, but I can't stand that bitch!' I stood there with my jaw hanging open. 'Hey, man, are you talking about your own mother like that?' Then he proceeded to tell me that Mary had abandoned him and his brother to go and become Al Capone's moll, and how he despised her for it.

"That same day, a large tree had toppled in our backyard, narrowly missing Nicky, who was a baby at the time. Redd spotted it and said, 'Man, fuck all that mother and father shit—look at all that good wood for carving in that felled tree.' Since that day, and from time to time, I try to carve something in wood."

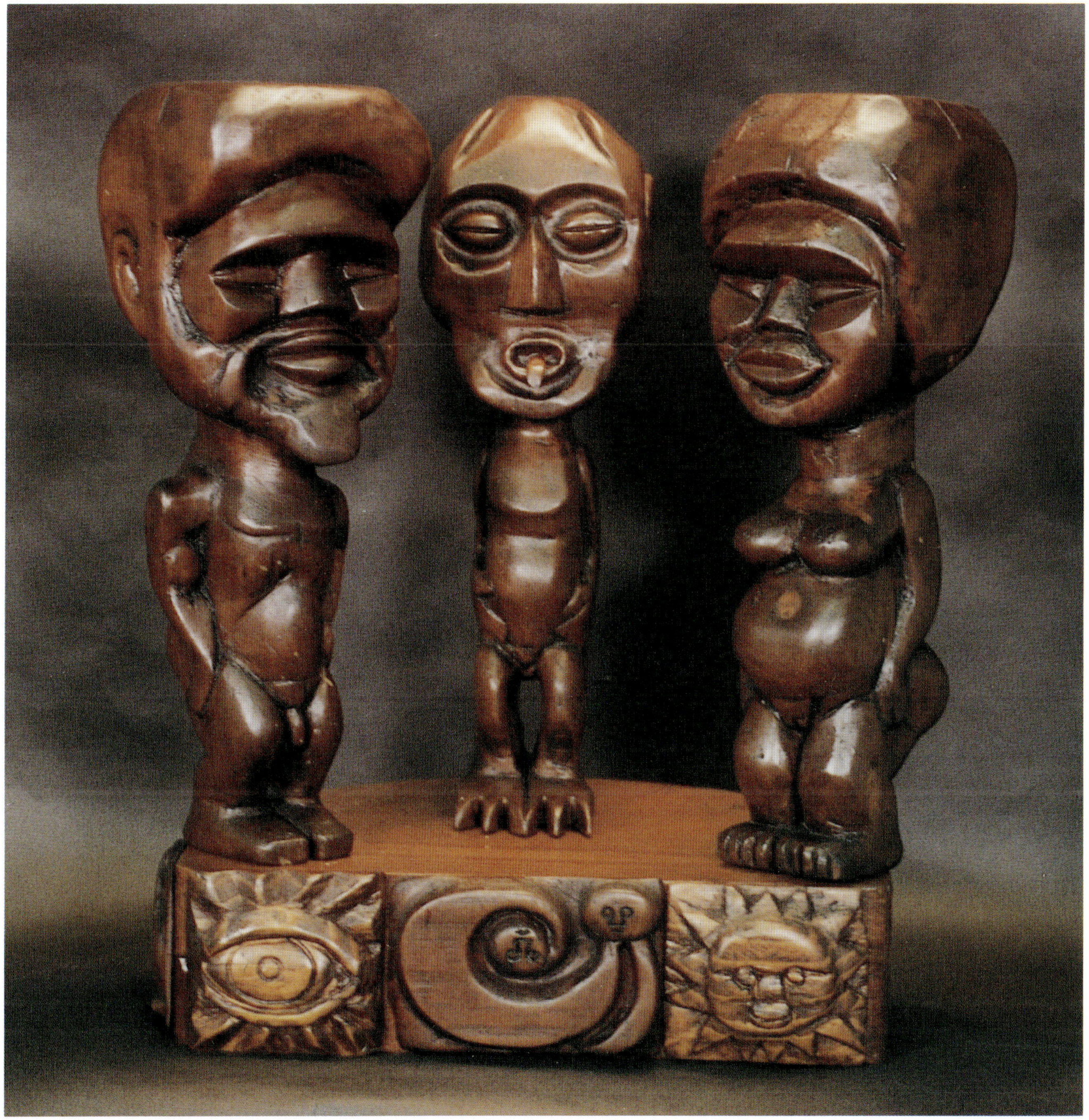

TEMPTATION c. 1975. Wood. Photograph by Johnny Otis.

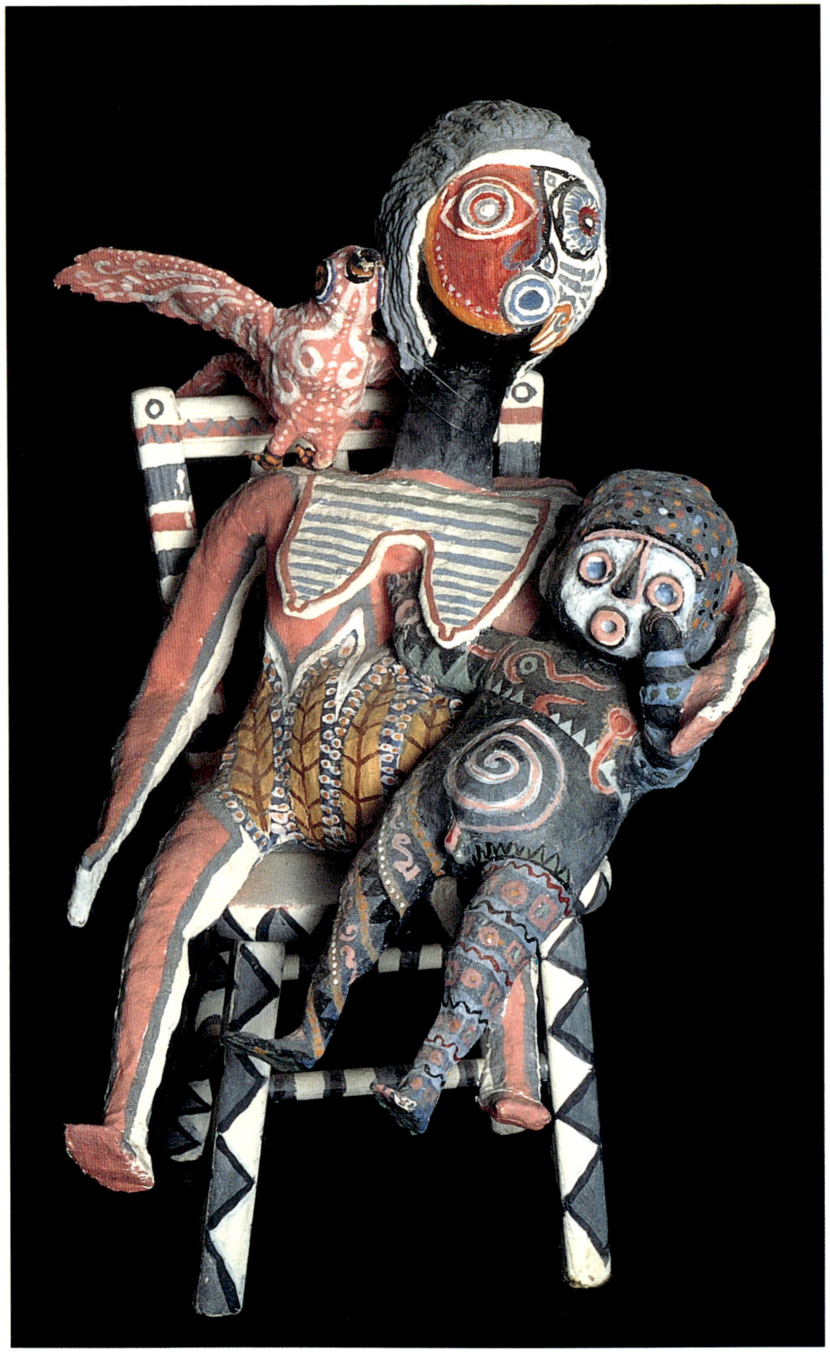

MOTHER AND CHILD 1985. Plaster, wood, acrylic. Photograph by Stephan Rockwerk.

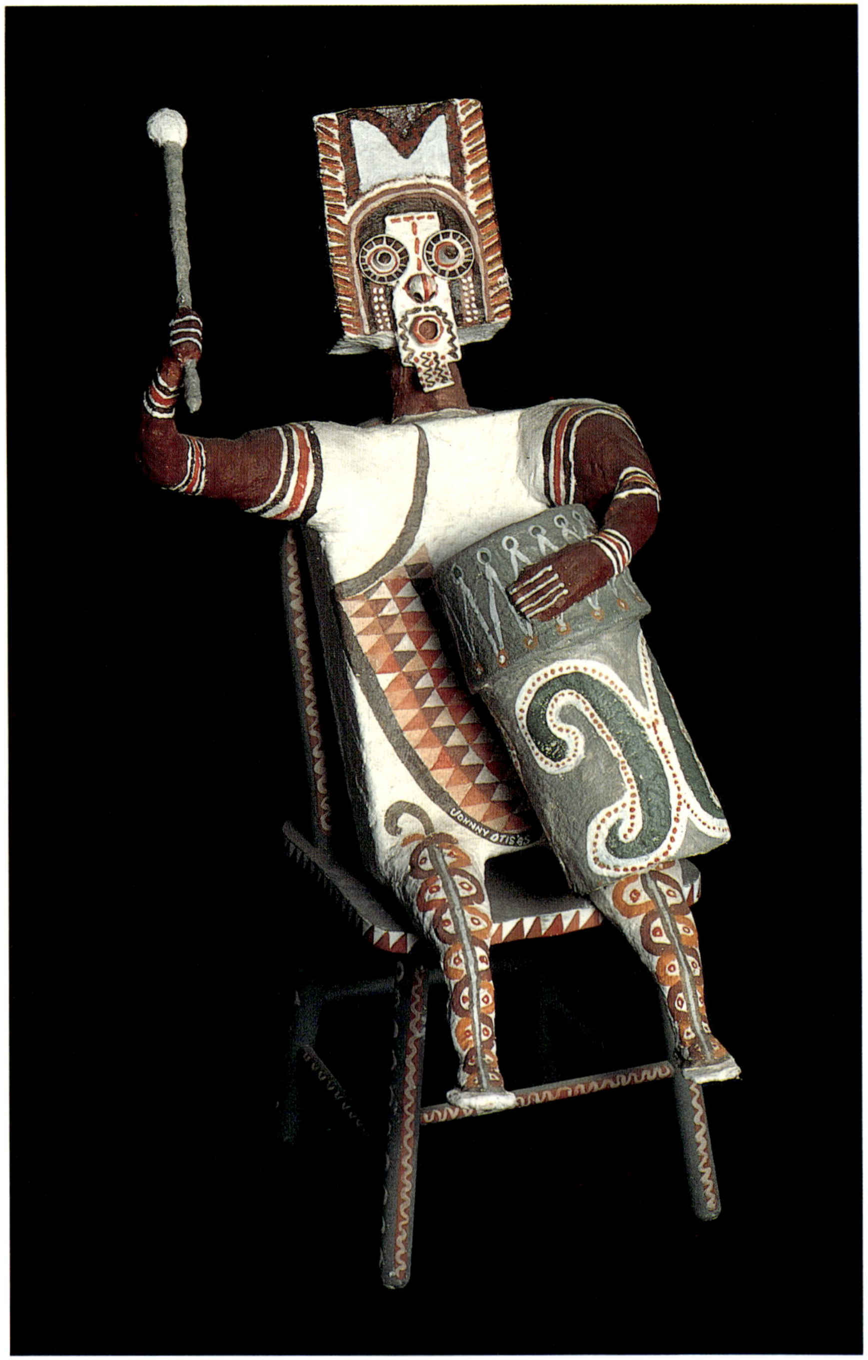

DRUMMER 1985. Plaster, wood, acrylic. Photograph by Stephan Rockwerk.

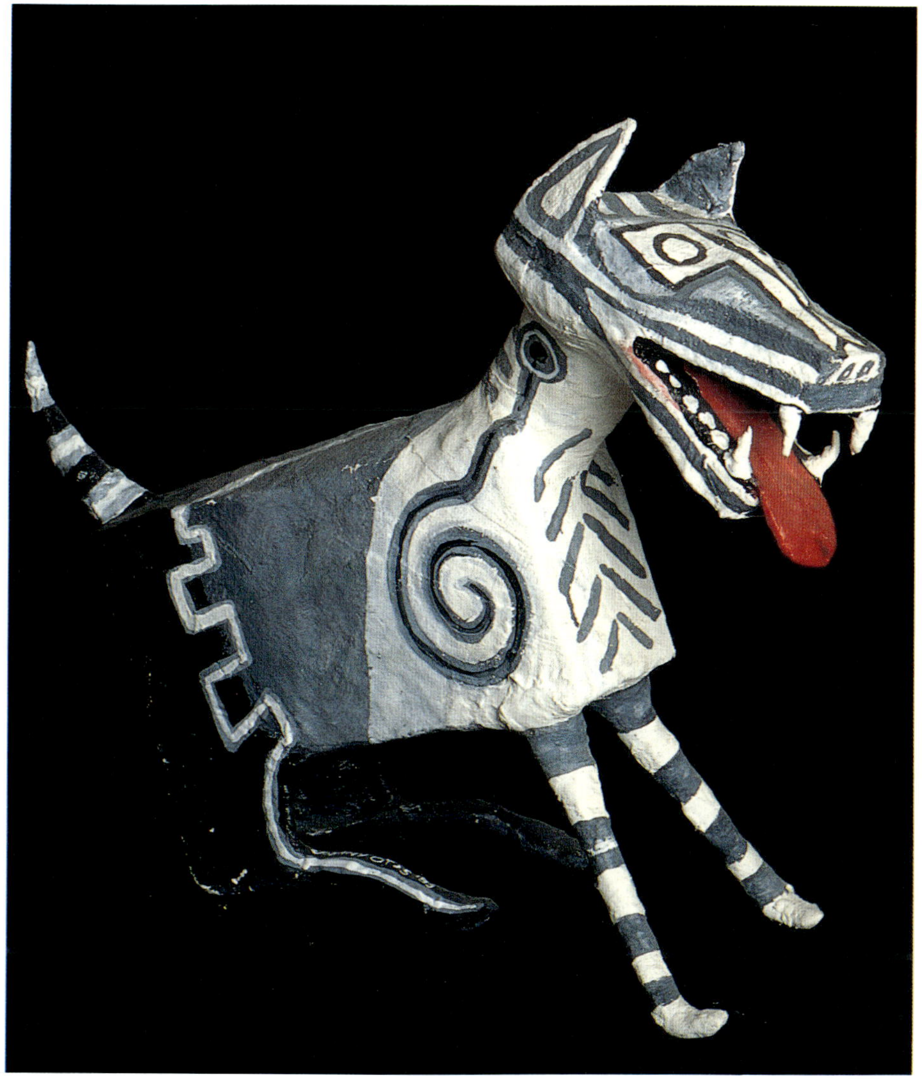

Grey Dog 1985. Plaster, wood, acrylic. Collection of Ben Myron. Photograph by Stephan Rockwerk.

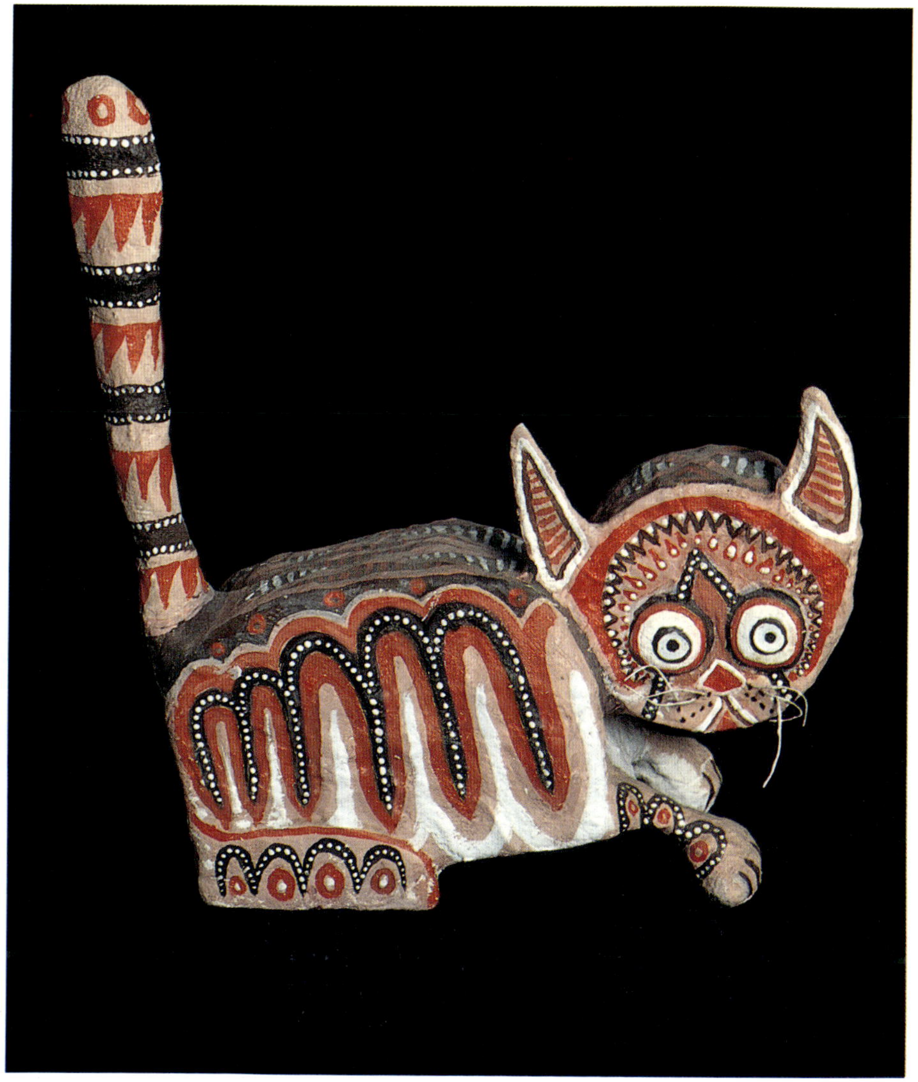

Orange Cat 1985. Plaster, wood, acrylic. Photograph by Stephan Rockwerk.

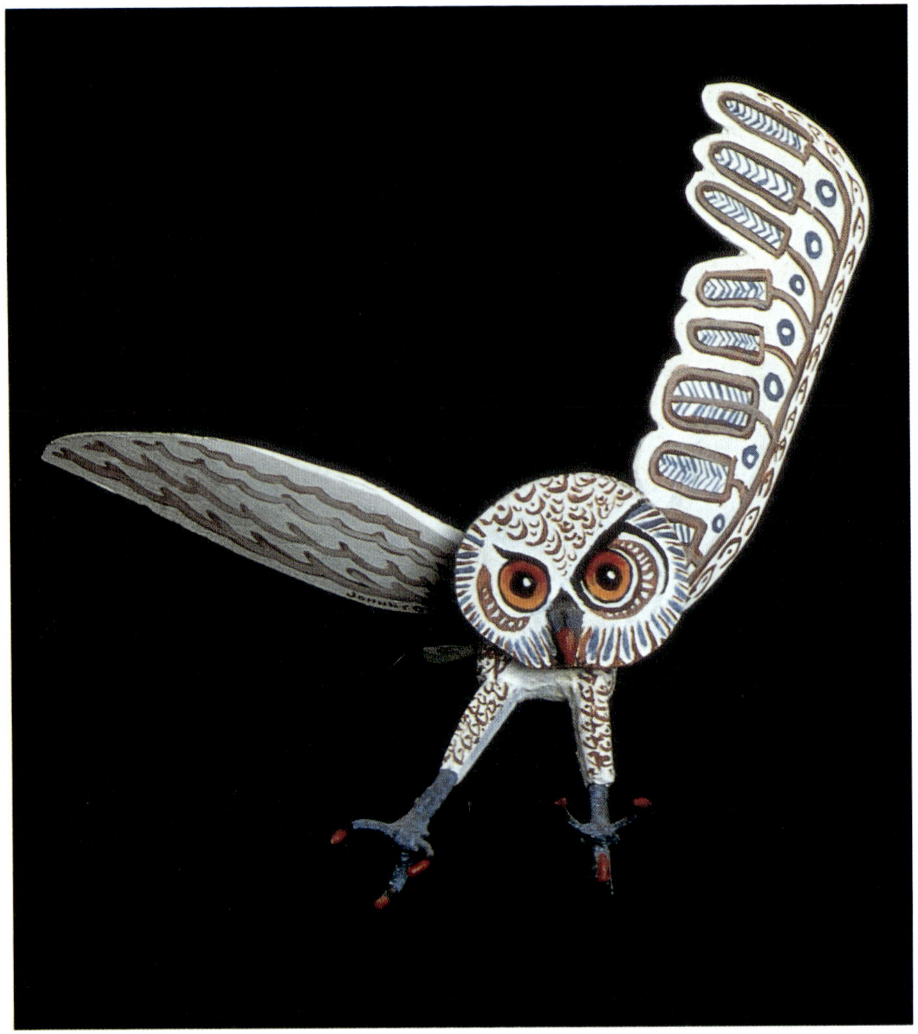

Owl 1986. Wood, acrylic. Photograph by Johnny Otis.

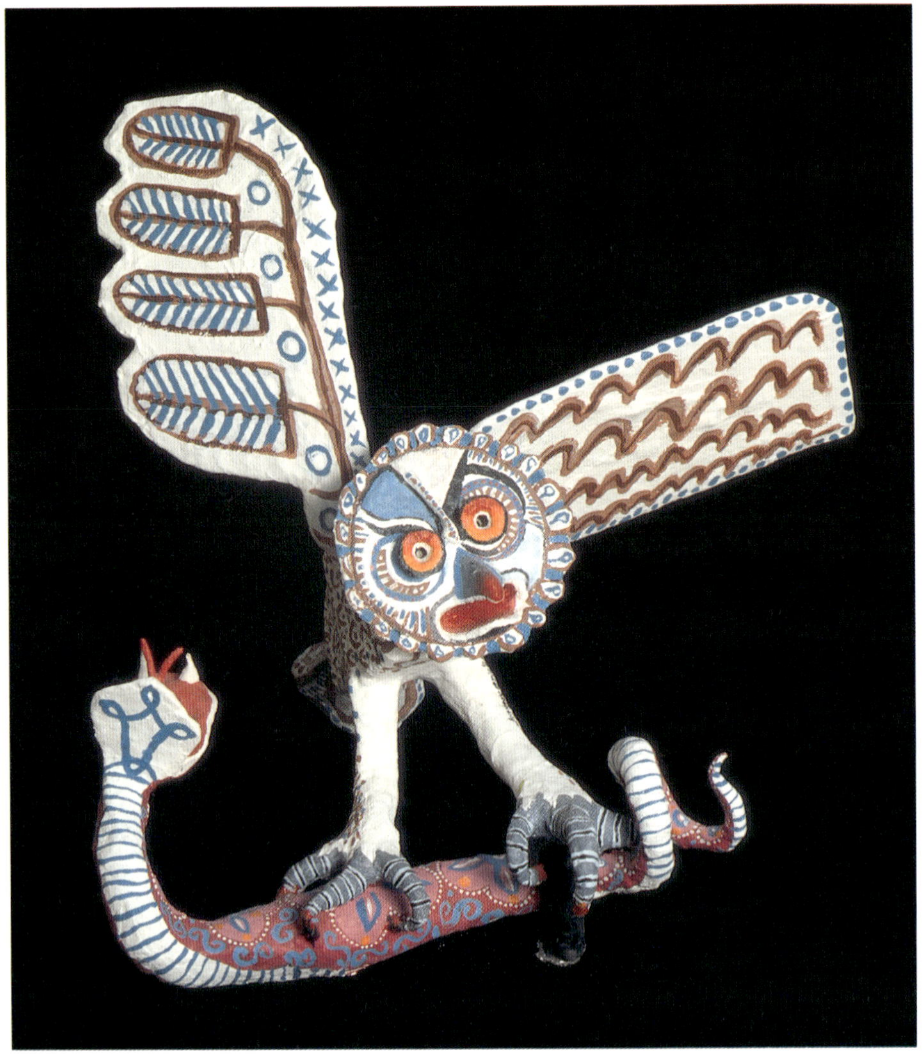

Owl Killing Snake 1986. Plaster, wood, acrylic. Photograph by Stephan Rockwerk.

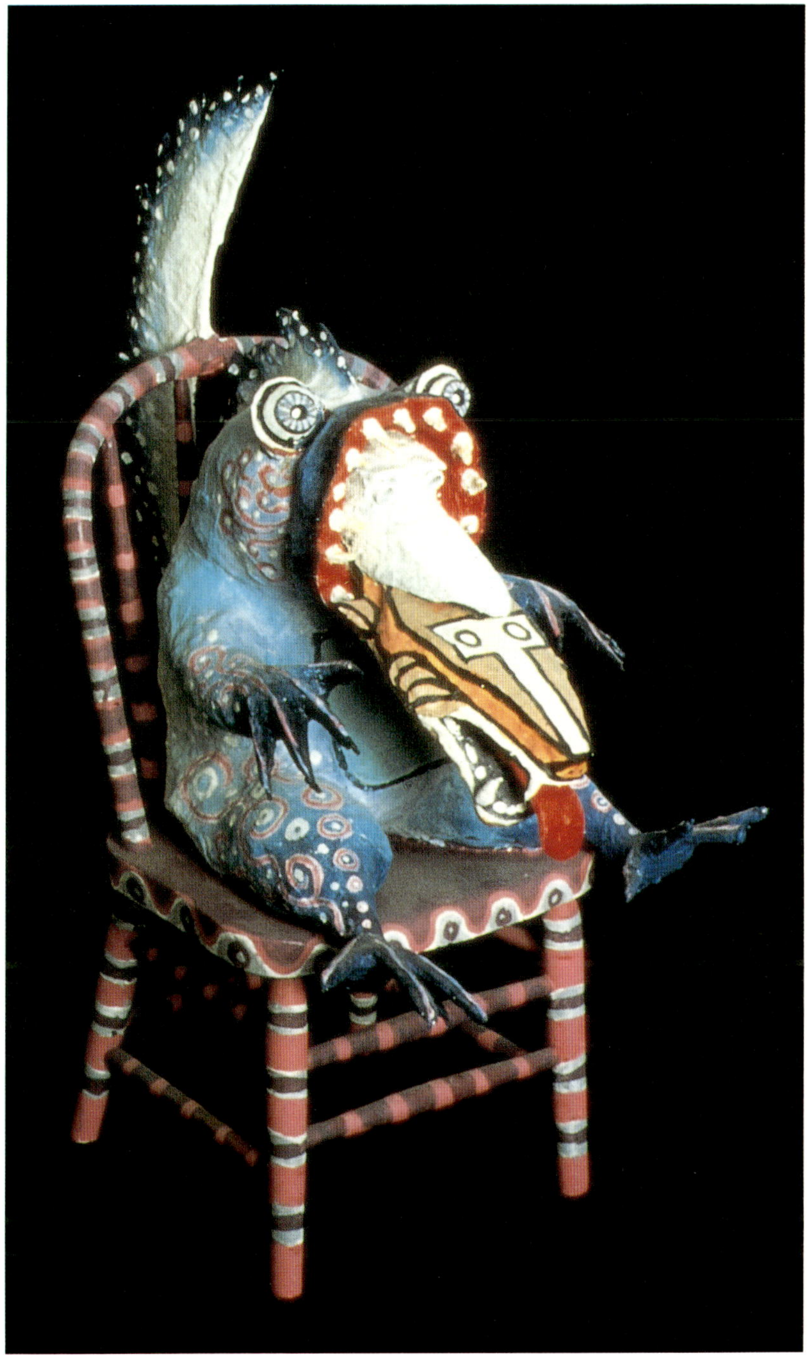

Humongous and Friends 1986. Plaster, wood, acrylic. Photograph by Stephan Rockwerk.

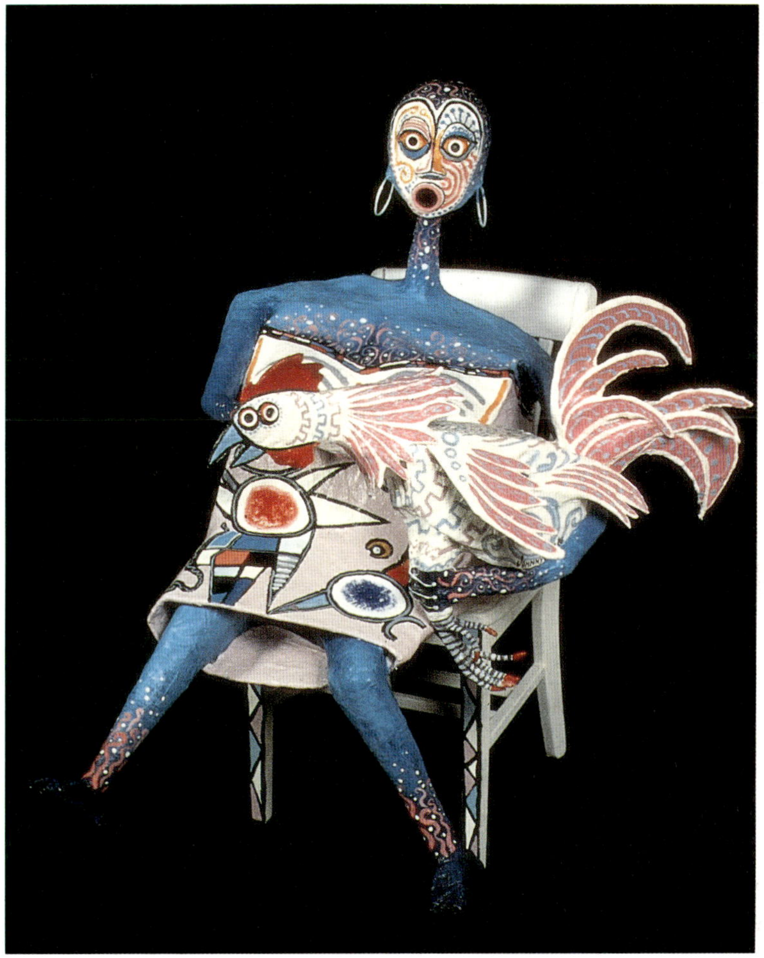

Mama Bought a Chicken 1986. Plaster, wood, acrylic. Photograph by Stephan Rockwerk.

"In Mama Bought a Chicken, I'm hearkening back to the old traditional jump blues song we used to do in the Count Otis Matthews band that goes, 'Mama bought a chicken, thought it was a duck, put him on the table with his legs stuck up. Here come sister with a spoon and glass, tryin' to stir the gravy from his yas, yas, yas—yas, yas, yes, I know.'"

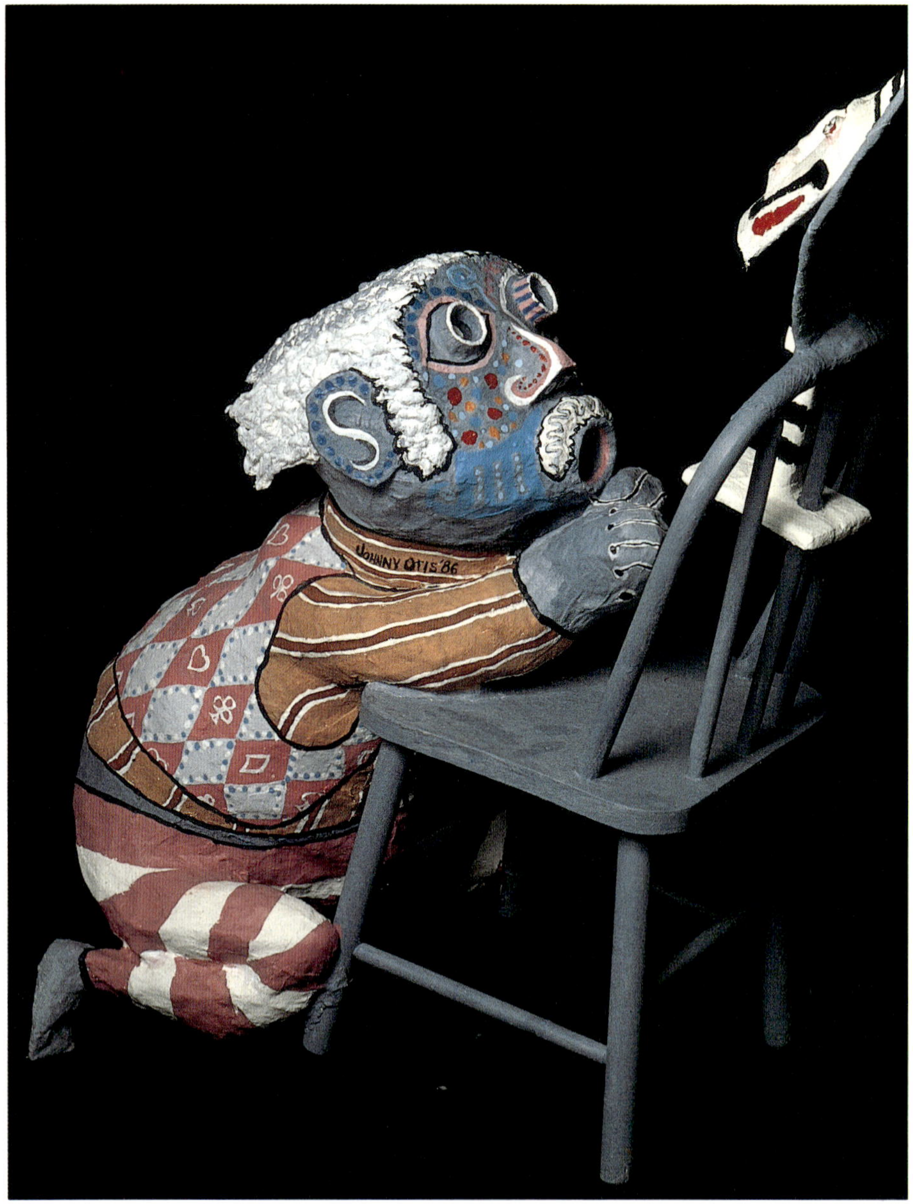

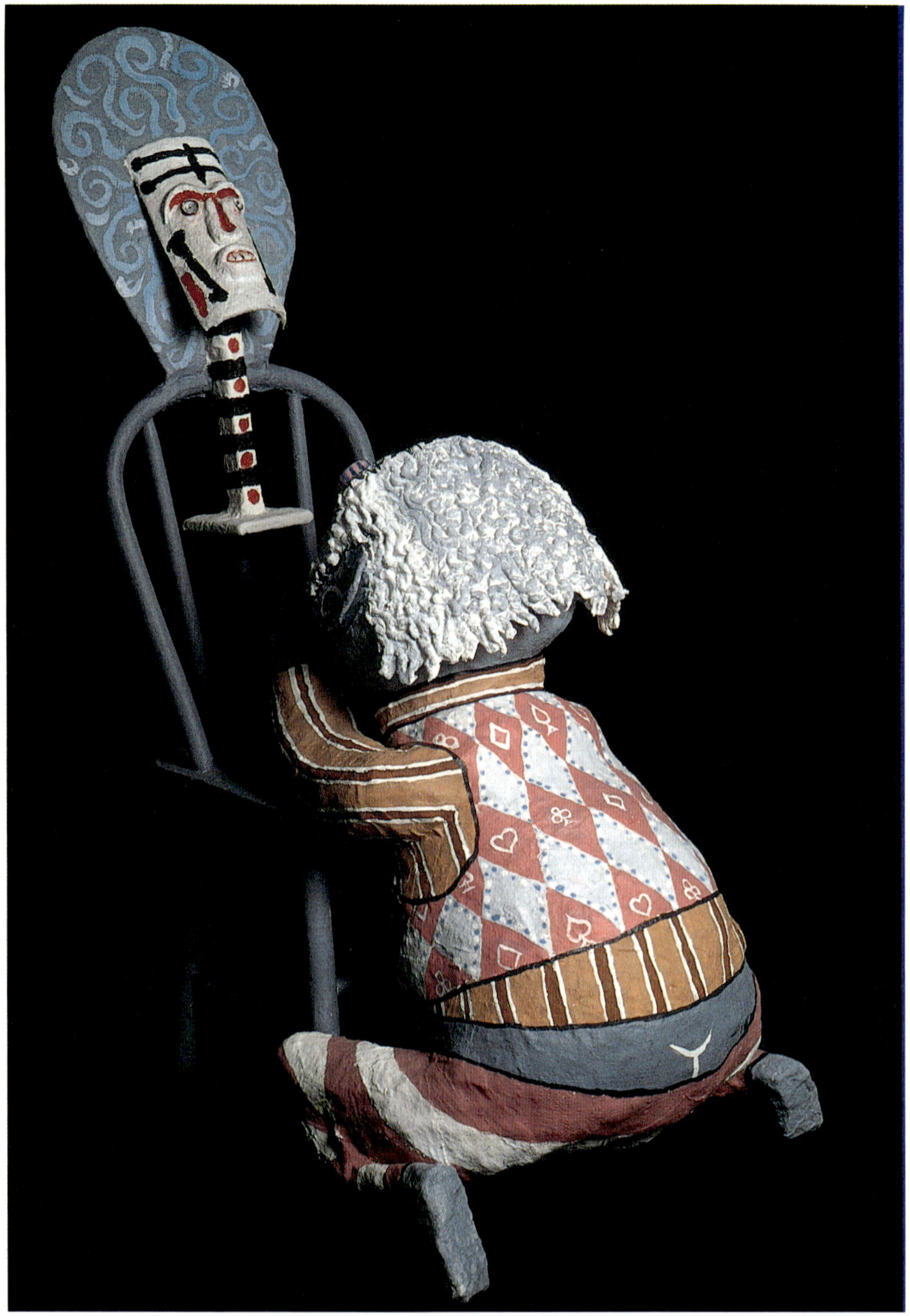

THE GREAT GOOGA MOOGA 1986 (2 views). Plaster, wood, acrylic. Photograph by Stephan Rockwerk.

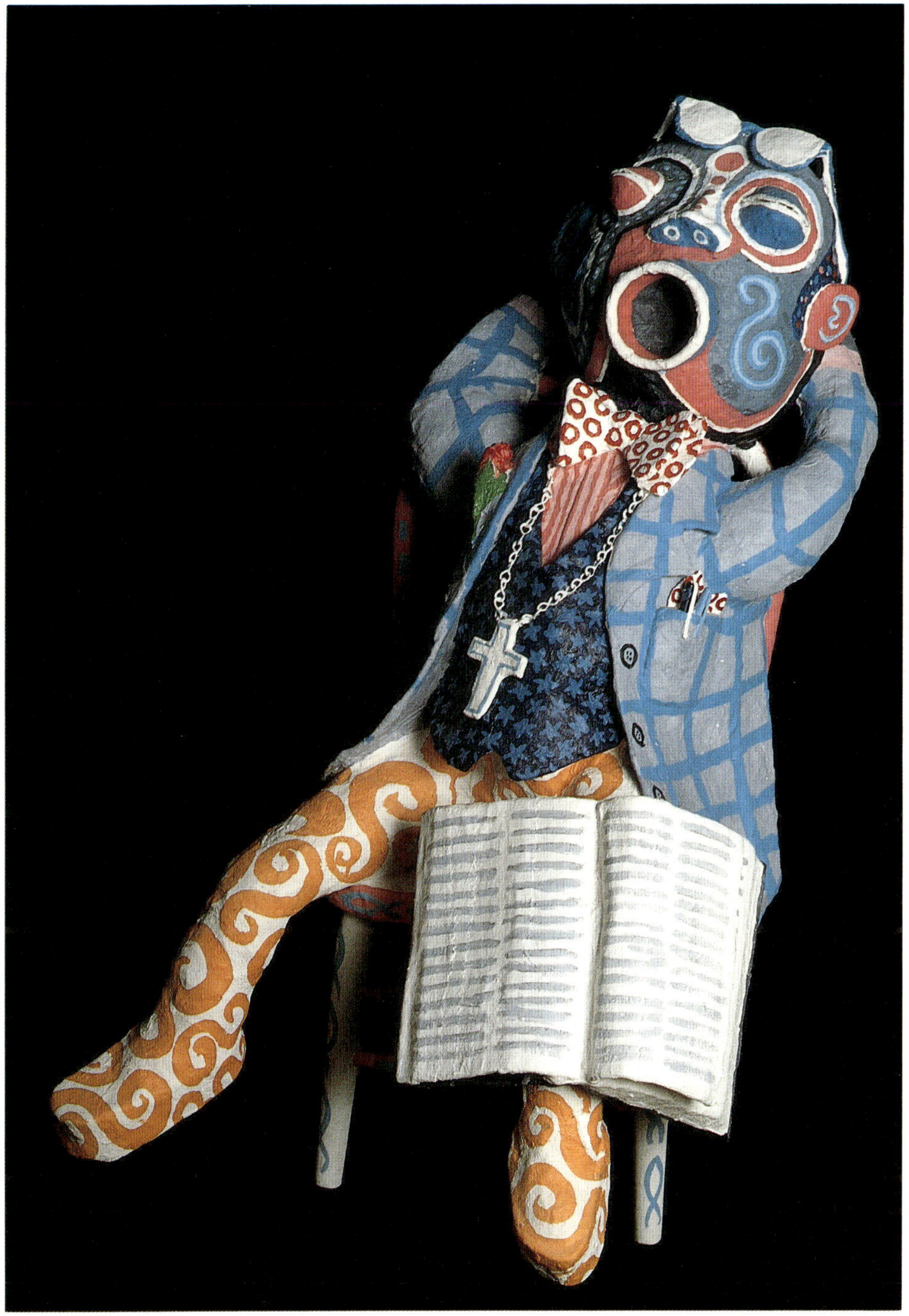

The Sleeping Preacher 1986. Plaster, wood, acrylic. Photograph by Stephan Rockwerk.

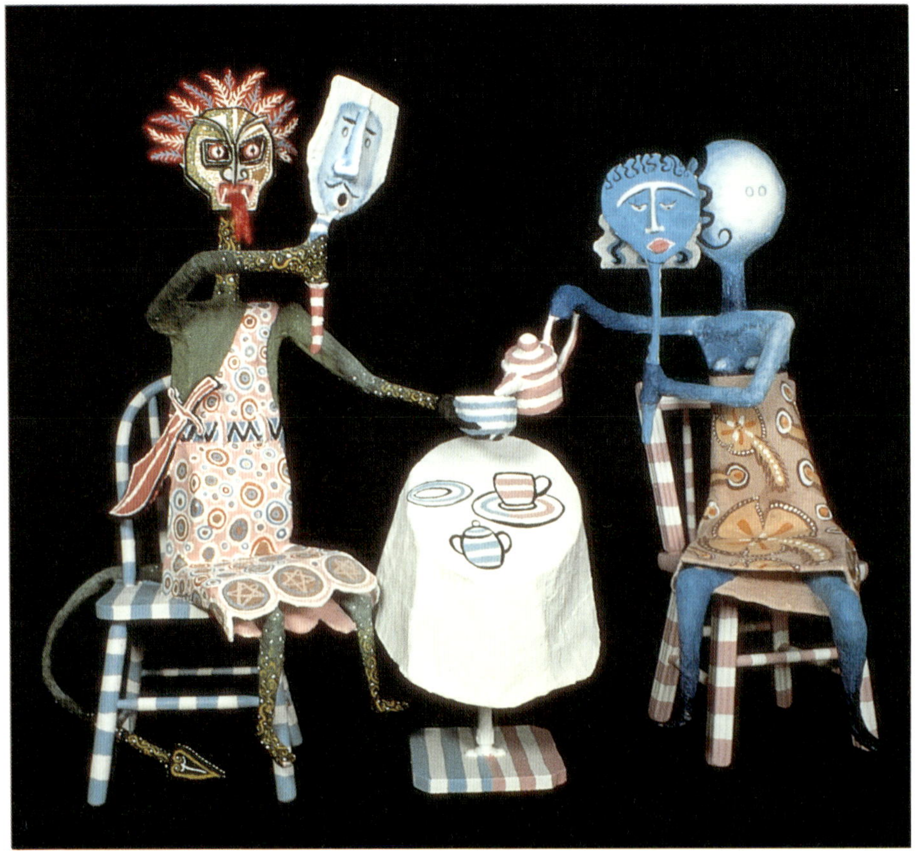

Two for Tea 1986. Plaster, wood, acrylic. Photograph by Stephan Rockwerk.

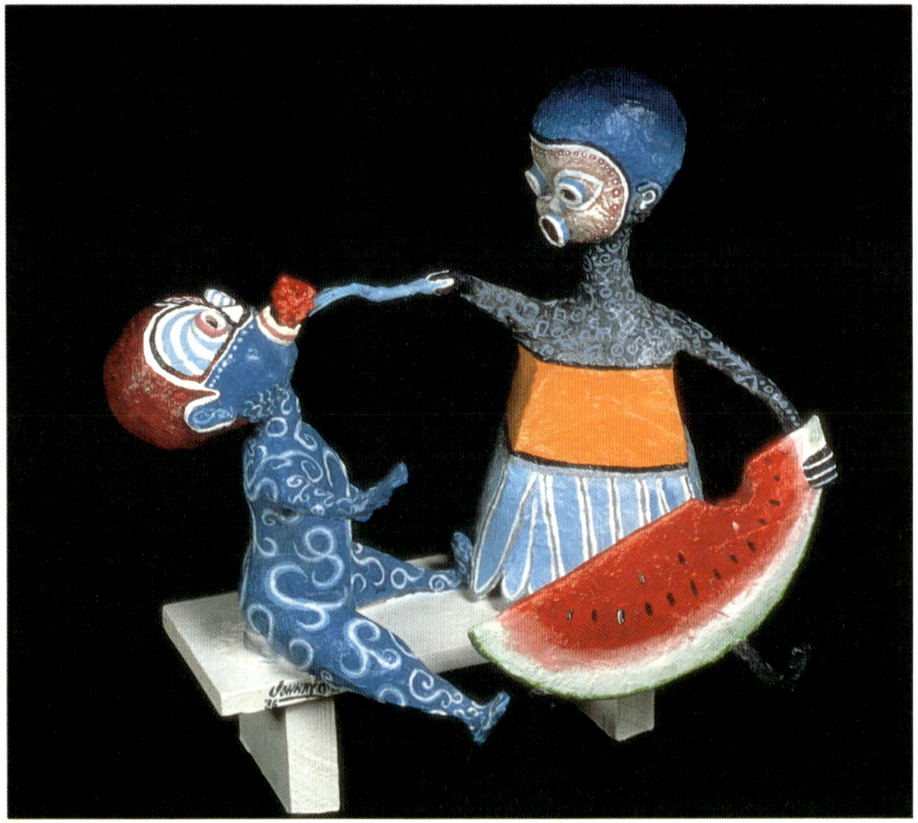

Children with Watermelon 1986. Plaster, wood, acrylic. Photograph by Stephan Rockwerk.

"When you've been in the band business as long as I have, you get to see all kind of stuff from the stage, couples meetin' and talking, everybody on their best behavior. But you see those same folks down the road in everyday settings and the phony masks have begun to slip and the real people behind the masks start to emerge. What I've shown behind the masks in *Two For Tea* are an evil male and an airhead female. This is a very extreme example of the masquerade games we play, but these artificial deceptions are consistently being played out."

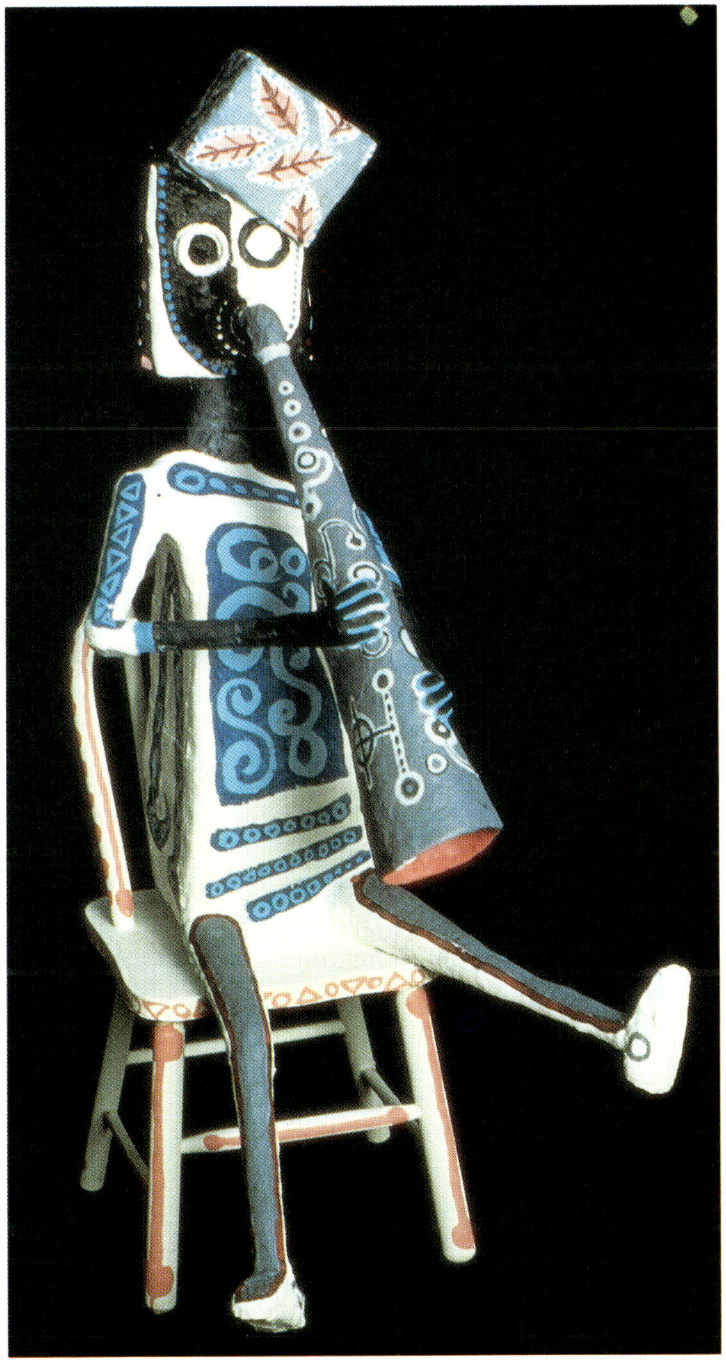

Horn Player 1986. Plaster, wood, acrylic. Photograph by Stephan Rockwerk.

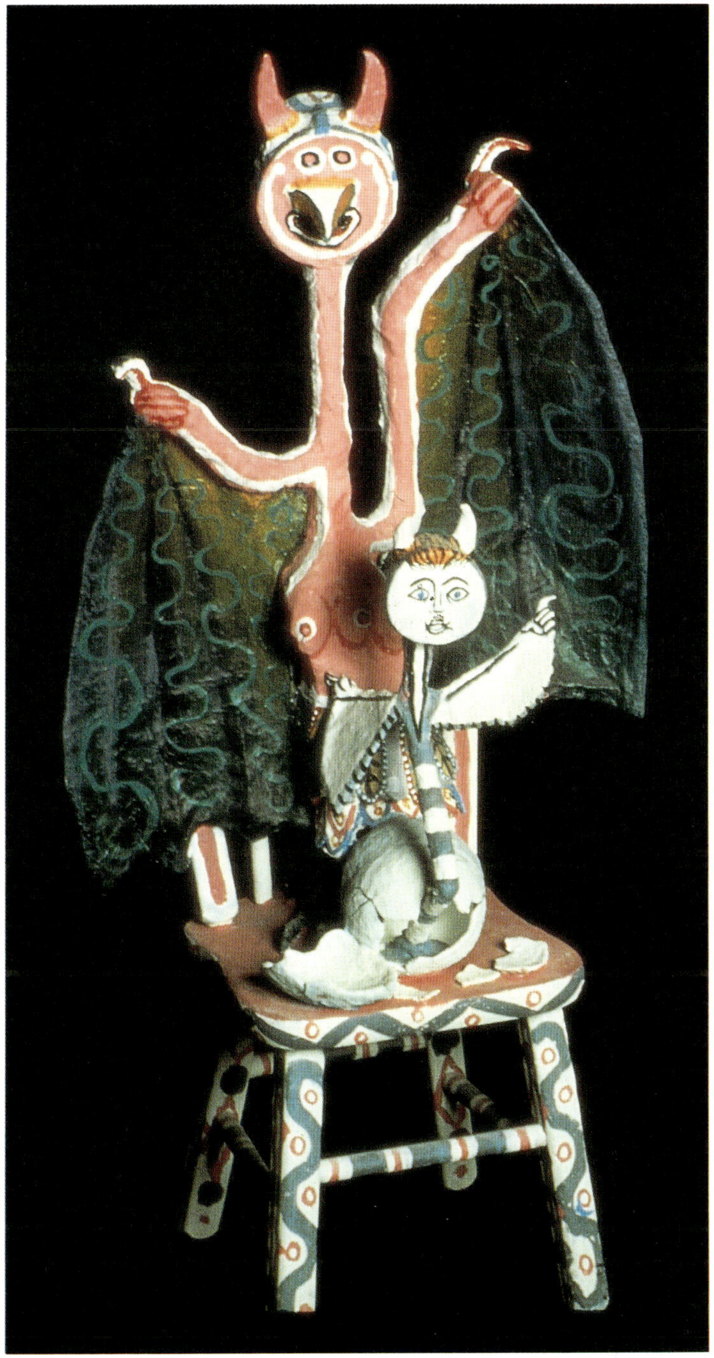

Demon Giving Birth to Western White Man (Hello World) 1986. Plaster, wood, acrylic. Photograph by Stephan Rockwerk.

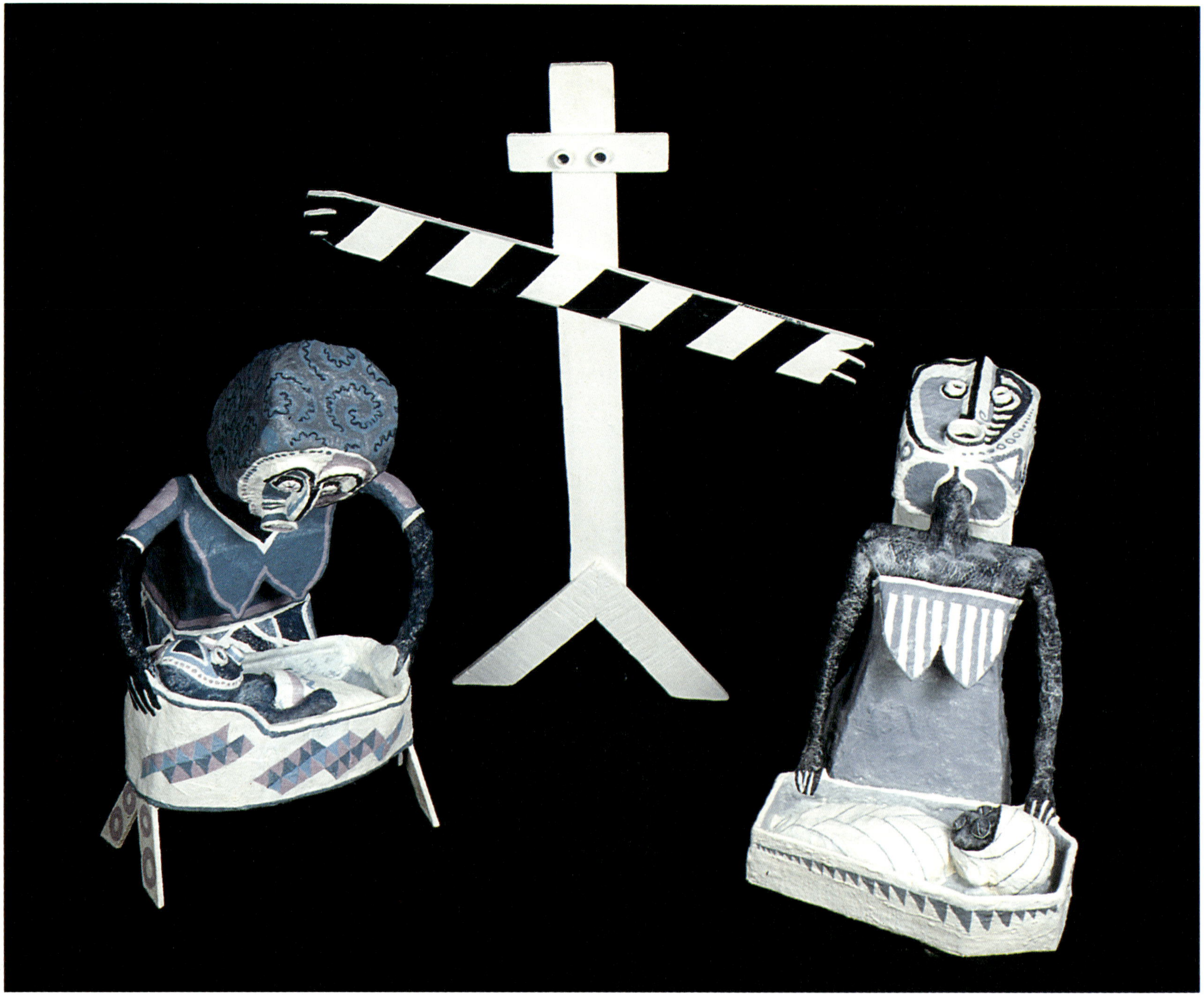

At the Crossroads 1986. Plaster, wood, acrylic. Photograph by Stephan Rockwerk.

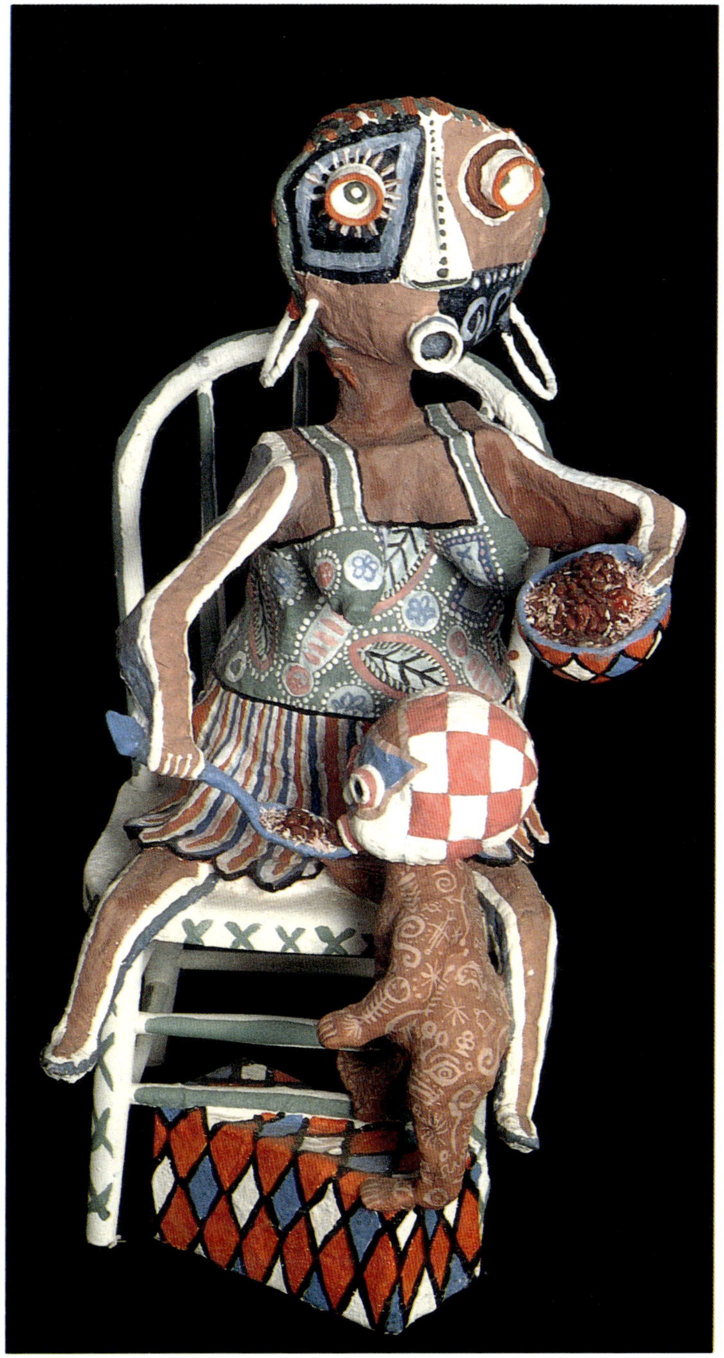

Red Beans and Rice 1986. Plaster, wood, acrylic. Photograph by Stephan Rockwerk.

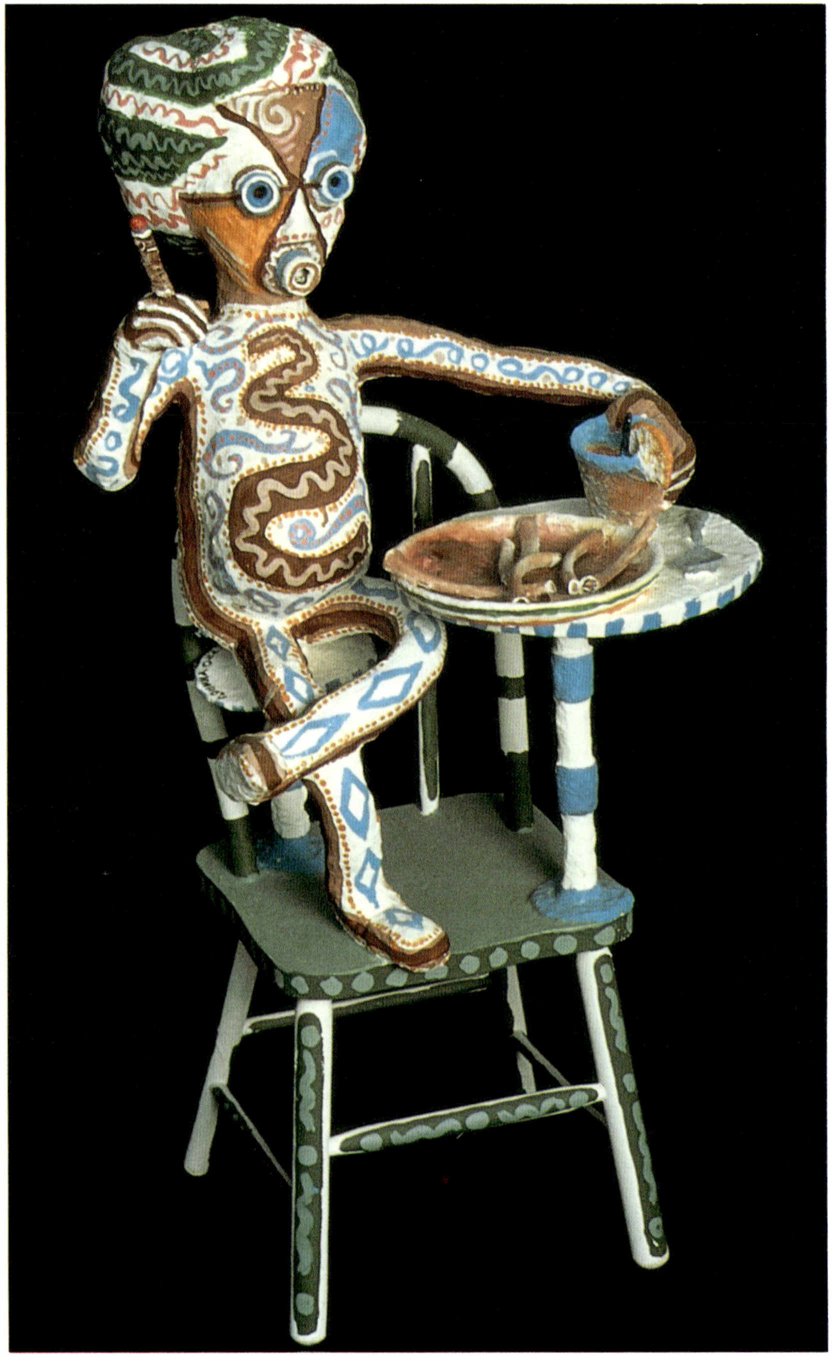

YOU GOTTA DIE OF SOMETHING 1986. Plaster, wood, acrylic. Photograph by Stephan Rockwerk.

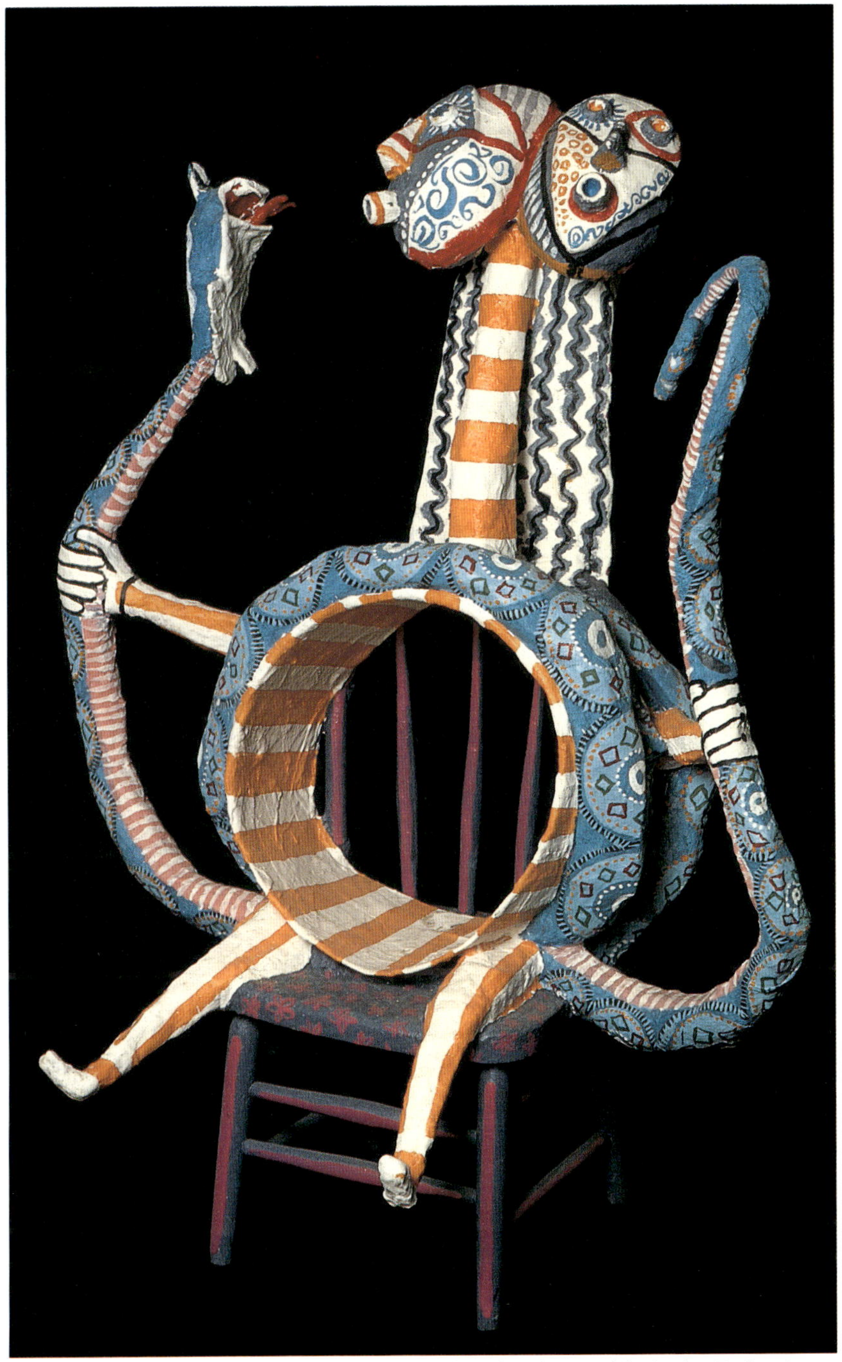

Two-Faced Woman 1986. Plaster, wood, acrylic. Photograph by Stephan Rockwerk.

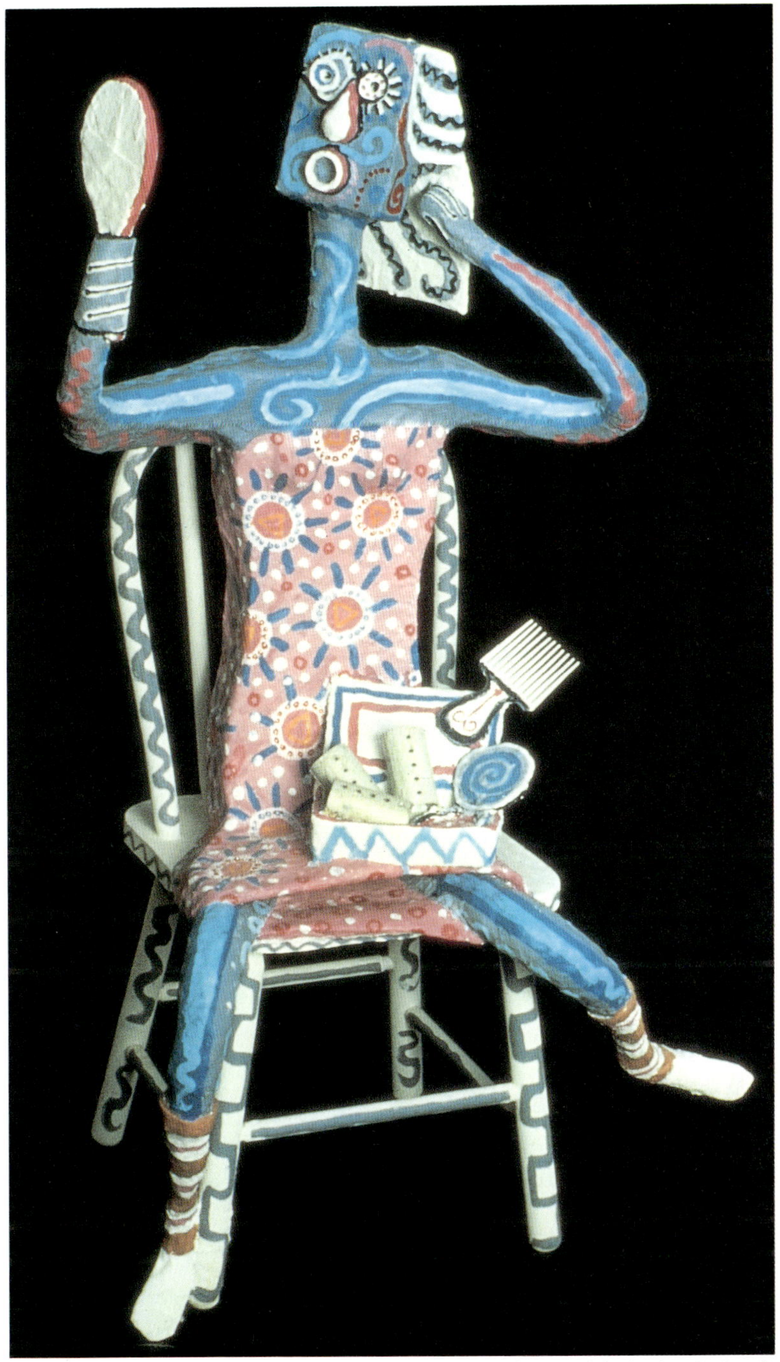

Woman with Mirror 1986. Plaster, wood, acrylic. Photograph by Stephan Rockwerk.

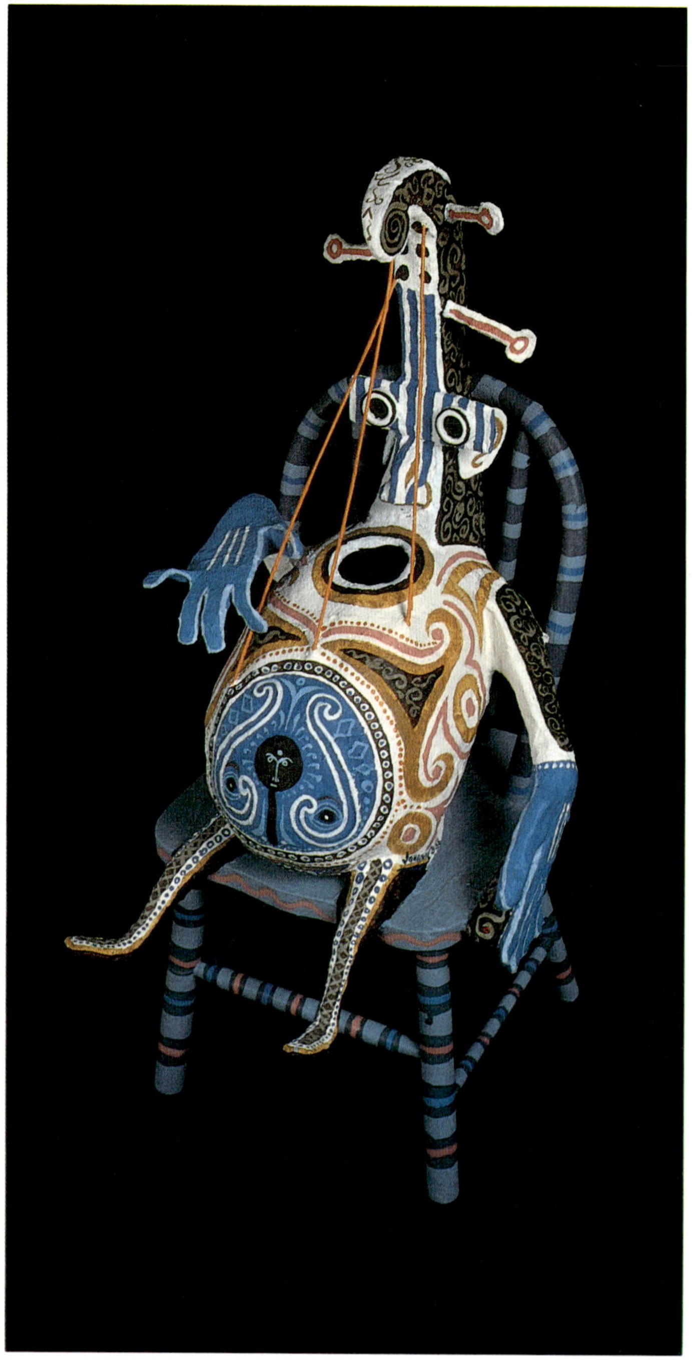

STRUNG OUT 1986. Plaster, wood, acrylic. Photograph by Stephan Rockwerk.

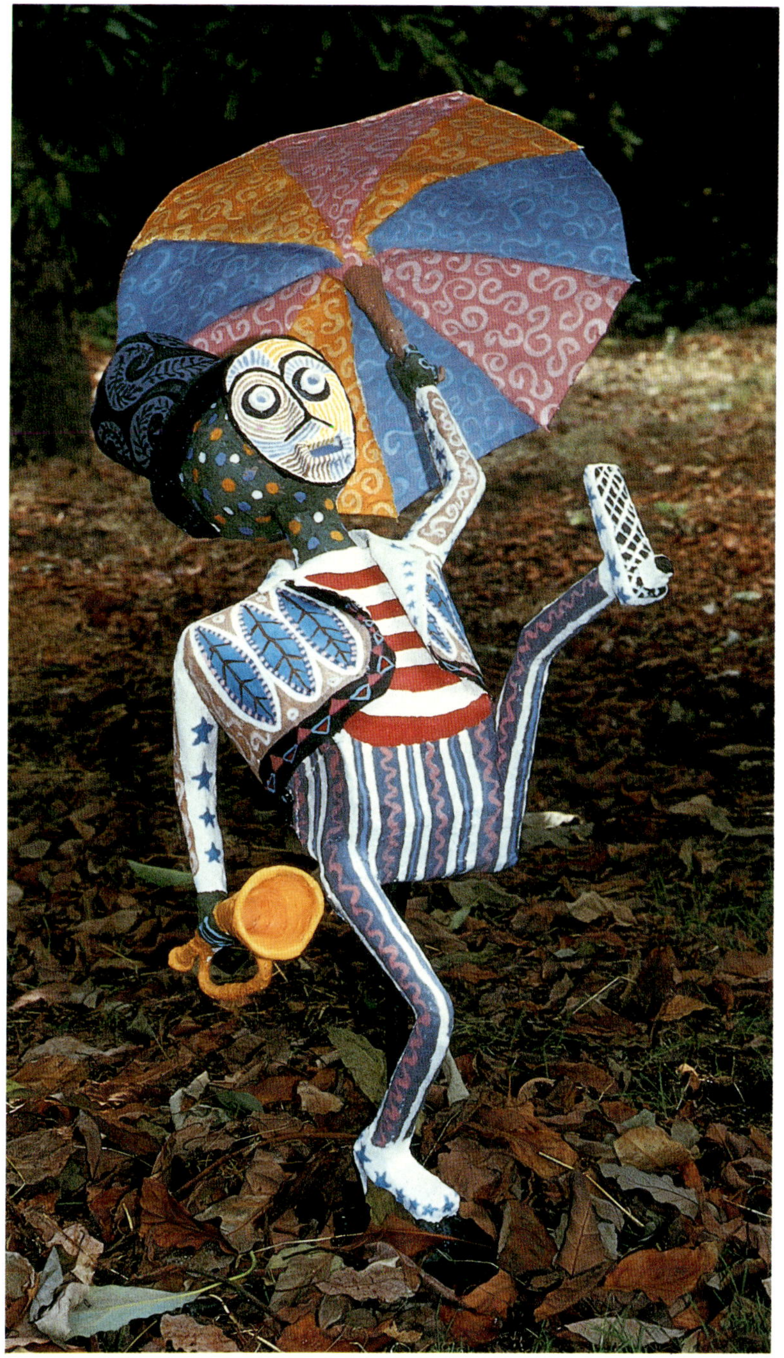

Louisiana Strut 1986. Plaster, wood, acrylic. Collection of Bob Dylan. Photograph by Johnny Otis.

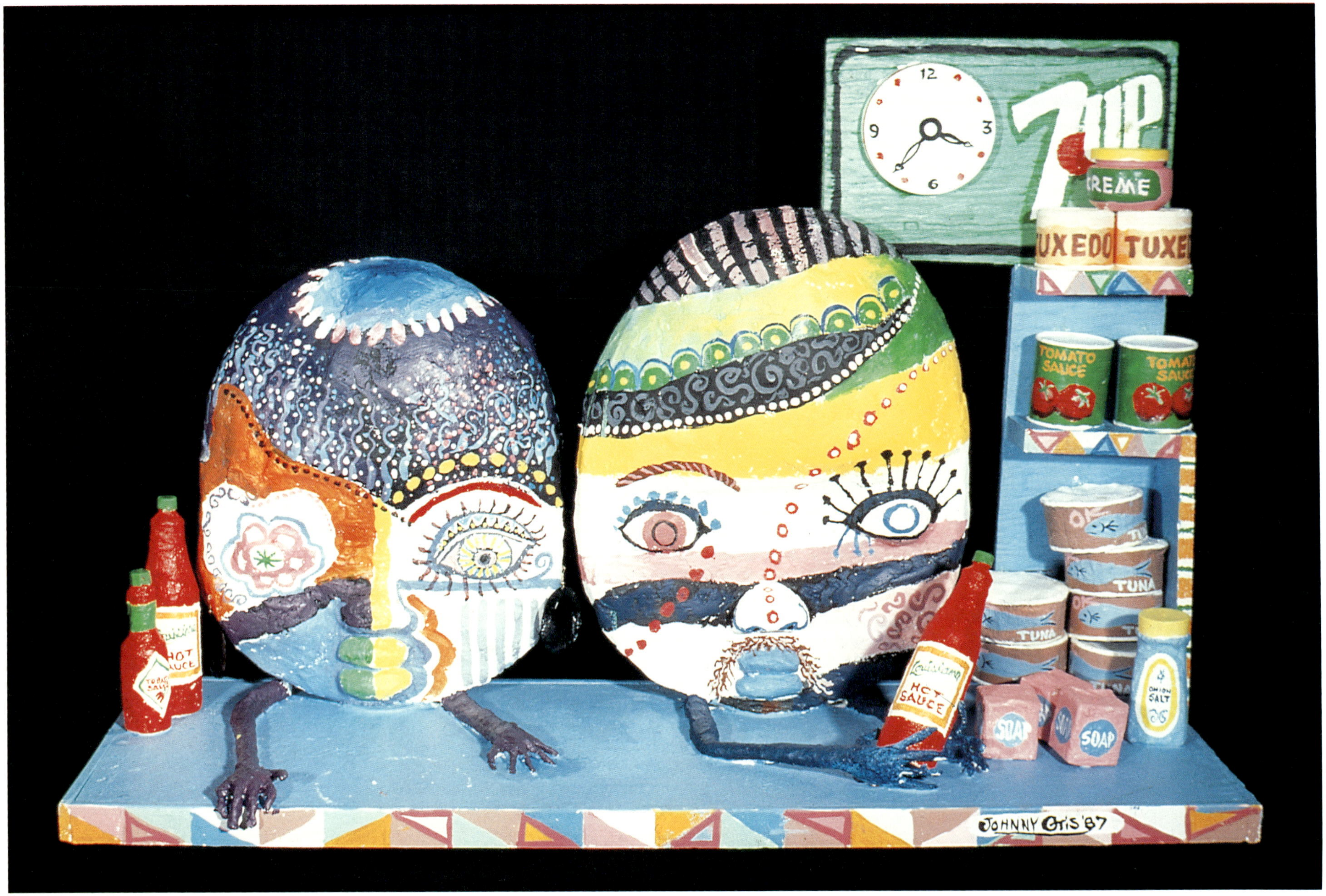

Mom and Pop Store II 1987. Plaster, wood, acrylic. Photograph by Stephan Rockwerk.

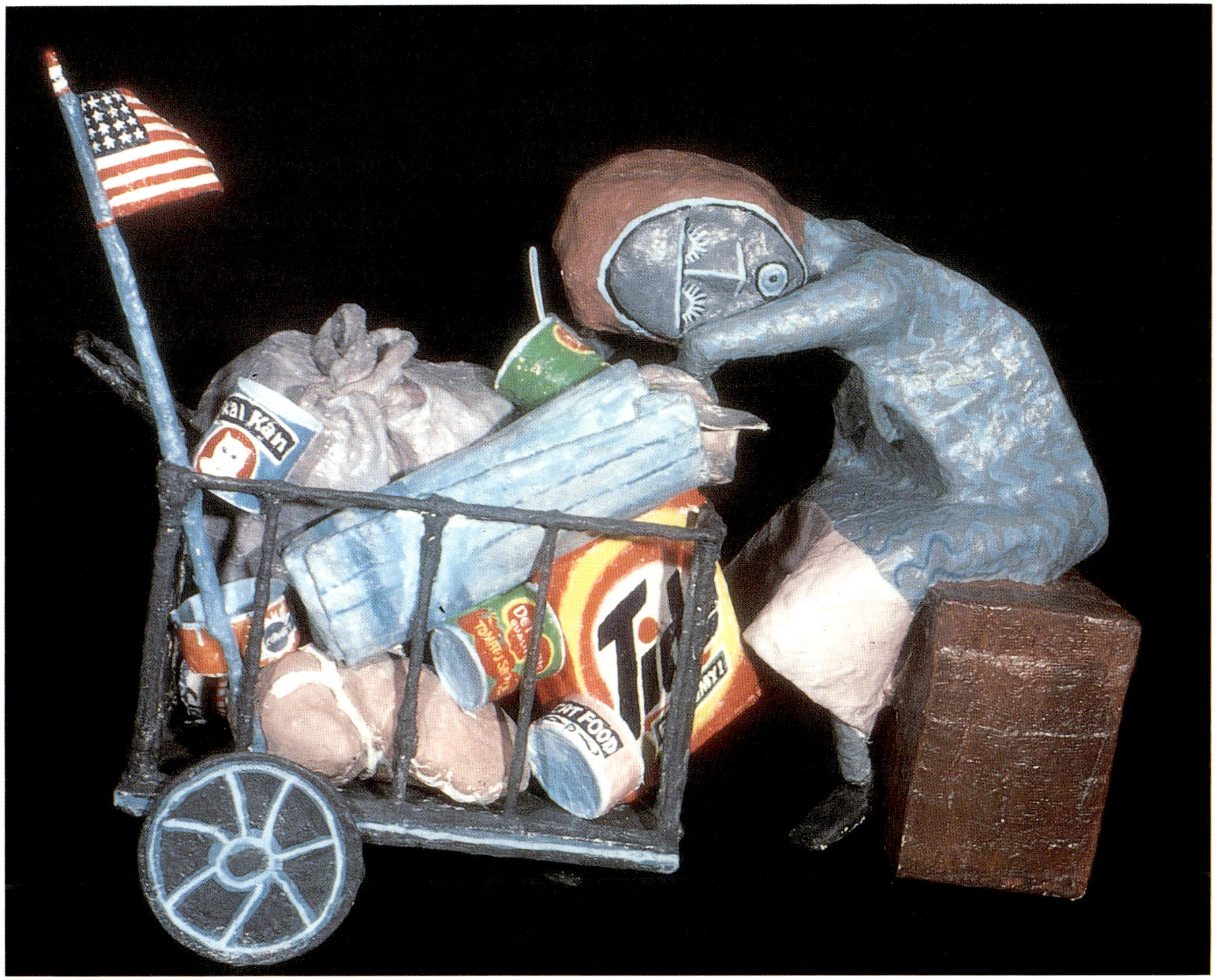

THROUGH THE CRACKS 1987. Plaster, wood, acrylic. Photograph by Stephan Rockwerk.

"DURING THE 1980S AT THE Los Angeles Landmark Church, we tried to feed and clothe as many homeless people as we could. In my eleven years as pastor at Landmark, I saw many heart-rending things, but nothing more poignant than the little homeless bag lady with the American flag tied to the shopping cart that contained all her worldly possessions. Impoverished, undernourished and emotionally unstable, she nonetheless kept her patriotism intact."

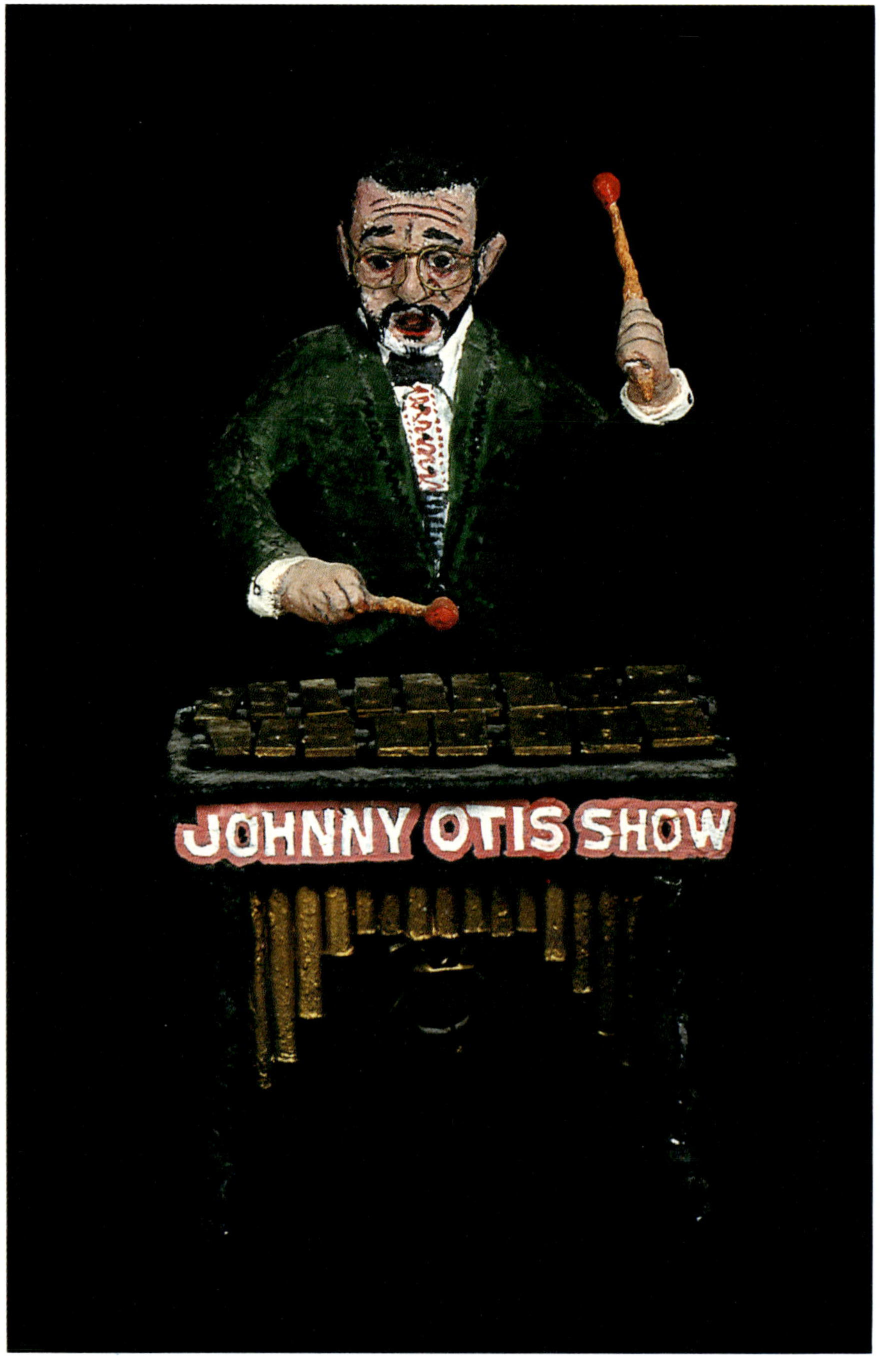

Self Portrait 1988. Plaster, wood, acrylic. Photograph by Stephan Rockwerk.

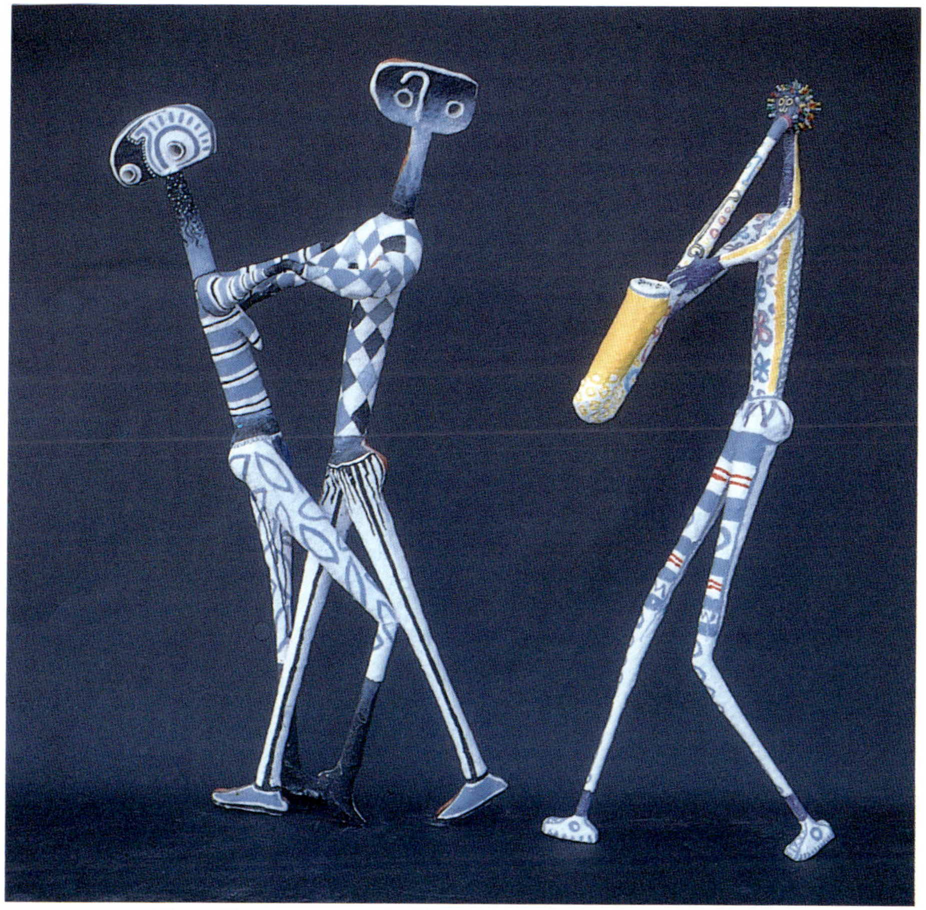

TWO DANCERS 1988, and **SAXOPHONE PLAYER** 1988.
Plaster, wood, acrylic. Photographs by Loren Faber and Johnny Otis.

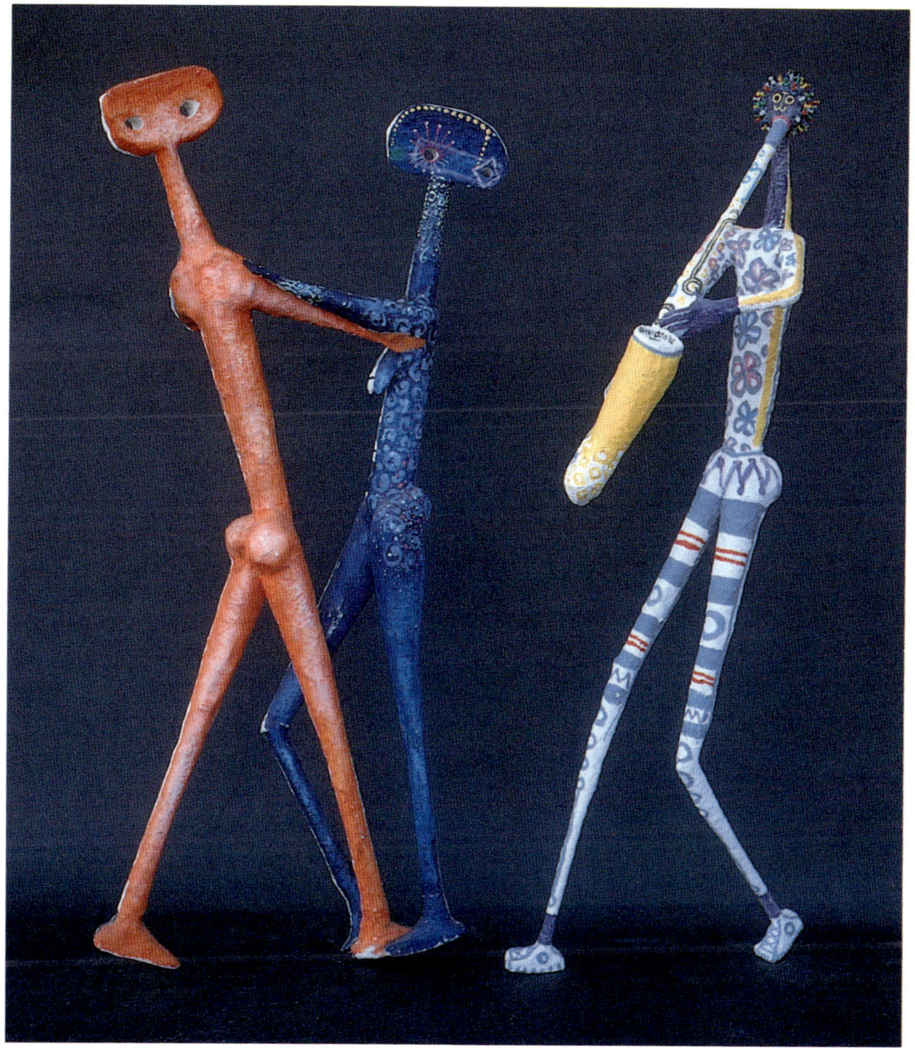

"THE LONG, STICK-FIGURED DANCING couple and sax player hang from my studio ceiling on springs. I put on some beautiful Duke Ellington music, give them a tug, and they dance for me."

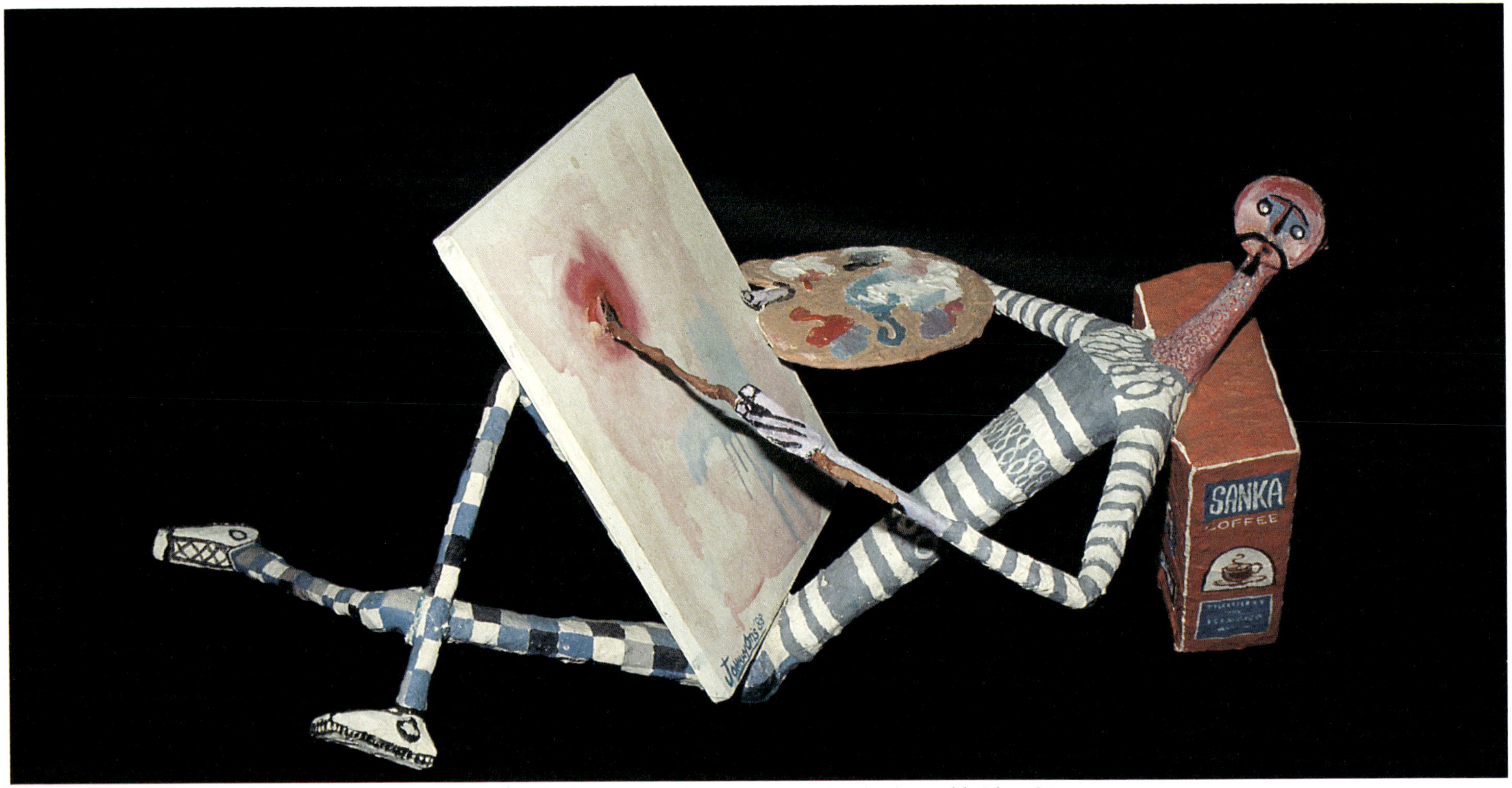

Trying To Get It Right 1989. Plaster, wood, acrylic. Photograph by Johnny Otis.

“**Recently, I was telling my** band members the story of the legendary Uncle Blue. Saxophonist Clifford Solomon was the only person in the band, besides me, who remembered the 1940s one-man band who performed as a street musician up and down Central Avenue and downtown L.A. He dressed in gunnysacks and rundown shoes; he played a motley collection of homemade instruments. Most of the time, Uncle Blue could be found working the streets of downtown Los Angeles, but occasionally, he would appear with his wagon load of homemade paraphernalia on Central Avenue.

“He would set up in front of the Dunbar Hotel or the Club Alabam, position his chamber pot kitty, sit on his stool, and wait stoically until enough coins had been put in the kitty. At this point, he would cause a telephone bell to ring, then he would answer the phone and say something like, ‘Hello, baby. Yeah, sure, I love you honey, but no, I ain’t got no money.’ Then somehow he’d have a smoke bomb explode—actually flour—and he would start singing, humming, scatting, tooting, strumming, and drumming. It was wonderful. How sad that Uncle Blue was never filmed or recorded. When he was found dead in his skid-row room, a Los Angeles policeman told us forty thousand dollars was discovered sewn into the gunnysack rags he wore. We were also told he was sending a daughter through medical school. In my sculpture of *Uncle Blue,* I used bright-colored clothing. Rather than showing him in threadbare tatters, I wanted to reflect the beauty of his spirited artistry.”

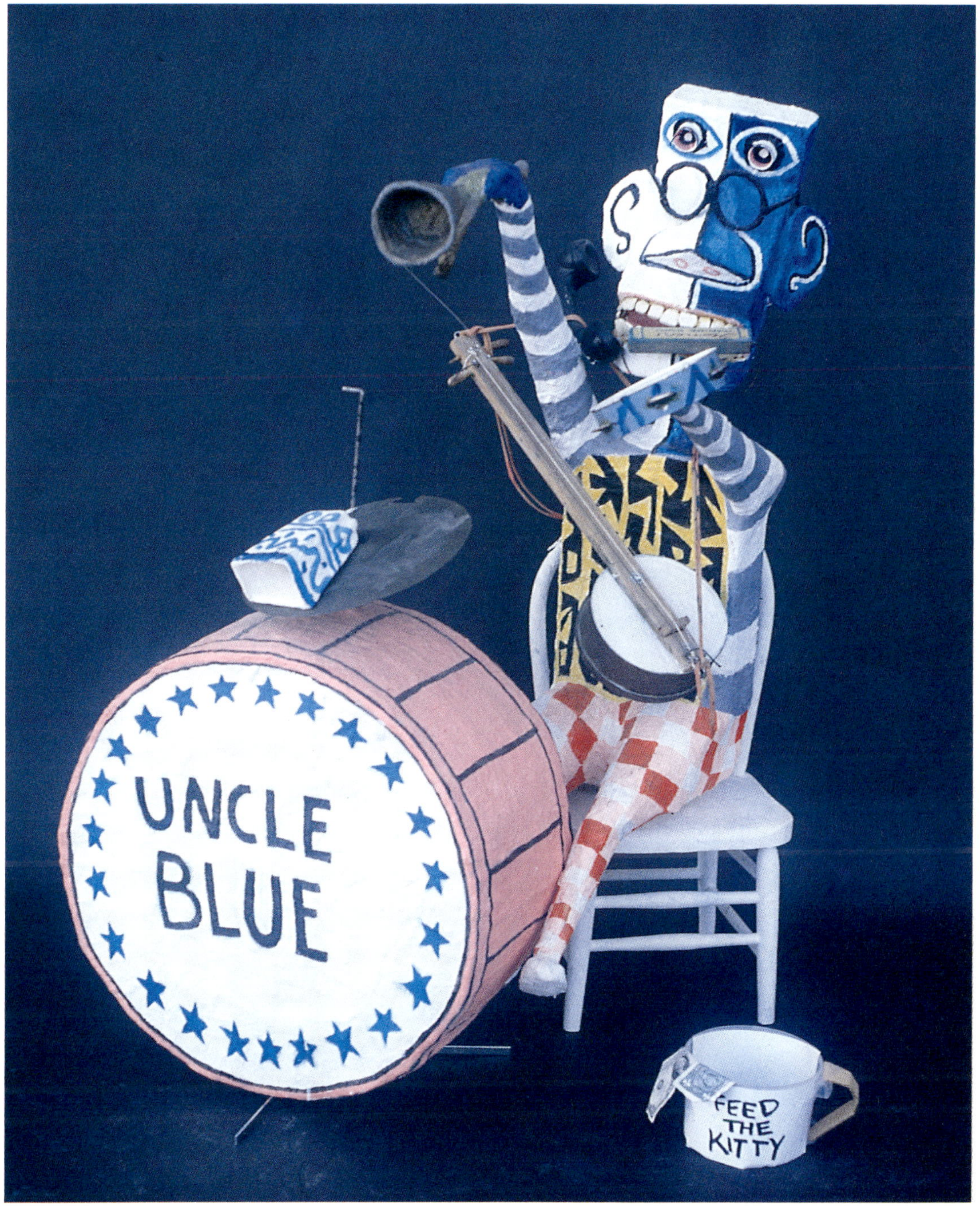

Uncle Blue 1989. Plaster, wood, acrylic. Photograph by Loren Faber and Johnny Otis.

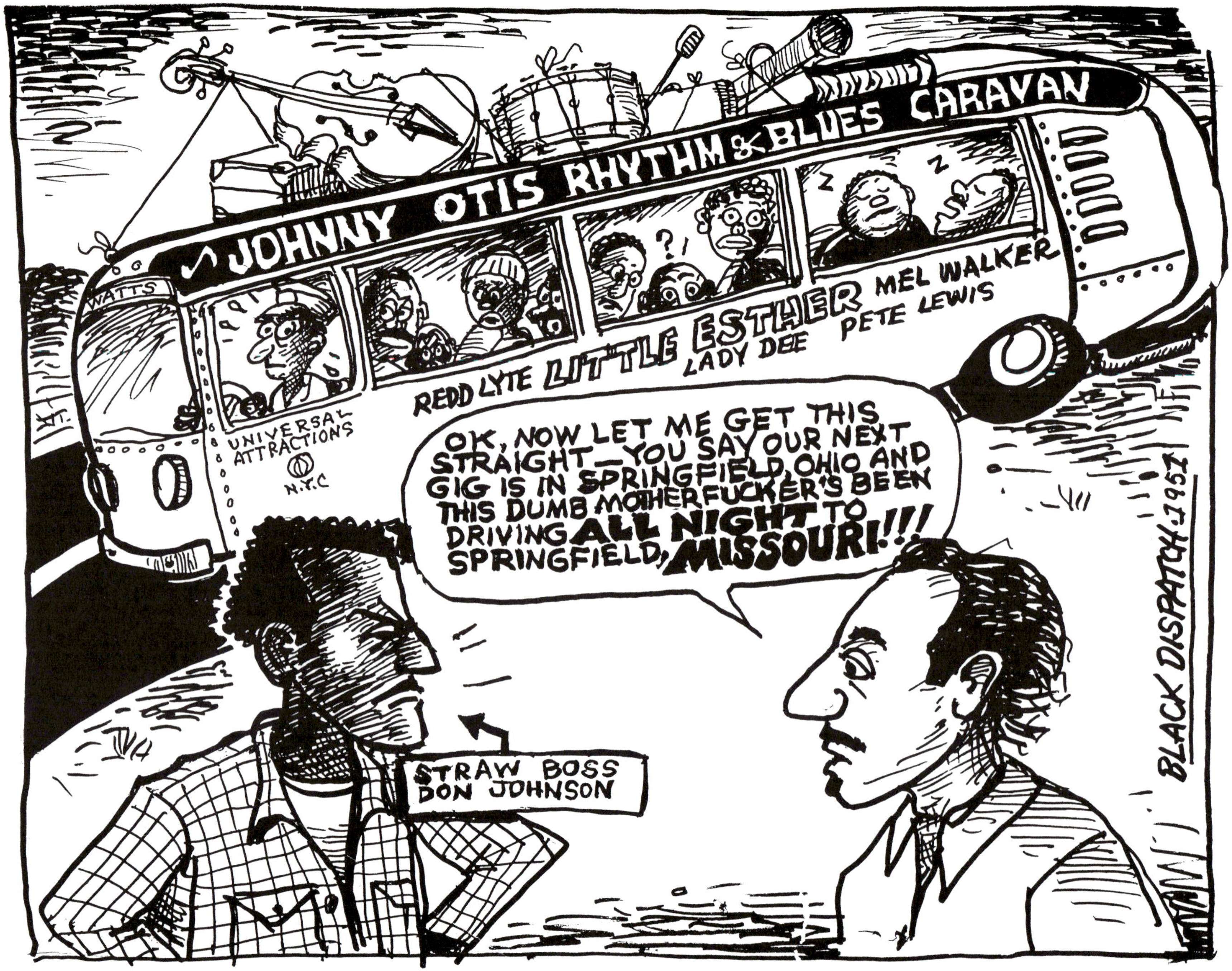
JOHNNY OTIS RHYTHM & BLUES CARAVAN
WATTS
MEL WALKER
PETE LEWIS
LITTLE ESTHER
LADY DEE
REDD LYTE
UNIVERSAL ATTRACTIONS N.Y.C
OK, NOW LET ME GET THIS STRAIGHT—YOU SAY OUR NEXT GIG IS IN SPRINGFIELD, OHIO AND THIS DUMB MOTHERFUCKER'S BEEN DRIVING ALL NIGHT TO SPRINGFIELD, MISSOURI!!!
STRAW BOSS DON JOHNSON
BLACK DISPATCH: 1951

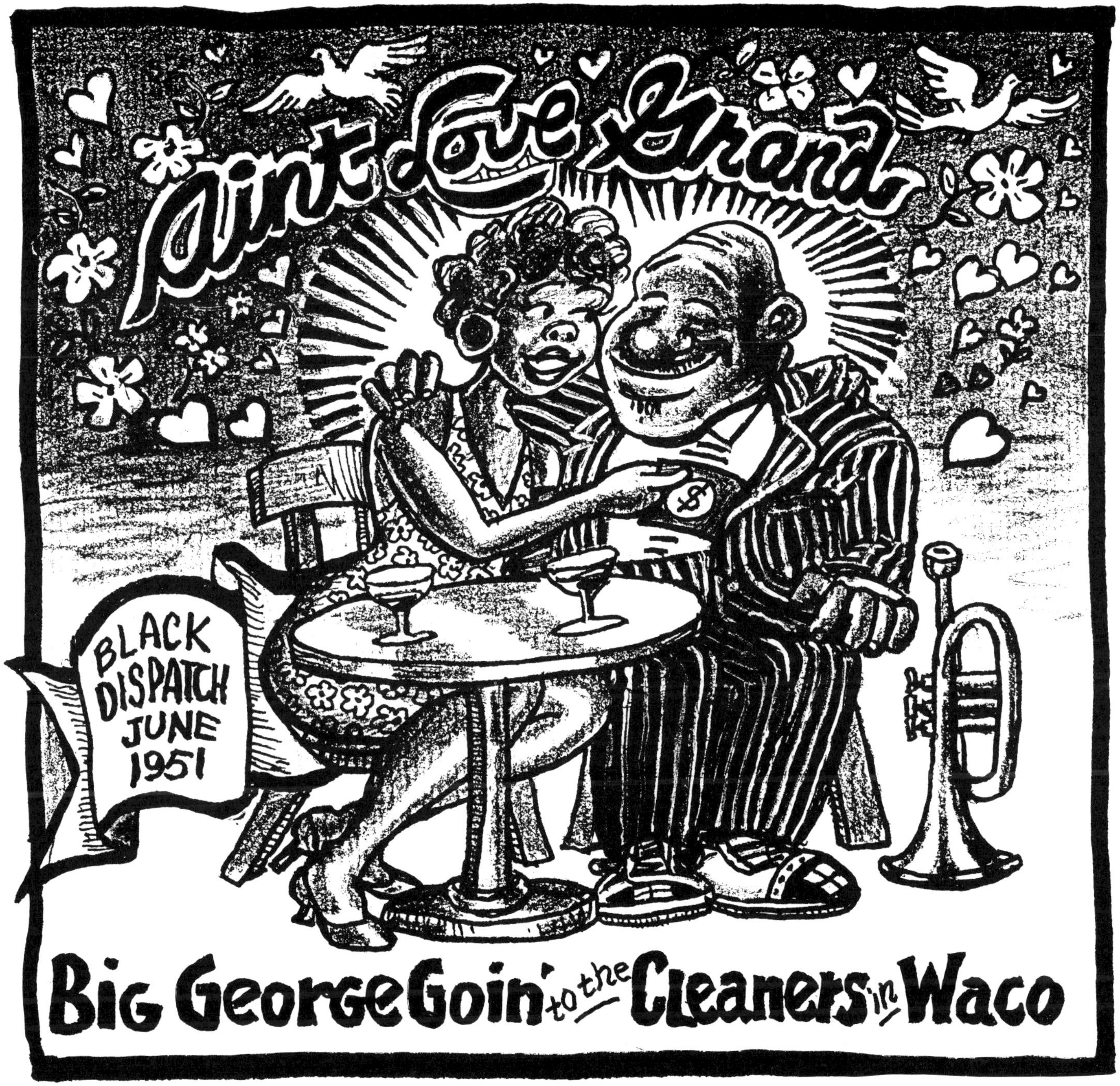
Aint Love Grand
BLACK DISPATCH JUNE 1951
Big George Goin' to the Cleaners in Waco

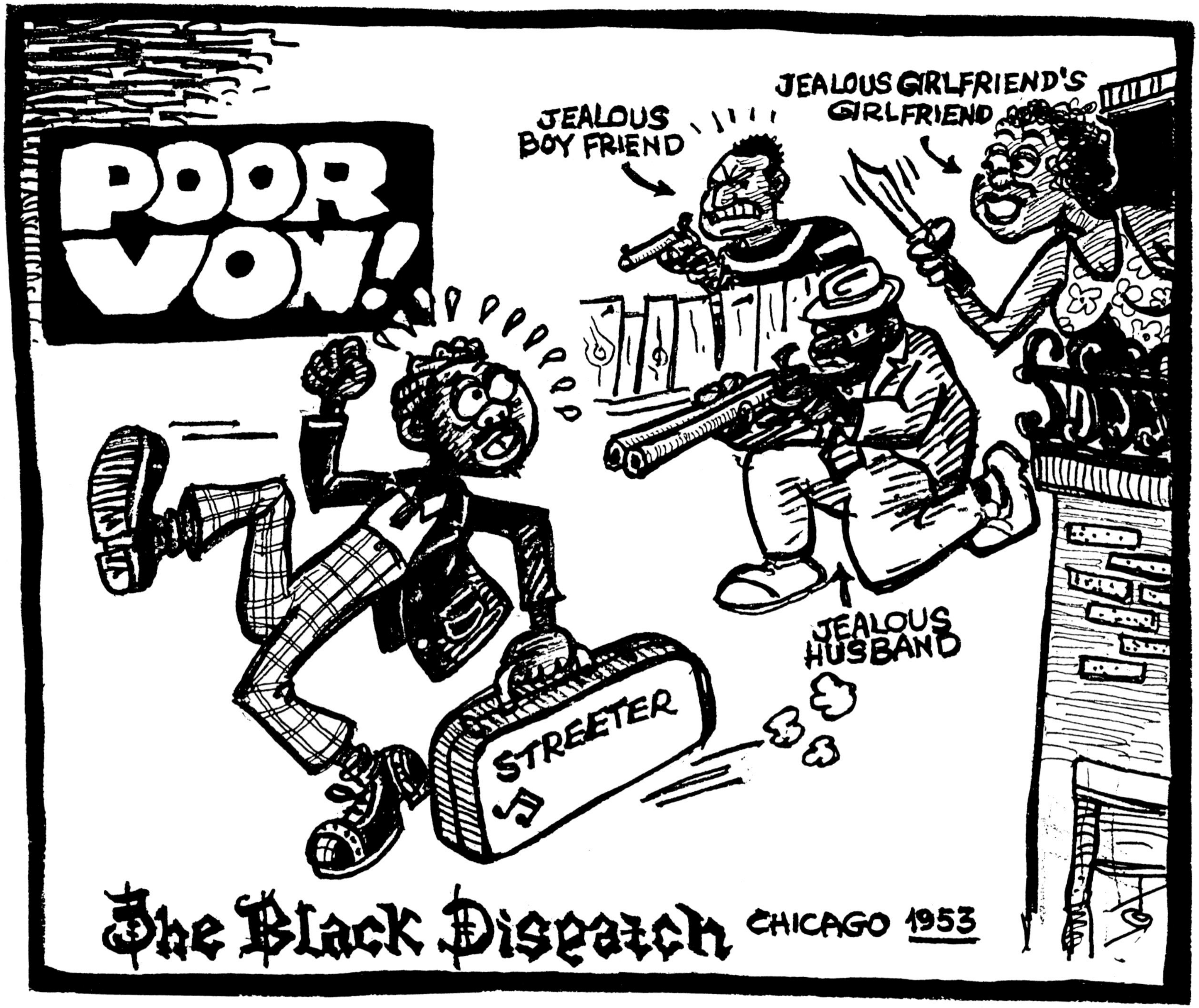
POOR VON!
JEALOUS BOY FRIEND
JEALOUS GIRLFRIEND'S GIRLFRIEND
JEALOUS HUSBAND
STREETER
The Black Dispatch
CHICAGO 1953

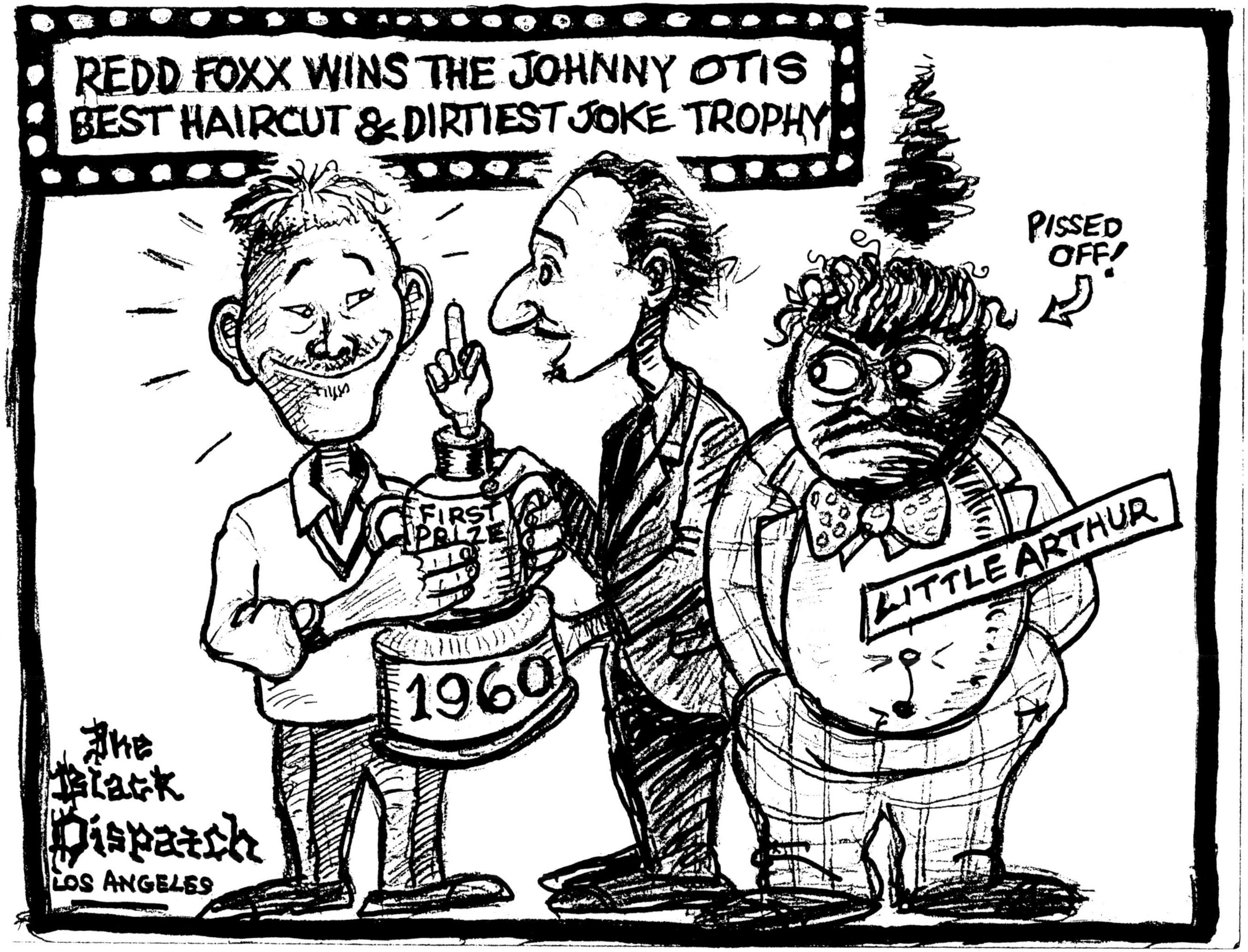
REDD FOXX WINS THE JOHNNY OTIS
BEST HAIRCUT & DIRTIEST JOKE TROPHY
PISSED OFF!
FIRST PRIZE
1960
LITTLE ARTHUR
The Black Dispatch
LOS ANGELES

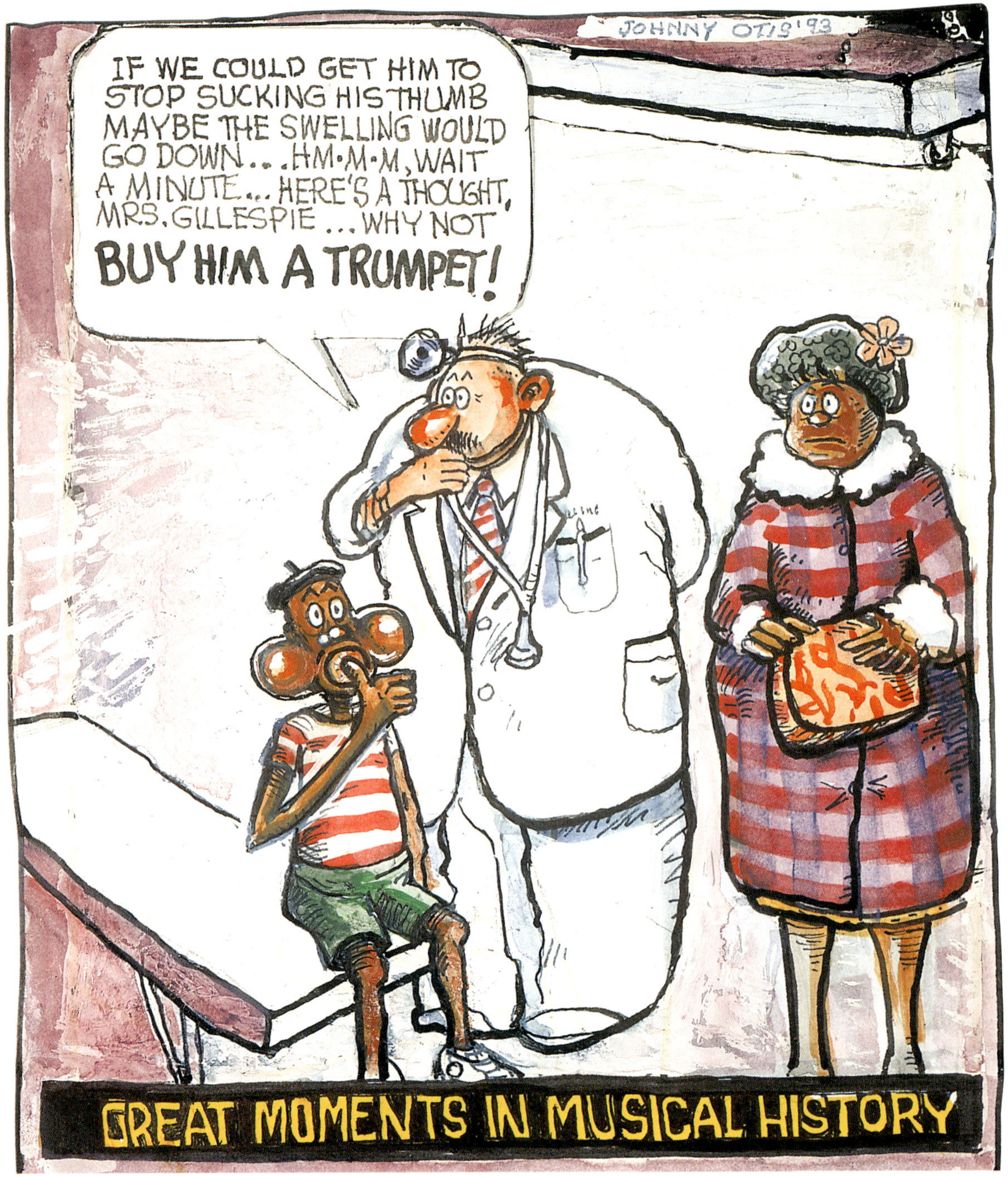
JOHNNY OTIS '93
IF WE COULD GET HIM TO STOP SUCKING HIS THUMB MAYBE THE SWELLING WOULD GO DOWN... .HM-M-M, WAIT A MINUTE... HERE'S A THOUGHT, MRS. GILLESPIE ... WHY NOT BUY HIM A TRUMPET!
GREAT MOMENTS IN MUSICAL HISTORY

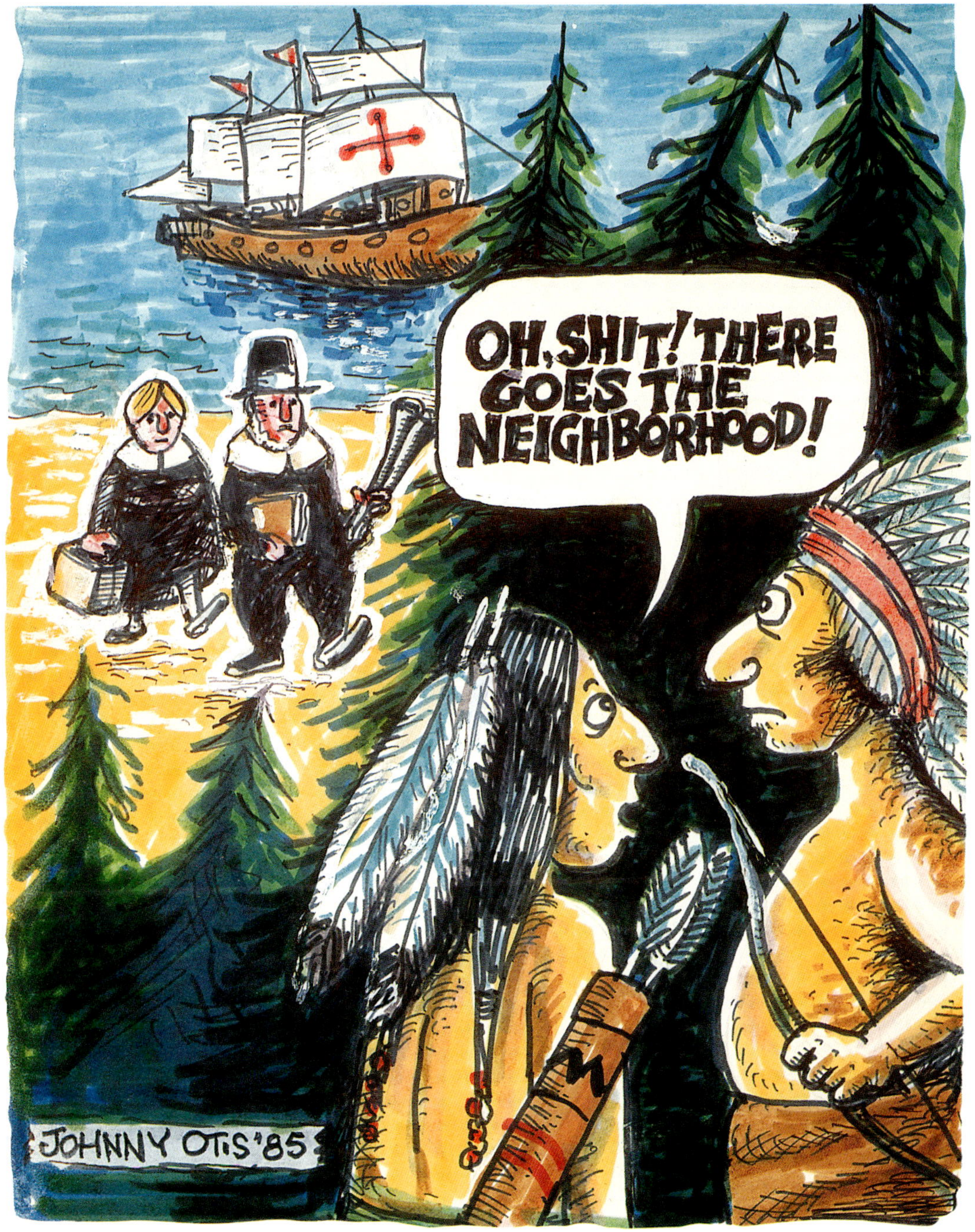
OH, SHIT! THERE GOES THE NEIGHBORHOOD!
JOHNNY OTIS '85

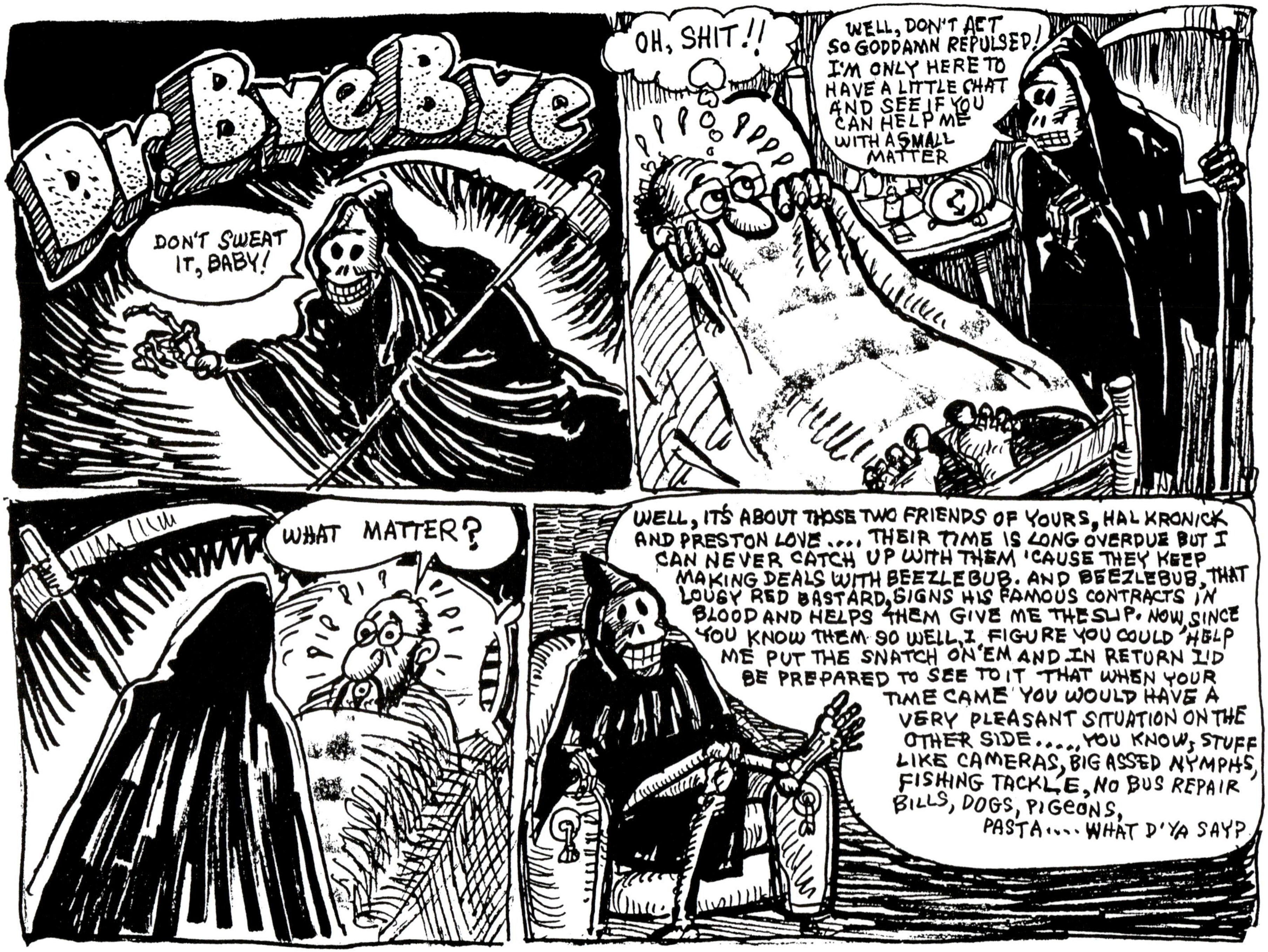
Dr. ByeBye
DON'T SWEAT IT, BABY!
OH, SHIT!!
WELL, DON'T ACT SO GODDAMN REPULSED! I'M ONLY HERE TO HAVE A LITTLE CHAT AND SEE IF YOU CAN HELP ME WITH A SMALL MATTER
WHAT MATTER?
WELL, IT'S ABOUT THOSE TWO FRIENDS OF YOURS, HAL KRONICK AND PRESTON LOVE.... THEIR TIME IS LONG OVERDUE BUT I CAN NEVER CATCH UP WITH THEM 'CAUSE THEY KEEP MAKING DEALS WITH BEEZLEBUB. AND BEEZLEBUB, THAT LOUSY RED BASTARD, SIGNS HIS FAMOUS CONTRACTS IN BLOOD AND HELPS THEM GIVE ME THE SLIP. NOW, SINCE YOU KNOW THEM SO WELL, I FIGURE YOU COULD HELP ME PUT THE SNATCH ON 'EM AND IN RETURN I'D BE PREPARED TO SEE TO IT THAT WHEN YOUR TIME CAME YOU WOULD HAVE A VERY PLEASANT SITUATION ON THE OTHER SIDE...., YOU KNOW, STUFF LIKE CAMERAS, BIG ASSED NYMPHS, FISHING TACKLE, NO BUS REPAIR BILLS, DOGS, PIGEONS, PASTA.... WHAT D'YA SAY?

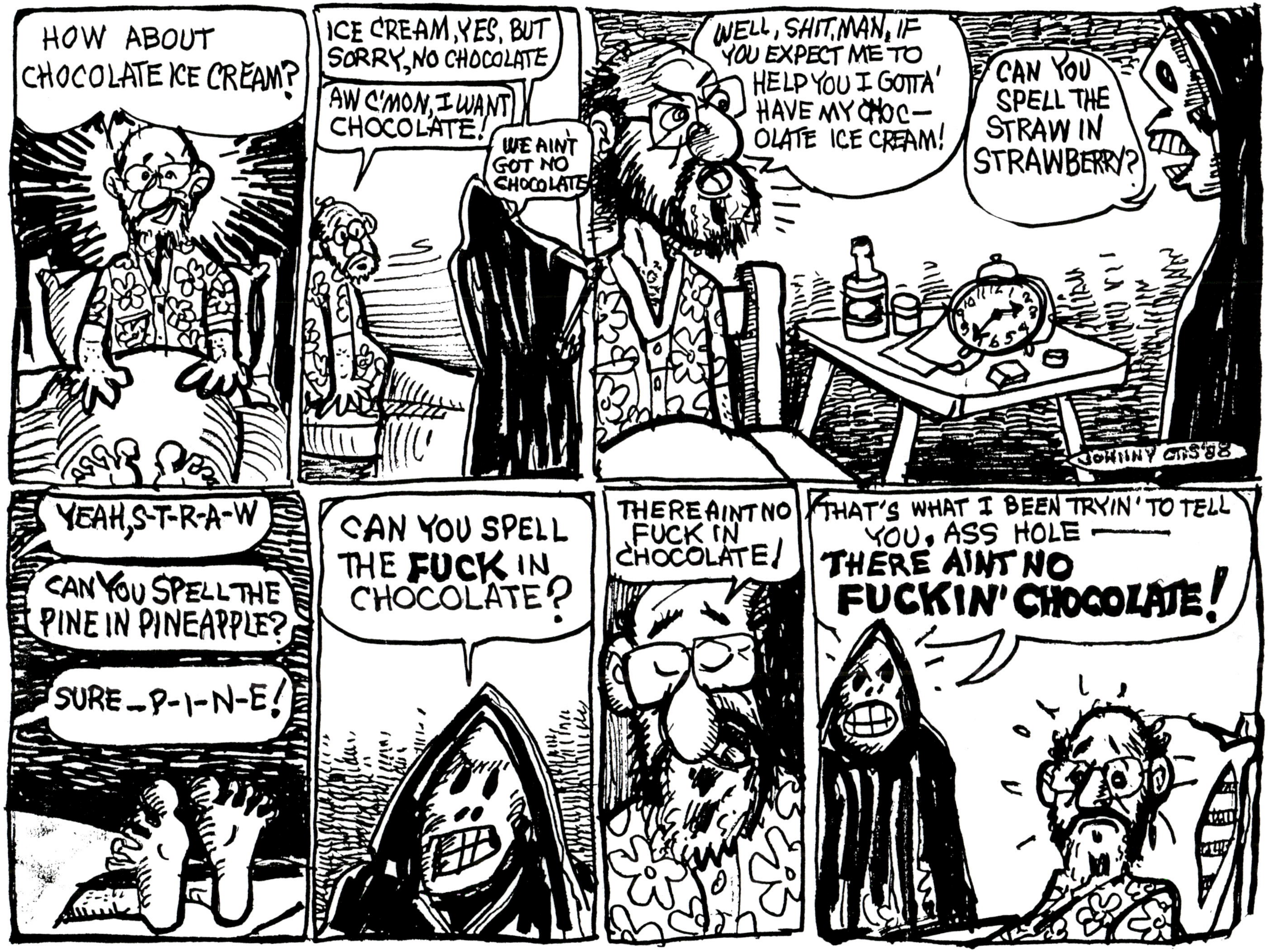
HOW ABOUT CHOCOLATE ICE CREAM?
ICE CREAM, YES, BUT SORRY, NO CHOCOLATE
AW C'MON, I WANT CHOCOLATE!
WE AIN'T GOT NO CHOCOLATE
WELL, SHIT, MAN, IF YOU EXPECT ME TO HELP YOU I GOTTA' HAVE MY CHOC-OLATE ICE CREAM!
CAN YOU SPELL THE STRAW IN STRAWBERRY?
JOHNNY OTIS '88
YEAH, S-T-R-A-W
CAN YOU SPELL THE PINE IN PINEAPPLE?
SURE — P-I-N-E!
CAN YOU SPELL THE FUCK IN CHOCOLATE?
THERE AINT NO FUCK IN CHOCOLATE!
THAT'S WHAT I BEEN TRYIN' TO TELL YOU, ASS HOLE —
THERE AINT NO FUCKIN' CHOCOLATE!

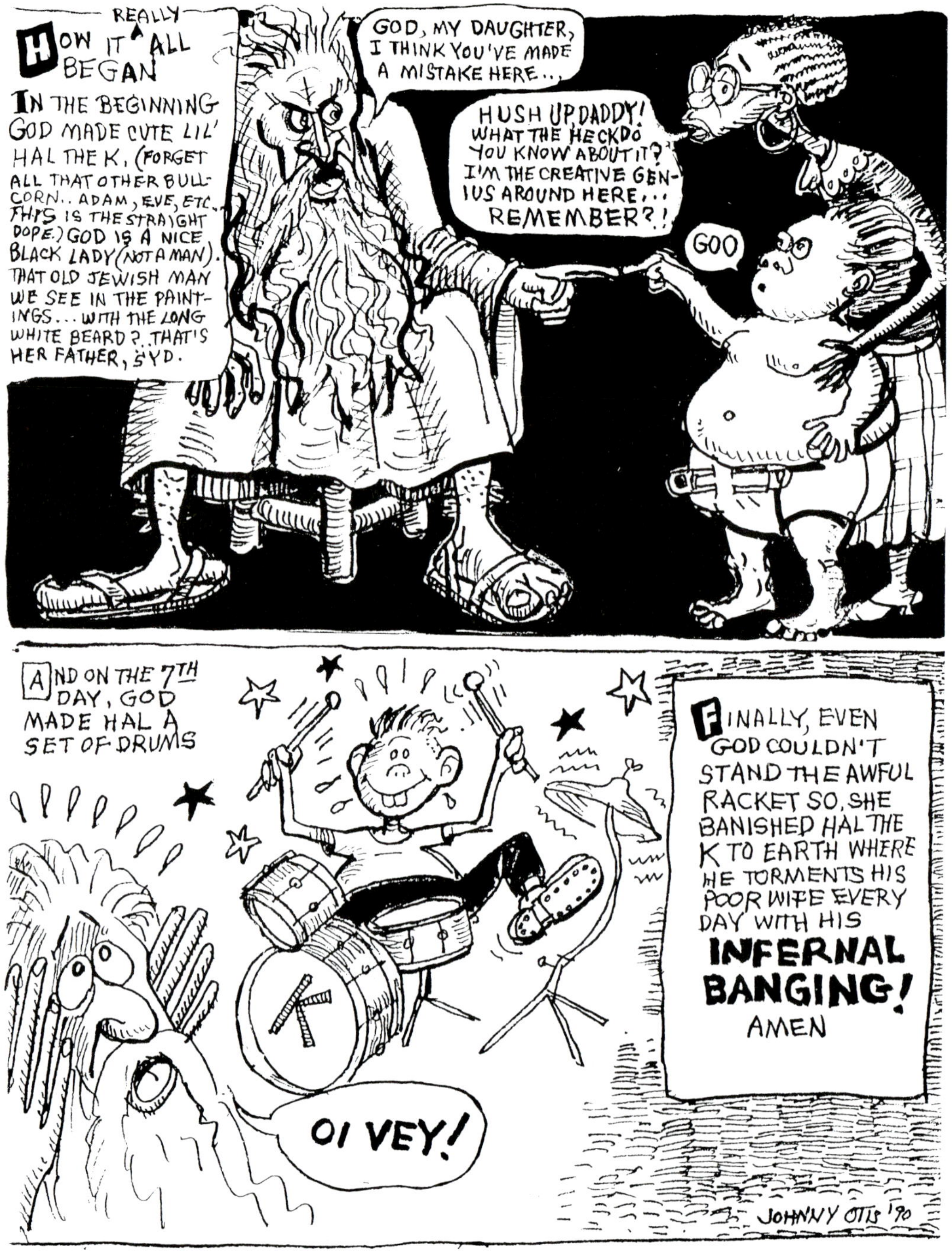

Pages 108–112: Five selections from a nine-page explanation of *Sid.*

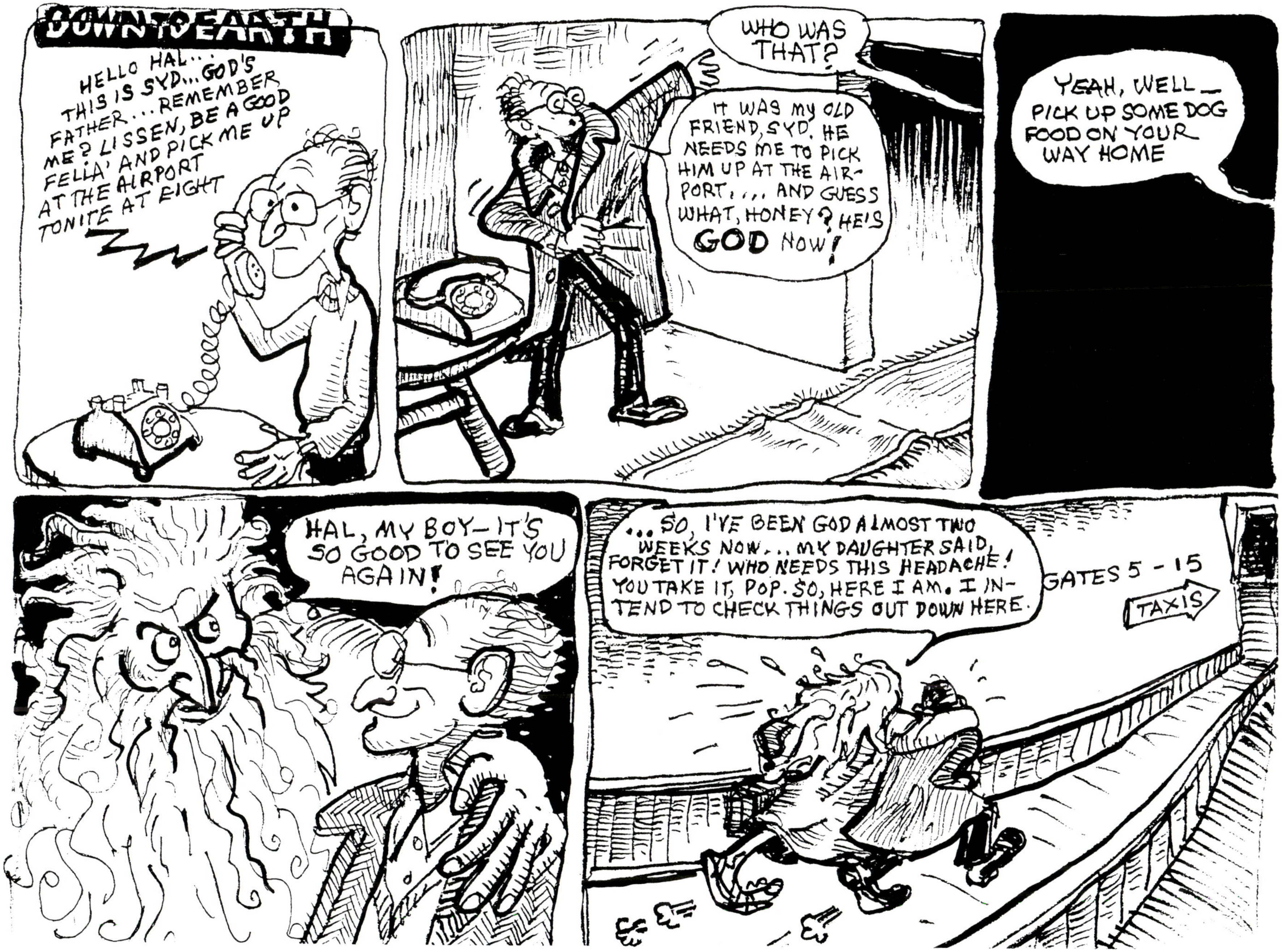
DOWN TO EARTH
HELLO HAL... THIS IS SYD... GOD'S FATHER... REMEMBER ME? LISSEN, BE A GOOD FELLA' AND PICK ME UP AT THE AIRPORT TONITE AT EIGHT
WHO WAS THAT?
IT WAS MY OLD FRIEND, SYD. HE NEEDS ME TO PICK HIM UP AT THE AIR-PORT.... AND GUESS WHAT, HONEY? HE'S GOD NOW!
YEAH, WELL_ PICK UP SOME DOG FOOD ON YOUR WAY HOME
HAL, MY BOY–IT'S SO GOOD TO SEE YOU AGAIN!
...SO, I'VE BEEN GOD ALMOST TWO WEEKS NOW... MY DAUGHTER SAID, FORGET IT! WHO NEEDS THIS HEADACHE! YOU TAKE IT, POP. SO, HERE I AM. I IN-TEND TO CHECK THINGS OUT DOWN HERE.
GATES 5 - 15
TAXIS

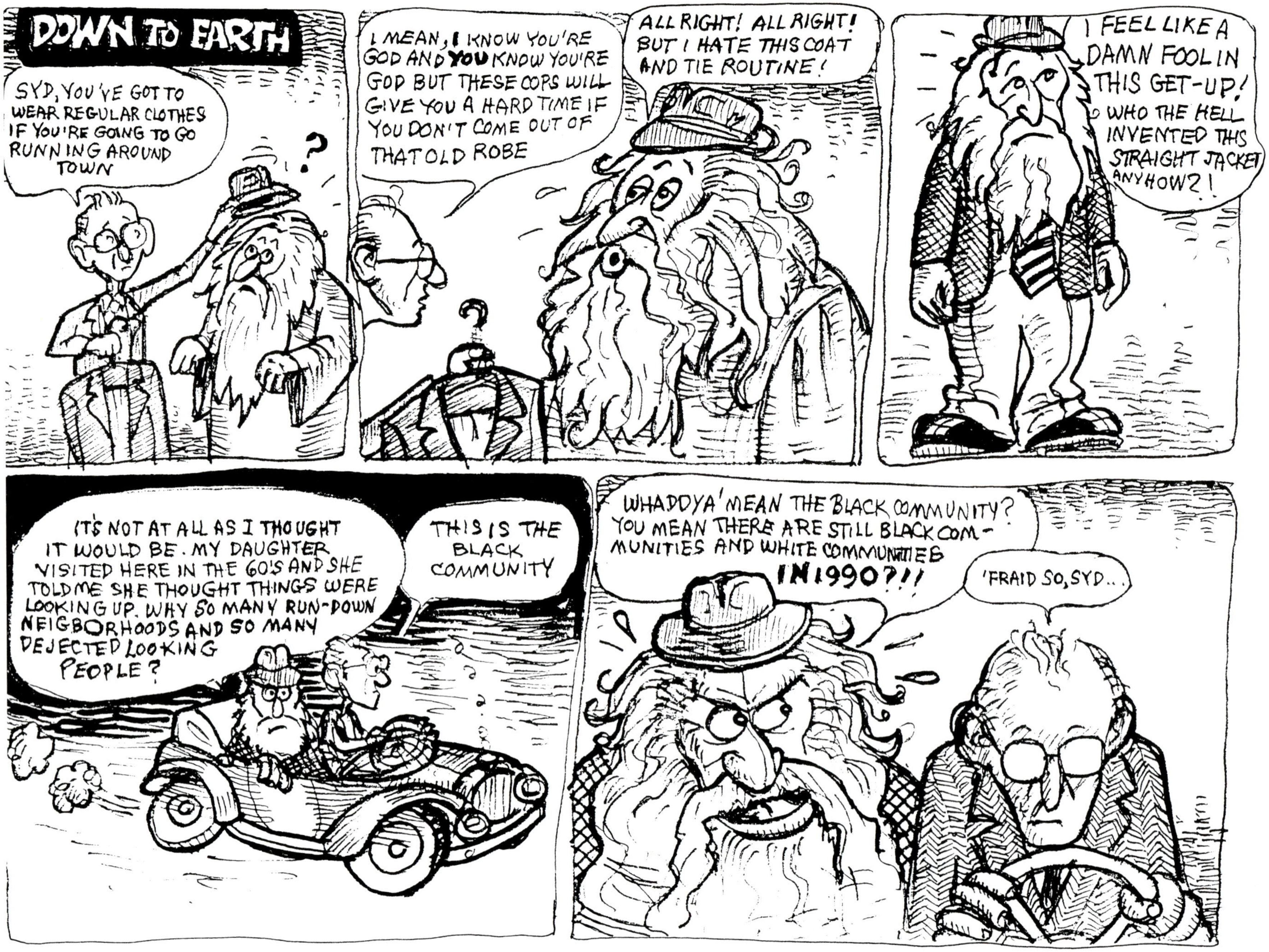
DOWN TO EARTH
SYD, YOU'VE GOT TO WEAR REGULAR CLOTHES IF YOU'RE GOING TO GO RUNNING AROUND TOWN
I MEAN, I KNOW YOU'RE GOD AND YOU KNOW YOU'RE GOD BUT THESE COPS WILL GIVE YOU A HARD TIME IF YOU DON'T COME OUT OF THAT OLD ROBE
ALL RIGHT! ALL RIGHT! BUT I HATE THIS COAT AND TIE ROUTINE!
I FEEL LIKE A DAMN FOOL IN THIS GET-UP! WHO THE HELL INVENTED THIS STRAIGHT JACKET ANYHOW?!
IT'S NOT AT ALL AS I THOUGHT IT WOULD BE. MY DAUGHTER VISITED HERE IN THE 60'S AND SHE TOLD ME SHE THOUGHT THINGS WERE LOOKING UP. WHY SO MANY RUN-DOWN NEIGBORHOODS AND SO MANY DEJECTED LOOKING PEOPLE?
THIS IS THE BLACK COMMUNITY
WHADDYA' MEAN THE BLACK COMMUNITY? YOU MEAN THERE ARE STILL BLACK COMMUNITIES AND WHITE COMMUNITIES IN 1990?!!
'FRAID SO, SYD...

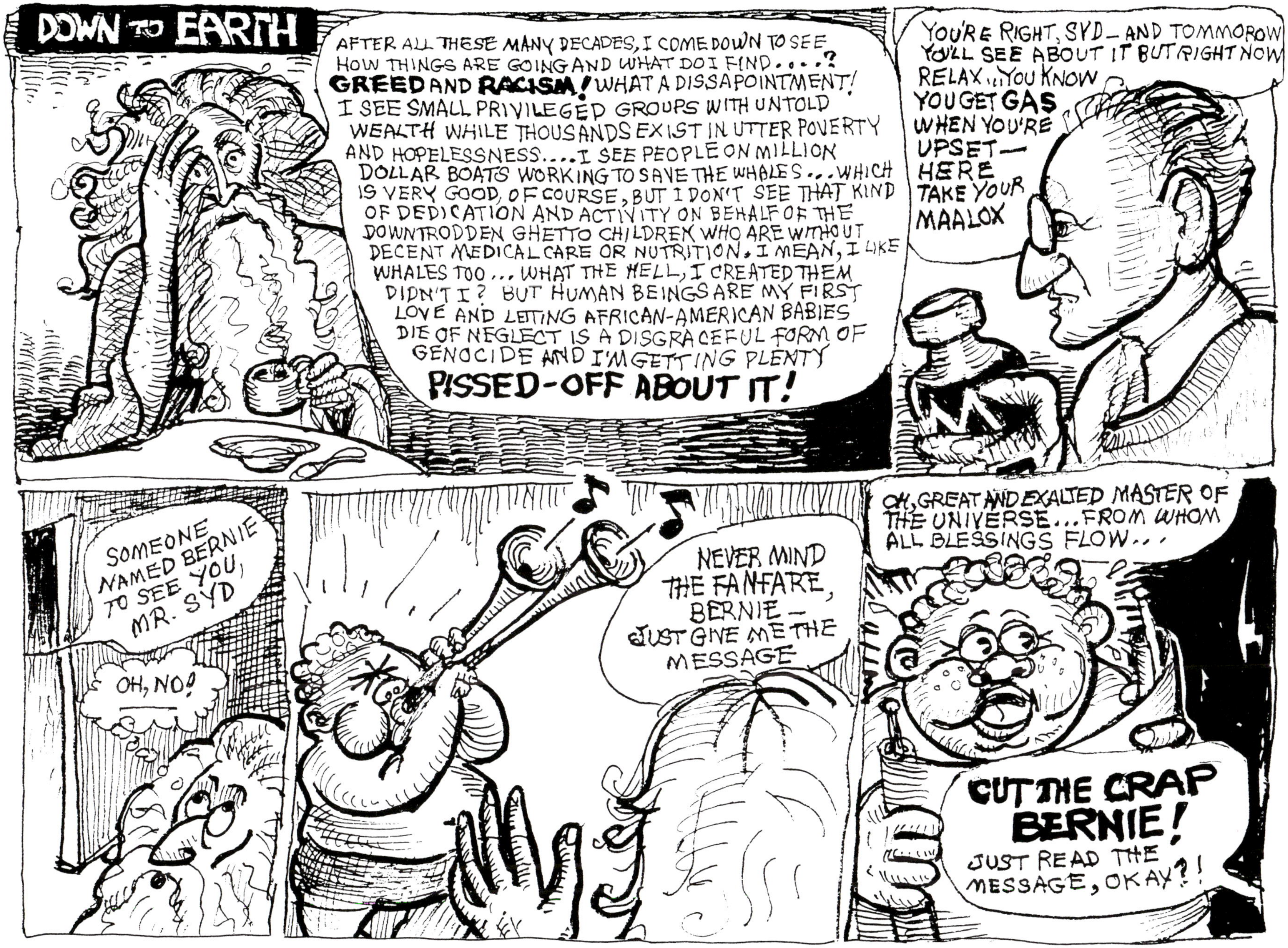
DOWN TO EARTH
AFTER ALL THESE MANY DECADES, I COME DOWN TO SEE HOW THINGS ARE GOING AND WHAT DO I FIND....? GREED AND RACISM! WHAT A DISSAPOINTMENT! I SEE SMALL PRIVILEGED GROUPS WITH UNTOLD WEALTH WHILE THOUSANDS EXIST IN UTTER POVERTY AND HOPELESSNESS.... I SEE PEOPLE ON MILLION DOLLAR BOATS WORKING TO SAVE THE WHALES... WHICH IS VERY GOOD, OF COURSE, BUT I DON'T SEE THAT KIND OF DEDICATION AND ACTIVITY ON BEHALF OF THE DOWNTRODDEN GHETTO CHILDREN WHO ARE WITHOUT DECENT MEDICAL CARE OR NUTRITION. I MEAN, I LIKE WHALES TOO... WHAT THE HELL, I CREATED THEM DIDN'T I? BUT HUMAN BEINGS ARE MY FIRST LOVE AND LETTING AFRICAN-AMERICAN BABIES DIE OF NEGLECT IS A DISGRACEFUL FORM OF GENOCIDE AND I'M GETTING PLENTY PISSED-OFF ABOUT IT!
YOU'RE RIGHT, SYD — AND TOMMOROW YOU'LL SEE ABOUT IT BUT RIGHT NOW RELAX... YOU KNOW YOU GET GAS WHEN YOU'RE UPSET — HERE TAKE YOUR MAALOX
SOMEONE NAMED BERNIE TO SEE YOU, MR. SYD
OH, NO!
NEVER MIND THE FANFARE, BERNIE — JUST GIVE ME THE MESSAGE
OH, GREAT AND EXALTED MASTER OF THE UNIVERSE... FROM WHOM ALL BLESSINGS FLOW...
CUT THE CRAP BERNIE! JUST READ THE MESSAGE, OKAY?!

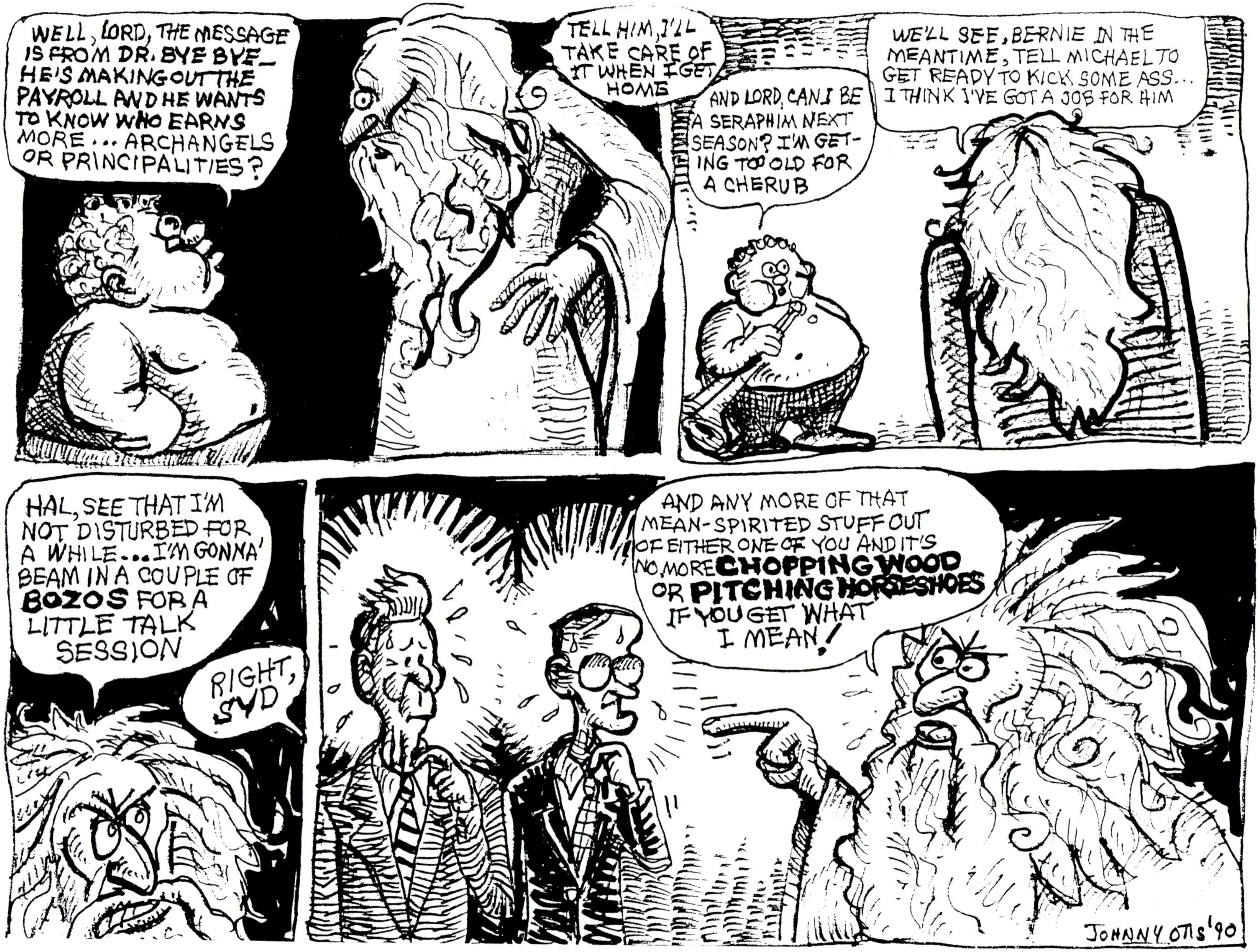
WELL, LORD, THE MESSAGE IS FROM DR. BYE BYE— HE'S MAKING OUT THE PAYROLL AND HE WANTS TO KNOW WHO EARNS MORE... ARCHANGELS OR PRINCIPALITIES?
TELL HIM, I'LL TAKE CARE OF IT WHEN I GET HOME
AND LORD, CAN I BE A SERAPHIM NEXT SEASON? I'M GETTING TOO OLD FOR A CHERUB
WE'LL SEE, BERNIE IN THE MEANTIME, TELL MICHAEL TO GET READY TO KICK SOME ASS... I THINK I'VE GOT A JOB FOR HIM
HAL, SEE THAT I'M NOT DISTURBED FOR A WHILE... I'M GONNA' BEAM IN A COUPLE OF BOZOS FOR A LITTLE TALK SESSION
RIGHT, SYD
AND ANY MORE OF THAT MEAN-SPIRITED STUFF OUT OF EITHER ONE OF YOU AND IT'S NO MORE CHOPPING WOOD OR PITCHING HORSESHOES IF YOU GET WHAT I MEAN!
JOHNNY OTIS '90

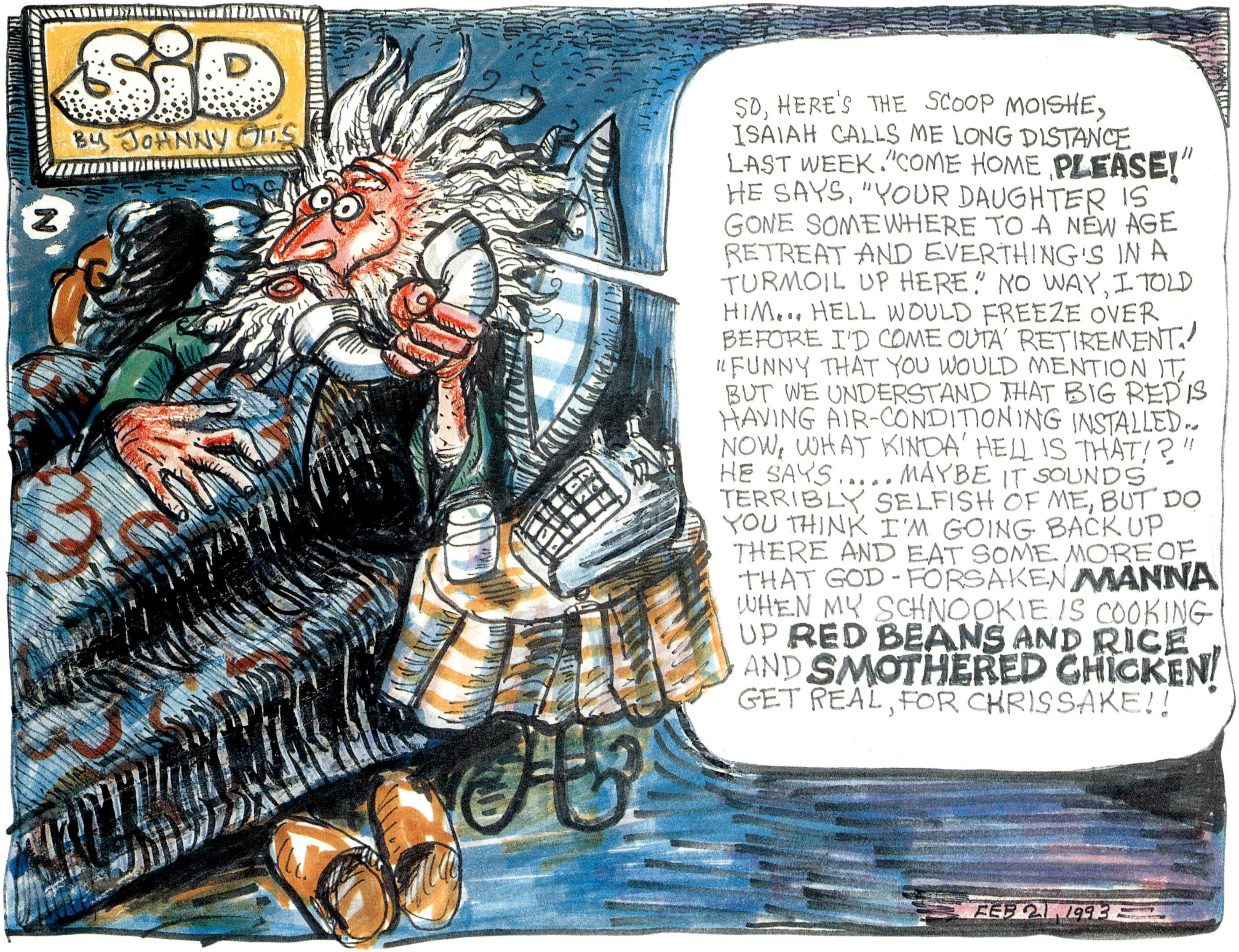
SID
BY JOHNNY OTIS
Z
SO, HERE'S THE SCOOP MOISHE, ISAIAH CALLS ME LONG DISTANCE LAST WEEK. "COME HOME, PLEASE!" HE SAYS, "YOUR DAUGHTER IS GONE SOMEWHERE TO A NEW AGE RETREAT AND EVERTHING'S IN A TURMOIL UP HERE." NO WAY, I TOLD HIM... HELL WOULD FREEZE OVER BEFORE I'D COME OUTA' RETIREMENT.' "FUNNY THAT YOU WOULD MENTION IT, BUT WE UNDERSTAND THAT BIG RED IS HAVING AIR-CONDITIONING INSTALLED.. NOW, WHAT KINDA' HELL IS THAT!?" HE SAYS..... MAYBE IT SOUNDS TERRIBLY SELFISH OF ME, BUT DO YOU THINK I'M GOING BACK UP THERE AND EAT SOME MORE OF THAT GOD-FORSAKEN MANNA WHEN MY SCHNOOKIE IS COOKING UP RED BEANS AND RICE AND SMOTHERED CHICKEN! GET REAL, FOR CHRISSAKE!!
FEB 21, 1993

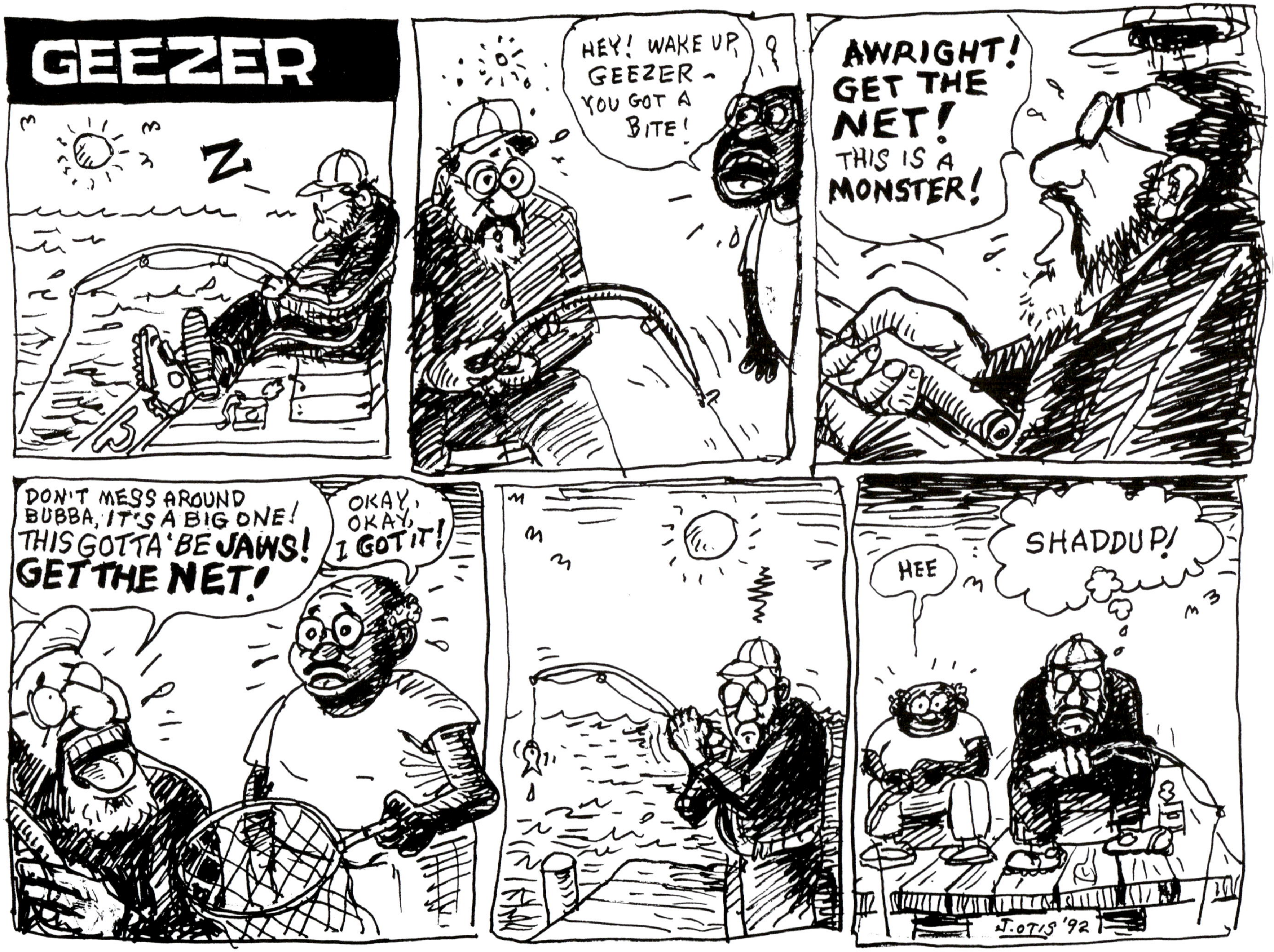
GEEZER
Z
HEY! WAKE UP, GEEZER - YOU GOT A BITE!
AWRIGHT! GET THE NET! THIS IS A MONSTER!
DON'T MESS AROUND BUBBA, IT'S A BIG ONE! THIS GOTTA' BE JAWS! GET THE NET!
OKAY, OKAY, I GOT IT!
HEE
SHADDUP!
J. OTIS '92

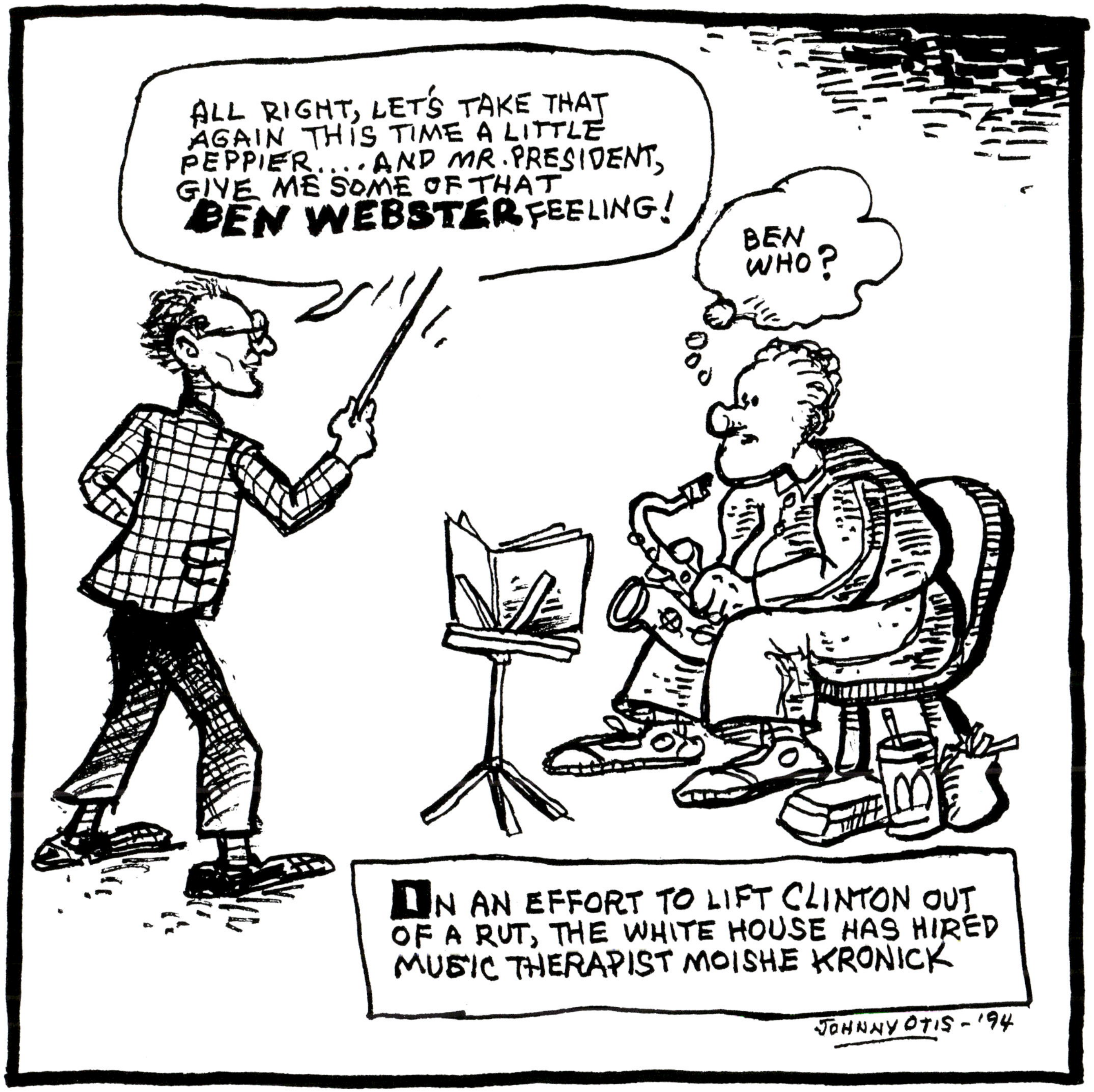
ALL RIGHT, LET'S TAKE THAT AGAIN THIS TIME A LITTLE PEPPIER....AND MR. PRESIDENT, GIVE ME SOME OF THAT BEN WEBSTER FEELING!
BEN WHO?
IN AN EFFORT TO LIFT CLINTON OUT OF A RUT, THE WHITE HOUSE HAS HIRED MUSIC THERAPIST MOISHE KRONICK
JOHNNY OTIS - '94

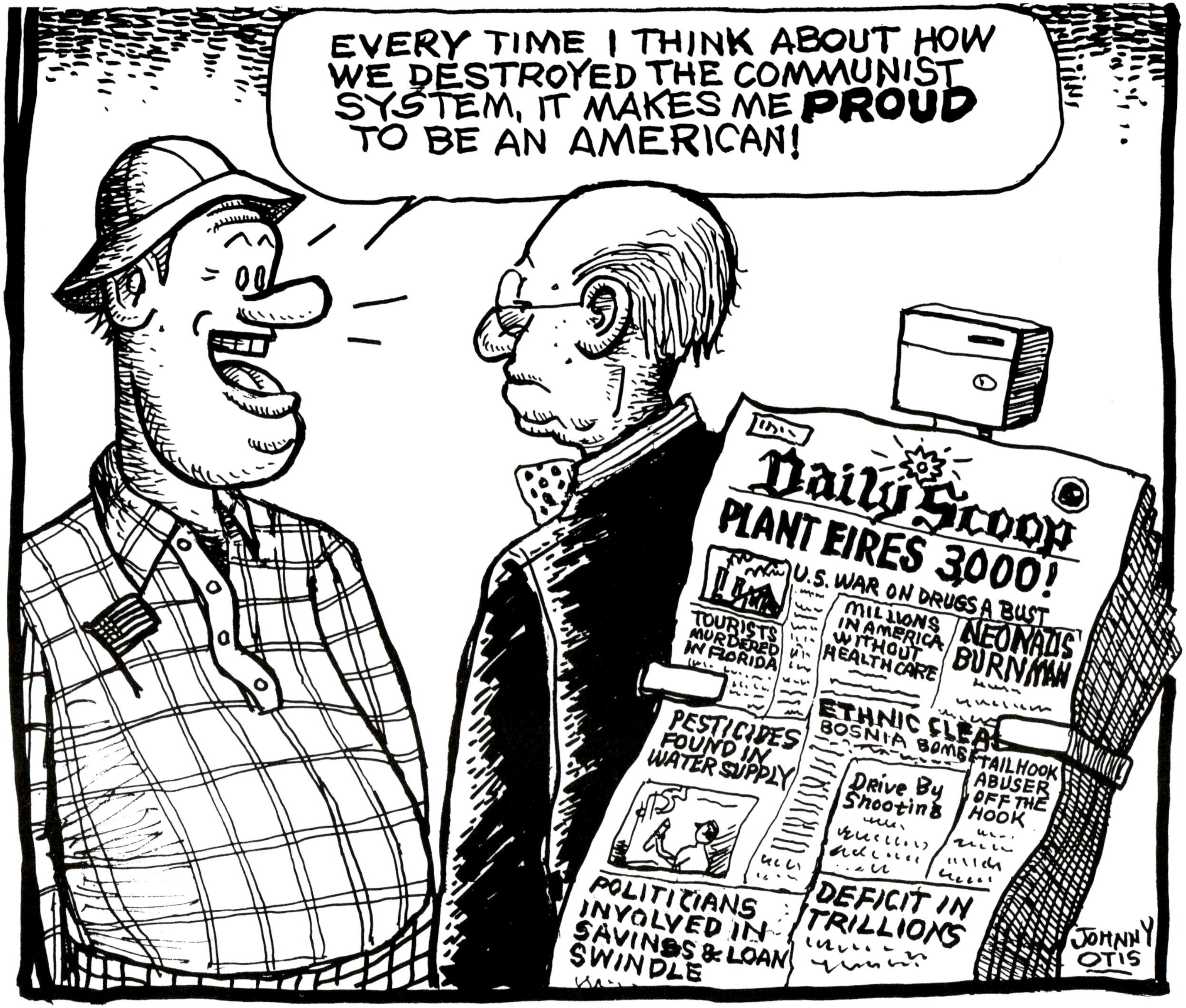
EVERY TIME I THINK ABOUT HOW WE DESTROYED THE COMMUNIST SYSTEM, IT MAKES ME **PROUD** TO BE AN AMERICAN!
Daily Scoop
PLANT FIRES 3000!
U.S. WAR ON DRUGS A BUST
TOURISTS MURDERED IN FLORIDA
MILLIONS IN AMERICA WITHOUT HEALTH CARE
NEONAZIS BURN MAN
ETHNIC CLEA
BOSNIA BOMB
PESTICIDES FOUND IN WATER SUPPLY
Drive By Shooting
TAILHOOK ABUSER OFF THE HOOK
POLITICIANS INVOLVED IN SAVINGS & LOAN SWINDLE
DEFICIT IN TRILLIONS
JOHNNY OTIS

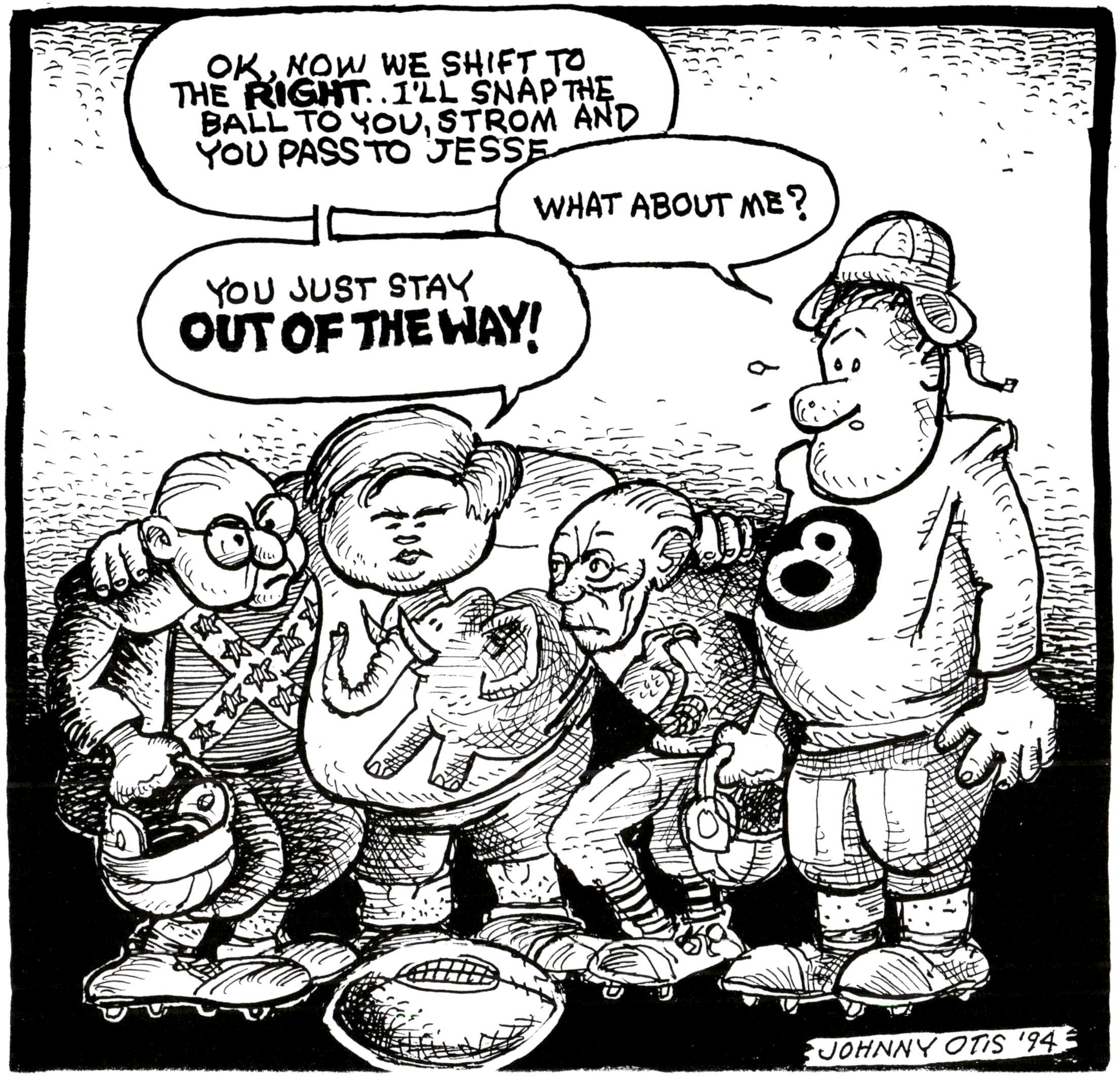
OK, NOW WE SHIFT TO THE RIGHT.. I'LL SNAP THE BALL TO YOU, STROM AND YOU PASS TO JESSE..
WHAT ABOUT ME?
YOU JUST STAY OUT OF THE WAY!
JOHNNY OTIS '94

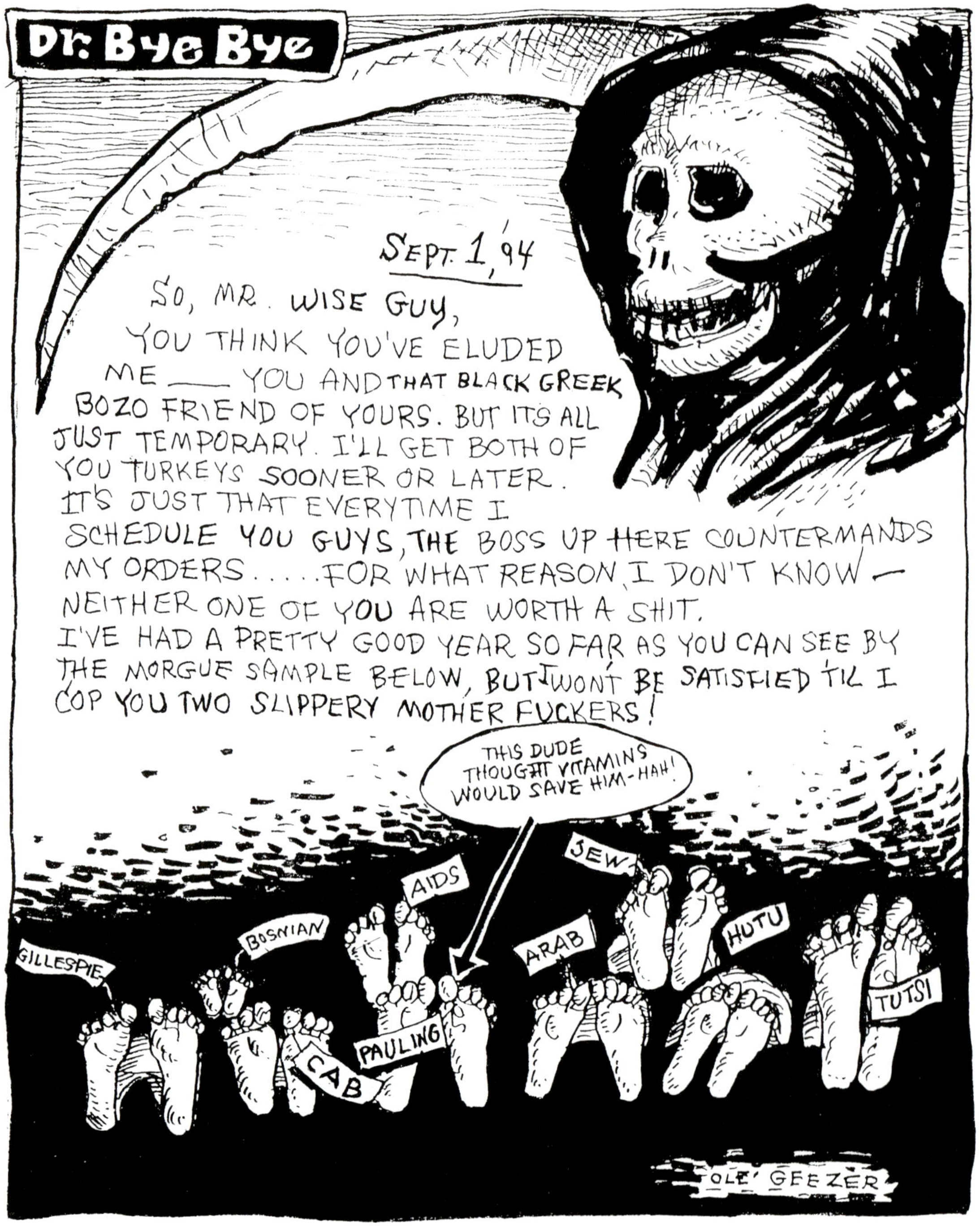
Dr. Bye Bye
SEPT. 1, '94
SO, MR. WISE GUY,
YOU THINK YOU'VE ELUDED ME ___ YOU AND THAT BLACK GREEK BOZO FRIEND OF YOURS. BUT ITS ALL JUST TEMPORARY. I'LL GET BOTH OF YOU TURKEYS SOONER OR LATER. IT'S JUST THAT EVERYTIME I SCHEDULE YOU GUYS, THE BOSS UP HERE COUNTERMANDS MY ORDERS.....FOR WHAT REASON, I DON'T KNOW — NEITHER ONE OF YOU ARE WORTH A SHIT.
I'VE HAD A PRETTY GOOD YEAR SO FAR AS YOU CAN SEE BY THE MORGUE SAMPLE BELOW, BUT I WON'T BE SATISFIED 'TIL I COP YOU TWO SLIPPERY MOTHER FUCKERS!
THIS DUDE THOUGHT VITAMINS WOULD SAVE HIM-HAH!
GILLESPIE
BOSNIAN
AIDS
CAB
PAULING
ARAB
JEW
HUTU
TUTSI
OLE' GEEZER

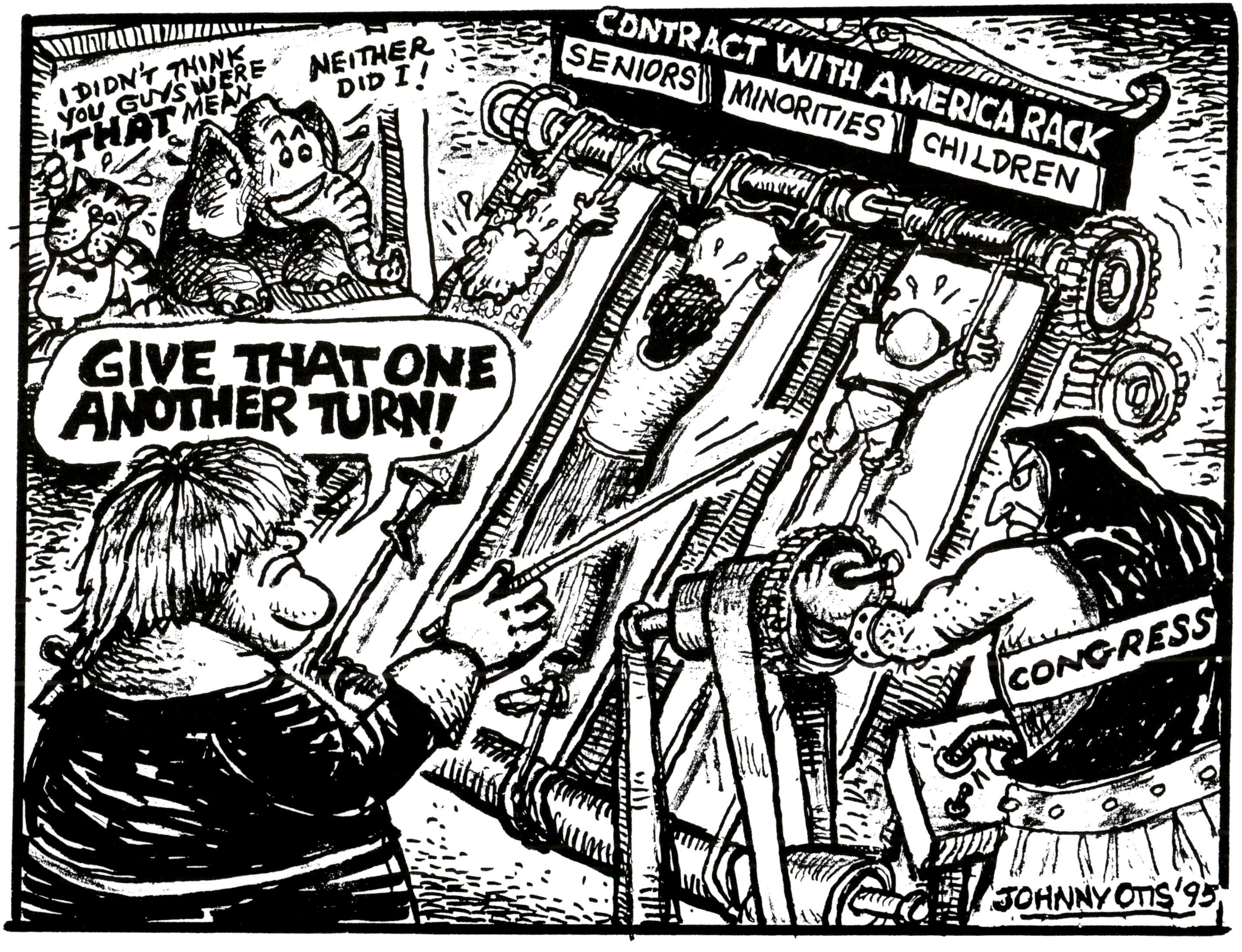
I DIDN'T THINK YOU GUYS WERE THAT MEAN
NEITHER DID I!
CONTRACT WITH AMERICA RACK
SENIORS
MINORITIES
CHILDREN
GIVE THAT ONE ANOTHER TURN!
CONGRESS
JOHNNY OTIS '95

Compiled by Lee Hildebrand from information provided by Johnny Otis, Dave Penny, Norbert Hess, Opal Louis Nations, Joel Selvin, and George Lipsitz. Dates that follow label and catalog number refer to year of recording and/or release. Album titles are indicated by italics.

I.
Recordings by Johnny Otis as primary artist of credit on label

(Note: Artist is usually listed as "Johnny Otis and His Orchestra" from 1945–1957 and as "The Johnny Otis Show" beginning with the 1957 Capitol sessions; featured vocalists are given in parentheses following song titles, by initials or abbreviations after first reference.)

My Baby's Business (v Jimmy Rushing)/Preston Love's Mansion (Excelsior 141) 1945

Jimmy's Round the Clock Blues (v JR)/Harlem Nocturne (Excelsior 142) 1945

One O'Clock Jump/Omaha Flash/He Was Tall, Dark, and Handsome (v Ivie Anderson)/S.K. Blues (v Joe Turner)/Jam Session Blues (v IA & JT)/One O'Clock Jump (Armed Forces Radio Jubilee 152) 1945

Omaha Flash/Jeff-Hi Stomp (Excelsior 152) 1946

Miss Mitchell/Ultra-Violet (Excelsior 156) 1946

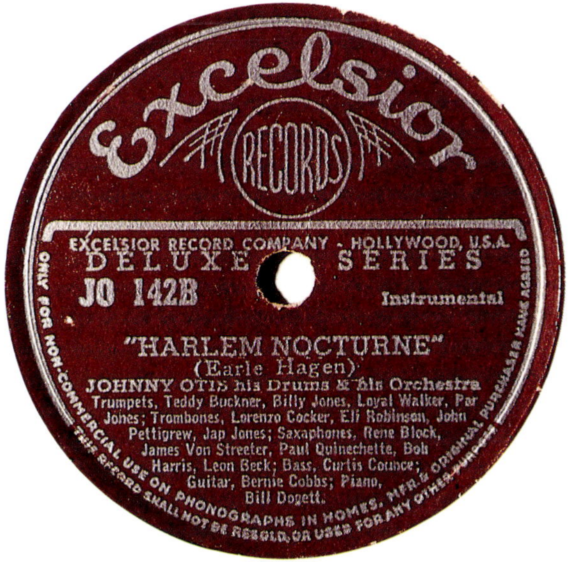

Sgt. Barksdale, Parts 1 and 2 (Excelsior 157) 1946

Love's Nocturne/Good Boo'di Goodie (v George Washington) (Excelsior 518) 1946

My Old Flame/La Boheme and Beans (Excelsior 519) 1946

Midnight at the Barrelhouse/Barrel House Stomp (Excelsior 536) 1947

Happy New Year Baby (v Lem Tally & Cathy Cooper)/Barrel House Stomp (Excelsior 536) 1947

Alimony Boogie (v CC)/Hog Jaws (Excelsior 537) 1947

Court Room Blues (v LT & Darby Hicks)/My Baby Done Told Me (v Four Bluebirds) (Excelsior 540) 1947

The Jelly Roll (v LT)/Pay Day Blues (v CC & Bardu Ali) (Excelsior 541) 1947

One O'Clock Jump/California Boogie/I Can't Believe That You're in Love with Me (v Barton)/Landlord Blues (v Jimmy Witherspoon)/Flying Home/One O'Clock Jump (Armed Forces Radio Jubilee 279) 1947

I Gotta Guy (v Little Esther)/Thursday Night Blues (Modern 20-715) 1949

Mean Ole Gal (v LE)/Good Ole Blues (Modern 20-748) 1949

If It's So Baby (v The Robins)/If I Didn't Love You So (v Rob) (Savoy 726) 1949

Ain't Nothin' Shakin' (v Roy Richards)/Double Crossing Blues (v LE, Bobby Nunn, & Rob) (Savoy 731) 1949

Goin' to See My Baby (v Redd Lyte)/The Little Red Hen (v RL) (Regent 1017) 1949

The Turkey Hop, Parts 1 and 2 (v Rob) (Savoy 7312) 1950

Misery (v LE)/Mistrustin' Blues (v LE, Mel Walker, & Rob) (Savoy 735) 1950

Our Romance Is Gone (v Rob)/Ain't No Use Beggin' (v Rob) (Savoy 738) 1950

Blues Nocturne/New Orleans Shuffle (Savoy 743) 1950

Helpless (v MWalk)/Dreamin' Blues (v MWalk) (Savoy 748) 1950

Cry Baby (MWalk & Rob)/I'm Falling in Love with You (v Devonia Williams & Rob) (Savoy 749) 1950

Cupid's Boogie (v LE & MWalk)/Just Can't Get Free (v LE & The Beltones) (Savoy 750) 1950

There's Rain in Your Eyes (v Rob)/I'm Livin' O.K. (v Rob) (Savoy 752) 1950

Lost Dream Blues (Lost in a Dream) (v LE)/ Deceivin' Blues (LE & MWalk) (Savoy 759) 1950

Freight Train Boogie/Good Time Blues (v MWalk) (Regent 1021) 1950

Lonely Blues (v MWalk)/Strange Woman (v MWalk) (Regent 1022) 1950

I'm Through (v Rob)/You're Fine, But Not My Kind (v Rob) (Savoy 762) 1950

Wedding Boogie (v LE, MWalk, & Lee Graves)/Far Away Blues (Faraway Christmas Blues) (v LE & MWalk) (Savoy 764) 1950

My Heart Tells Me (v MWalk)/Rockin' Blues (v MWalk) (Savoy 766) 1950

Head Hunter/Cool and Easy (v RL) (Savoy 774) 1950

Love Will Break Your Heart (v LE & MWalk)/I Don't Care (v LE) (Savoy 775) 1951

Gee Baby (v MWalk)/Mambo Boogie (Savoy 777) 1951

Doggin' Blues (v Linda Hopkins)/Living and Loving You (v LH) (Savoy 780) 1951

New Love (v MWalk)/All Night Long (v GW & Johnny Otis) (Savoy 788) 1951

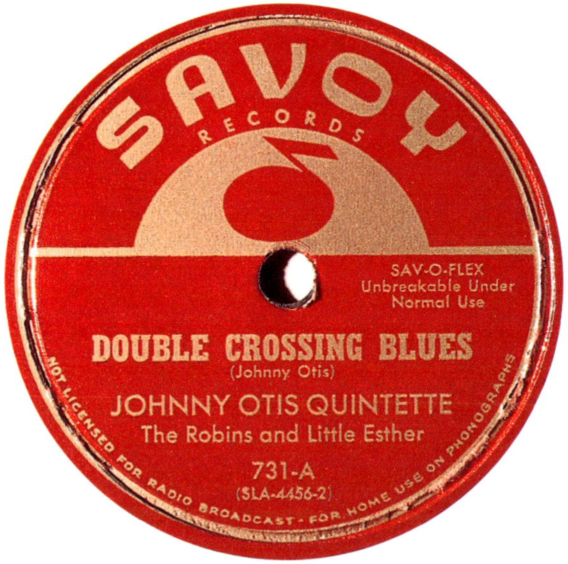

Hangover Blues/I Dream (v LE & MWalk) (Savoy 787) 1951

Warnin' Blues (v LH)/I'll Ask My Heart (v LH) (Savoy 812) 1951

Sunset to Dawn (V MWalk)/Feel Like Crying Again (v MWalk) (Savoy 821) 1951

Get Together Blues (v LE & Junior Ryder)/Chittlin' Switch (v The Vocaleers) (Savoy 824) 1951

Heartache Here I Come (v MWalk)/Help Me Blues (v MWalk) (Savoy 849) 1951

It Ain't the Beauty (v GW)/Gonna Take a Train (v RL) (Savoy 855) 1951

Oopy Doo (v JO)/Stardust (Mercury 8263) 1951

One Nighter Blues/Goomp Blues (Mercury 8273) 1951

Call Operator 210 (v MWalk)/Baby Baby Blues (v MWalk) (Mercury 8289) 1952

Gypsy Blues (v MWalk)/The Candle's Burnin' Low (v MWalk) (Mercury 8295)

Why Don't You Believe Me (v Ada Wilson)/Wishing Well (v AW) (Mercury 70038) 1952

The Love Bug Boogie (v MWalk & AW)/Brown Skin Butterball (v MWalk) (Mercury 70050) 1952

Rock Me Baby (v JO)/Young Girl (v JO & The Peacocks) (Peacock 1625) 1953

I Won't Be Your Fool No More (v JO)/Shake It (v JO) (Peacock 1636) 1954

Sittin' Here Drinkin' (v JO)/You Got Me Crying (Down by the River) (v JO) (Peacock 1648) 1954

Boom Diddy Wa Wa (v JR & Marie Adams (Peacock 1649) 1955

Butterball (v JO)/Sandy's Boogie (Peacock 1675) 1956

Hey! Hey! Hey! Hey! (v JO)/Let the Sunshine in My Life (v JO) (Dig 119) 1957

The Midnight Creeper, Parts 1 and 2 (Dig 122) 1957

Tough Enough (v JR)/The Blooper (Dig 131) 1957

Turtle Dove (v JO)/My Eyes Are So Full of Tears (v JO) (Dig 132) 1957

Wa Wa, Parts 1 and 2 (Dig 134) 1957

The Night Is Young (And You're So Fine) (v JO)/Stop, Look, and Love Me (v JO) (Dig 139) 1957

Rock and Roll Hit Parade (v JO, Arthur Lee Maye, Mel Williams) (Dig LP-104) 1957

Can't You Hear Me Callin' (v JO)/Hum Ding a Ling (v JO) (Capitol 3799) 1957

Ma, He's Makin' Eyes at Me (v MA & Three Toys of Joy)/(Romance) In the Dark (MA & TTJ) (Capitol 3800) 1957

Tell Me So (v MWill)/Stay with Me (v MWill) (Capitol 3801) 1957

It's Too Soon to Know (v Jeannie Sterling & The Moonbeans)/Star of Love (v JS & Moon) (Capitol 3802) 1957

The Johnny Otis Show (v JO, MA, TTJ, MWill, JS, Moon) (Capitol T-940) 1958

Good Golly (v JO)/Bye Bye Baby (v JO) (Capitol 3852) 1958

Well, Well, Well (v JO)/You Just Kissed Me Goodbye (v JO) (Capitol 3889) 1958

Ring-A-Ling (v JO)/Willie and the Hand Jive (v JO) (Capitol 3966) 1958

Willie Did the Cha Cha Cha (v JO)/Crazy Country Hop (v JO) (Capitol 4060) 1958

A Fool in Love (v MA)/What Do You Want to Make Those Eyes at Me For (v MA) (Capitol 4108) 1959

My Dear (v MWill)/You (v MWill) (Capitol 4156) 1959

Telephone Baby (v JO & Marci Lee)/Castin' My Spell (v JO) (Capitol 4168) 1959

I'll Do the Same Thing for You (v JO & ML)/Three Girls Named Molly, Doin' the Hully-Gully (v JO & ML) (Capitol 4226) 1959

Baby, Just You (v JO)/Let the Sun Shine in My Life (v JO) (Capitol 4260) 1959

Hey Baby, Don't You Know (v JO)/Mumblin' Mosie (v JO) (Capitol 4326) 1959

The Jelly Roll (v JO)/The New Bo Diddley (v JO) (Eldo 106) 1960

Baby, I Got News for You (v JO)/Hand Jive One More Time (v JO) (King 5581) 1961

It Must Be Love (v JO)/She's All Right (v JO and The Kelly Brothers) (King 5606) 1961

Darling I'll Be There (v JO)/Wilted Rose Bud (v JO) (King 5633) 1962 (issued as by "The Interludes")

Queen of the Twist (v JO)/I Know My Love Is True (v JO) (King 5634) 1962

Early in the Morning Blues (v JO)/The Hey, Hey, Hey, Hey Song (v JO) (King 5690) 1962

Somebody Call the Station (v JO)/Yes (v JO) (King 5707) 1962

Bye Bye Baby (I'm Leaving You) (v JO)/The Hash (King 1790) 1962

Keep the Faith, Parts 1 and 2 (Eldo 152) 1966

Long Distance (v Sugar Rainge)/Banana Peels (Eldo 153) 1967

Cold Shot (v JO, Delmar Evans, Don "Sugarcane" Harris) (Kent KST-534) 1968

Country Girl (v JO)/Bye Bye Baby (v JO) (Kent 509) 1968

Cuttin' Up (v JO, DE, DSH, Margie Evans) (Epic BN-26524) 1969

The Watts Breakaway (v JO)/You Can Depend on Me (v JO) (Okeh 4-7332) 1969

The Johnny Otis Show Live at Monterey! (v JO, DE, ME, Esther Phillips, Eddie "Cleanhead" Vinson, Joe Turner, Ivory Joe Hunter, Roy Milton, Roy Brown, Pee Wee Crayton) (Epic EG-30473) 1970

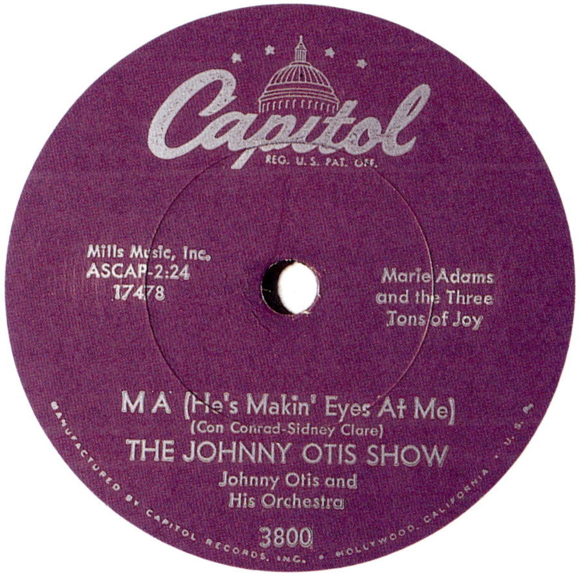

Willie and the Hand Jive (v JO)/Goin' Back to L.A. (v JO & DE) (Epic 5-10757) 1970

Snatch and the Poontangs (v DE) (Kent KST-557X) c. 1971 (issued as by "Snatch and the Poontangs")

Great Rhythm & Blues Oldies, Volume 3 (v JO, DE) (Blues Spectrum BS 103) c. 1974

Great Rhythm & Blues Oldies, Volume 8 (v JO, DE) (Blues Spectrum BS 108) 1977

Great Rhythm & Blues Oldies, Volume 13 (v JO, DE) (Blues Spectrum BS 113) c. 1977

Back to Jazz (v Barbara Morrison) (Jazz World JW 707) 1977

The New Johnny Otis Show (v JO, DE, Charles Williams, Linda Dorsey, Vera Hamilton, Wendell D. Perry) (Alligator AL 4726) 1981

Johnny Otis! Johnny Otis! The 1984 Johnny Otis Show (v JO, DE, BM, CW) (Hawksound, # unavailable) 1984

Otisology (v JO, DE, BM, CW) (Kent KLP 8001) 1986

Good Lovin' Blues (v JO, Ramona, La Dee Streeter, Jackie Payne) (Ace CH 299) 1990

Spirit of the Black Territory Bands (v JO, BM, JP) (Arhoolie CD 384) 1992

II.
Recordings by Johnny Otis as bandleader with other artists and/or as producer of other artists

JOHNNY ACE:

Saving My Love for You/Yes Baby (with Willie Mae Thornton) (Duke 118) 1953

Please Forgive Me/You've Been Gone So Long (Duke 128) 1954

Pledging My Love (Duke 136) 1954

Anymore (Duke 144) 1954

So Lonely (Duke 148) 1954

Still Love You So (Duke 154) 1954

MARIE ADAMS:

I'm Gonna Latch On (Peacock 1631) 1954

In Memory (A Tribute to Johnny Ace) (Peacock 1649) 1955

TONY ALLEN:

Check Yourself/It Hurts Me So (Ultra 104) 1955

I'm Dreaming/I Found an Angel (Dig 109) 1956

MR. "GOOGLE EYES" AUGUST:

Oh What a Fool/Play the Game (Duke 117) 1953

Lead Us On/Oh Ho Doodle Lu (Duke 156) 1954

JEANNIE BARNES:

My Love Song/Can't Get Out of Your Mind (Aladdin 3300) 1955

H.B. BARNUM:

Love Lost/Hallelujah (Eldo 111) 1961

RICHARD BERRY:

Great Rhythm & Blues Oldies, Volume 12 (Blues Spectrum BS 112) c. 1977

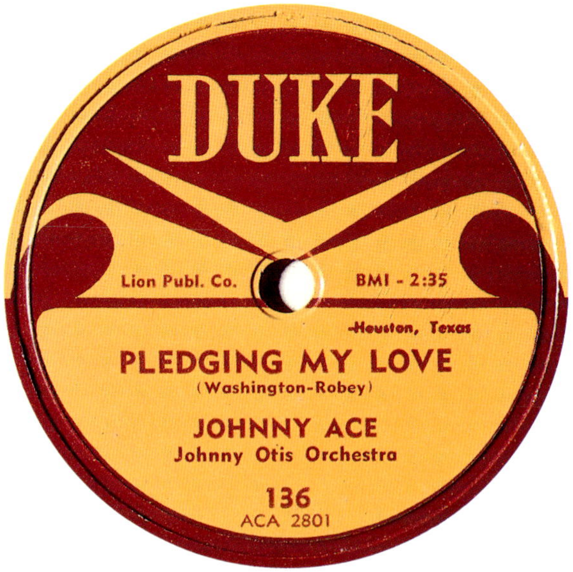

BIP & BOP:

Ding Dong Ding/Du Wada Du (Du Tra De Du) (Alladin 3287) 1955

CLIFFORD "FAT MAN" BLIVENS:

Korea Blues/Fat Man Boogie (Fat Man Blues) (Swing Time 236) 1949

ELOISE BROOKS & THE DREAMERS:

My Plea/Charles, My Darling (Aladdin 3303) 1955

CHARLES BROWN:

Great Rhythm & Blues Oldies, Volume 2 (Blues Spectrum BS 102) c. 1974

CALIFORNIA GOSPEL CARAVAN

(Billy Preston, Spiritual Trojans, Mel Carter, The Cavaliers, Rev. Claude Keller, Burma Floyd, Los Angeles All-Stars, The Angel Aires):

Gospel Anthology No. 1 (Gospel Tone GT 104) 1963

THE CLICK CLACKS:

Gospel Contrast (Gospel Tone GT 103) 1963

BUDDY COLLETTE:

Tanganyika (Dig LP-101) 1956

JOHNNY CRAWFORD:

Love Contractor's Blues/Big Daddy Blows (Down Beat 101) c. 1946

Texas Woman/Caldonia's Boogie (Down Beat 102) c. 1946

PEE WEE CRAYTON:

Great Rhythm & Blues Oldies, Volume 5 (Blues Spectrum BS 105) c. 1974

DESSARAY:

Ain't Gonna Tell/Daddy (7-11 2103) c. 1956

THE DING DONGS:

Ding Dongs/Sweet Thing (Eldo 109) 1960

BO DIDDLEY:

Where It All Began (Chess CH-50020) 1971

DOROTHY ELLIS:

Slowly Going Out of My Mind/He's Gone (Federal 12062) 1952

Drill, Daddy, Drill/Must Go Out to Play (Religion Blues) (Federal 12070) 1952

CELL FOSTER & THE AUDIOS:

I Prayed for You/Honest I Do (Ultra 105) 1955

JOE "PAPOOSE" FRITZ:

Honey Honey/The Woman I Love (Peacock 1627) 1953

GENE & EUNICE:

Kokomo (I Love You So)/You and Me (Aladdin 3276) 1955

Move It Over Baby/This Is My Story (Aladdin 3282) 1955

Flim Flam/Can We Forget It (Aladdin 3292) 1955

The Gladiators:

My Baby Doll/Girl of My Heart (Dig 135) 1957

Lee Graves:

Cloudy Weather Blues/Papa Said Yes, Mama Said No No No (Mercury 8214) 1950

I'm from Texas/Sixty Years and a Day (Mercury 8222) 1950

Slim Green:

My Woman Done Quit Me (Dig 142) 1957

Stone Down Blues (Kent KST-549) c. 1970

Don "Sugarcane" Harris:

They Say You Never Can Miss/Elim Stole My Baby (Boo Hoo) (Eldo 103) 1960

Sugar Cane (Epic E-30027) 1970

Little Julian Herrara & The Tigers:

Long Lonely Nights/In Exchange for Your Love (Dig 118) 1957

Here in My Arms/Symbol of Heaven (Dig 137) 1957

Henry Hill:

Wondering Blues/Sunday Morning Blues (Federal 12030) 1951

Hold Me Baby/Since You've Been Away (Federal 12037) 1951

If you Love Me/What's the Matter, Mama (Federal 12044) 1951

My Baby's Back Home/Give Me Something Called Love (Federal 12053) 1951

Ron Holden:

I'll Be Happy/I'll Always Love You (Eldo 117) c. 1961

Earl Jackson:

Take Out the Squeal (If You Want a Meal)/If I Had One (Supreme 1527) 1947

A Woman Don't Want a Good Man No More/So Help Me (Supreme 1532) 1947

Kansas City Jumps/Talking to Myself (Supreme 1537) 1947

Etta James & The Peaches:

The Wallflower/Hold Me Squeeze Me (Modern 947) 1954

Louis Jordan

Great Rhythm & Blues Oldies, Volume 1 (Blues Spectrum BS 101) c. 1974

The Lamplighters:

Part of Me/Turn Me Loose (Federal 12149) 1953

Be-Bop Wino/Give Me (Federal 12152) 1953

Smoochie/I Can't Stand It (Federal 12166) 1953

You Hear (Federal 12192) 1954

Yum Yum/Goody Good Things (Federal 12197) 1954

Lovey Lewis:

Alright Baby/Take a Chance with Me (Duke 126) 1953

Pete "Guitar" Lewis:

Louisiana Hop/Crying with the Rising Sun (Federal 12066) 1952

Raggedy Blues/Harmonica Boogie (Federal 12076) 1952

Ooh Midnight/Scratchin' (Federal 12103) 1952

The Blast/Chocolate Pork Chop Man (Federal 12113) 1952

Goin' Crazy/Back Door Troubles (Peacock 1624) 1953

Richard Lewis:

Hey Little Girl/Richard's Boogie (Aladdin 3238) 1955

I Wish You Love (with Dolores Gibson)/Let's Love Tonight (with Dolores Gibson) (Aladdin 3239) 1955

Joe Liggins:

Great Rhythm & Blues Oldies, Volume 6 (Blues Spectrum BS 106) c. 1974

Lilly of the Valley:

I Had a Sweet Dream/Blue Mood (Eldo 151) 1966

Little Esther:

Other Lips, Other Arms/The Deacon Moves In (with The Dominoes) (Federal 12016) 1950

Looking for a Man (To Satisfy Me)/Heart to Heart (with The Dominoes) (Federal 12036) 1950

Don't Make a Fool Out of Me/I'm a Bad, Bad Girl (with Mel Walker) (Federal 12023) 1951

Cryin' and Singin' the Blues/Tell Him That I Need Him (Federal 12042) 1951

Ring-A-Ding-Doo (with Mel Walker)/The Crying Blues (Federal 12055) 1951

Summertime/The Storm (Federal 12063) 1952

I'll Be There/Better Beware (Federal 12065) 1952

Bring My Lovin' Back to Me/Aged and Mellow Blues (Federal 12078) 1952

Somebody New/Ramblin' Blues (Federal 12090) 1952

Saturday Night Daddy (with Bobby Nunn & The Robins)/Mainliner (with The Robins) (Federal 12100) 1952

Last Laugh Blues (with Little Willie Littlefield)/ Flesh, Blood, and Bones (Federal 12108) 1952

Hollerin' and Screamin'/Turn the Lamps Down Low (with Little Willie Littlefield) (Federal 12115) 1952

You Took My Love Too Fast (with Bobby Nunn)/ Street Lights (Federal 12122) 1952

I Paid My Dues (Federal 12344) 1952

Little Richard:

Directly from My Heart to You/Little Richard's Boogie (Peacock 1658) 1953

Maybe I'm Right/I Love My Baby (Peacock 1673) 1953

Preston Love:

Wondering/Voodoo (Federal 12038) 1951

Unconscious Blues/Twilight Blues (Federal 12043) 1951

September Song/Wango Blues (Federal 12069) 1952

Like a Ship at Sea/Strictly Cash (Federal 12085) 1952

Strange Land Blues/Crying for My Baby (Spin 101) 1952

Kissin' Boogie/Jumpin' for Charles (Spin 102) 1952

Feel So Good/Huckle Boogie (Spin 103) 1952

You Got Me Drinking/Stay by My Side (Federal 12132) 1953

Suicide Blues/My Love Is Draggin' (Federal 12145) 1953

Boom Diddy Wawa Baby/A Man Goin' Crazy (Federal 12216) 1955

If You Ever Get Lonesome/Groove Juice (Ultra 101) 1955

That's All Right, Baby/Ali Baba's Boogie (Ultra 103) 1955

Dog Face Boy, Parts 1 and 2 (Dig 110) 1956

Country Boogie (Dig 116) 1956

Omaha Bar-B-Q (Kent KST-540) c. 1969

Sydney Maiden:

Hand Me Down Baby (Dig 138) 1957

Billy Mann:

Lost Angel/Find Yourself Another Guy (Dig 111) 1956

A Million Heartaches Ago/Just Like Before (Dig 120) 1957

Little Arthur Matthews:

Bad Bad Bulldog/Hot Diggitty Dog (Dig 117) 1956

Arthur Lee Maye & The Clowns:

Honey, Honey/This Is the Night for Love (Dig 124) 1957

Whispering Wind/A Fool's Prayer (Dig 133) 1957

Amos Milburn:

Great Rhythm & Blues Oldies, Volume 10 (Blues Spectrum BS 110) c. 1977

Mighty Flea (Gene Connors):

Ode to Billy Joe, Parts 1 and 2 (Eldo 155) 1967

Music to Think By (Eldo 156) 1968

Roy Milton:

Roots of Rock (Kent KST-554) c. 1970

Great Rhythm & Blues Oldies, Volume 9 (Blues Spectrum BS 109) c. 1977

Abe Moore:

S & J/Moore Boogie (Dig 125) 1957

Gatemouth Moore:

Great Rhythm & Blues Oldies, Volume 7 (Blues Spectrum BS 107) c. 1977

Moose John (Johnny "Moose John" Walker):

Wrong Doin' Woman/Talkin' 'Bout Me (Ultra 102) 1955

The Nic Nacs:

Gonna Have a Merry Christmas/I Found Me a Sugar Daddy (RPM 313) 1950

You Didn't Want My Love/I Found Me a Sugar Daddy (RPM 316) 1950

Bobby Nunn & The Robins

Rockin'/That's What the Good Book Says (Modern 20-807) 1951

Laura Otis & The Satinettes:

I'm Gonna Make You Love Me/Bye Bye Soldier Boy (Mexie 102) c. 1961

Shuggie Otis

Here Comes Shuggie Otis (Epic BN-26511) 1969

Freedom Flight (Epic KE-30752) 1970

Strawberry Letter 23/Ice Cold Daydream (Epic 5-10798) 1970

Lawanda Page (comedy):

Mutha (Laff, # unavailable) c. 1971

The Penguins:

Universal Twist/To Keep Our Love (Eldo 119) c. 1961

The Premiers:

New Moon/Baby (Dig 106) 1956

Have a Heart/My Darling (Dig 113) 1956

Little Billy Robbins:

Bring Her Back to Me/Baby, Please Come Home (Dig 127) 1957

The Robins:

Don't Like the Way You're Doing/Come Back Baby (Aladdin 3031) 1949

'Round About Midnight/You Sure Look Good to Me (Score 4010) 1949

The Royals:

Every Beat of My Heart/All Night Long (Federal 12064) 1952

I Know I Love You So/Starting from Tonight (Federal 12077) 1952

Big Daddy Rucker:

This Is My Song/He Made You Mine (Hawksound 101) 1971

Junior Ryder:

Sad Story (with The Peacocks)/Better Stop (Duke 119) 1953

Don't Tell Noboby/Every Star I See (Duke 139) 1954

The Safaris:

Image of a Girl/Four Steps to Love (Eldo 101) 1960

Sailor Boy (Alex Spearman):

Country Home (Dig 116) 1956

What Have I Done Wrong? Parts 1 and 2 (Dig 126) 1957

Marilyn Scott (The Carolina Blues Girl):

Beer Bottle Boogie/Uneasy Blues (Regent 1025) 1950

I Want to Die Easy/I Really Believe (Regent 1029) 1950 (issued as by "Mary DeLoach")

The Sheiks:

So Fine/Sentimental Heart (Federal 12337) 1955

Al Simmons (with Slim Green):

Old Folks' Boogie (Dig 138) 1957

You Ain't Too Old (Dig 142) 1957

Skillet & Leroy (comedy):

2 or 3 Times a Day (Laff A131) c. 1971

Burglar in the Bedroom (Laff, # unavailable) c. 1971

Julie Stevens & The Premiers:

Blue Mood/Crazy Bells (Dig 115) 1956

I Don't Want to Know/Take My Heart (Dig 129) 1957

Lawrence Stone:

Everytime/Until the Real Thing Comes Along (Dig 130) 1957

Sugar Pie & Hank (Sugar Pie DeSanto and Henry Houston):

Please Be True/I'm So Lonely (Federal 12217) 1955

The Sultans:

How Deep Is the Ocean?/Good Thing Baby (Duke 125) 1954

I Cried My Heart Out/Baby Don't Put Me Down (Duke 133) 1954

Joe Swift:

That's Your Last Boogie/What's Your Name? (Exclusive 51X) 1948

I'll Just Laugh (While You Cry)/Lovin' Baby Blues (Exclusive 64X) 1948

Crazy 'Bout Your Cookin'/Right Now Baby (Exclusive 80X) 1948

Nightmare/Alligator Meat (Exclusive 85X) 1948

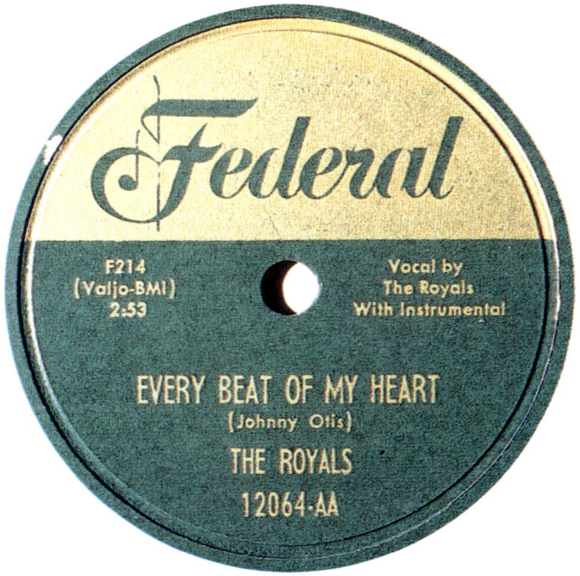

The Tears:

Until the Day I Die/Nothing but Love (Dig 112) 1956

Willie Mae "Big Mama" Thornton:

Hound Dog/Nightmare (Peacock 1612) 1952

They Call Me Big Mama (Peacock 1621) 1952

I Ain't No Fool Either/The Big Change (Peacock 1626) 1953

I've Searched the Whole World Over/I Smell a Rat (Peacock 1632) 1952

Walking Blues/Rock A Bye Baby (Peacock 1647) 1952

Just Like a Dog (Barking Up the Wrong Tree)/My Man Called Me (Peacock 1681) 1957

Joe Turner:

Great Rhythm & Blues Oldies, Volume 4 (Blues Spectrum BS 104) c. 1974

The Twilighters:

Nothin'/Do You Believe (Eldo 115) c. 1961

Eddie "Cleanhead" Vinson:

Great Rhythm & Blues Oldies, Volume 11 (Blues Spectrum BS 111) c. 1977

Larry Waters:

Don't Tell Me That You Love Me/Full Grown Woman (Dig 108) 1956

I Wonder, I Wonder/I Wish I Didn't Love You So (Dig 121) 1957

Johnny "Guitar" Watson:

Cold, Cold Heart/That's the Chance You've Got to Take (King 5716) 1962

I Say I Love You/You Better Love Me (King 5833) 1962

In the Evenin'/Gangster of Love (King 5774) 1962

Gerald Wiggins:

Wiggin' with Wig (Dig LP-102) 1956

Mel Williams:

Here at My Phone/Talk to Me (Dig 107) 1956

Hold Me/Here in My Heart (Dig 114) 1956

My Love/Don't Cry Baby (Dig 123) 1957

I Cried a Million Tears/All Through the Night (Dig 128) 1957

I Got Eyes/It's You (Dig 136) 1957

Stand There, Mountain/I Don't Care if the Sun Don't Shine (Dig 140) 1957

All Through the Night (Dig LP-103) 1957

III.
Recordings by Johnny Otis as sideman

A. Drums with

Wynonie Harris:

Around the Clock, Parts 1 and 2 (Philo 103) 1945

Cock-A-Doodle-Doo/Yonder Comes My Baby (Philo 104) 1945

The Jacquerabbits (Illinois and Russell Jacquet):

Ladies Lullaby/Illinois Stomp (American Recording Artists 144) 1945

Illinois Jacquet:

Jammin' the Blues (Armed Forces Radio Service Jubilee 125) 1945

Flying Home, Parts 1 and 2 (Philo 101) 1945

Uptown Boogie/Throw It Out of Your Mind, Baby (Philo 102) 1945

Johnny Moore's Three Blazers:

Drifting Blues/Groovy (Philo 112) 1945

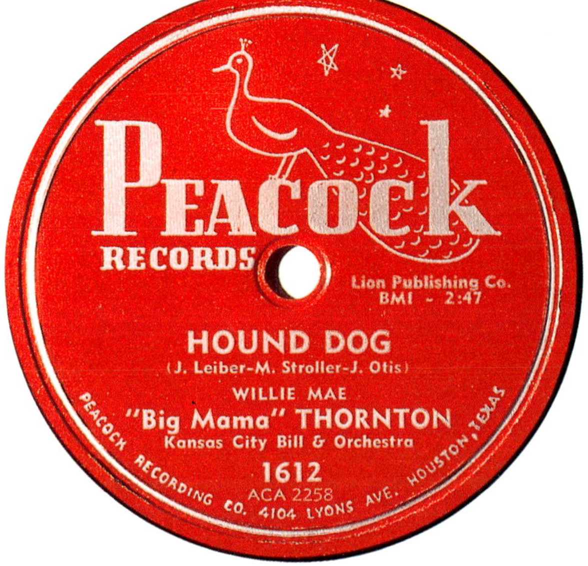

Timmie Rogers & Stomp Russell Trio:

Fla-Ga-La-Pa/Drop Another Nickle in the Jukebox (Excelsior 136) 1945

Daddy-O/Hep Paderewski from Basin Street (Excelsior 138) 1945

Lester Young:

It's Only a Paper Moon/After You're Gone (Philo 127) 1946

Lover Come Back to Me/Jammin' with Lester (Philo 128) 1946

B. Piano and tambourine with

Frank Zappa:

Hot Rats (Bizarre RS-6358) 1969

C. Vibraharp with

Charles Brown:

Charles Brown's Cool Christmas Blues (Bullseye Blues CD BB 9561) 1994

Jimmy McCracklin:

A Taste of the Blues (Bullseye Blues CD BB 9535) 1994

IV.
Reissue compilations of Johnny Otis recordings (selected)

The Original Johnny Otis Show (Savoy SJL 2230) 1978 (contains Excelsior and Savoy material, 1945–1951)

The Original Johnny Otis Show, Volume 2 (Savoy SJL 2252) 1980 (contains Excelsior and Savoy material, 1945–1951)

Start to Jump Because It's Jubilee (Swingtime ST 1009) 1986 (contains Armed Forces Radio Service Jubilee material, 1945)

Midnight at the Barrel House (B&E 102) c. 1978 (contains Excelsior, Exclusive, Regent, Mercury, Duke, and Peacock material, 1945–1954)

Be Bop Baby Blues (Night Train CD 7003) 1991 (contains Down Beat, Supreme, Exculsive, and Swing Time material, 1946–1949)

Barrelhouse Stomp (Jukebox Lil JB-611) 1983 (contains Excelsior, Exclusive, and Mercury material, 1947–1952)

Gee Baby (Jukebox Lil JB-617) 1986 (contains Excelsior, Savoy, and Mercury material, 1947–1952)

Johnny Otis Presents the Robins, Little Esther, the Nic Nacs (Ace CH88) 1983 (contains Modern and RPM material, 1949–1951)

Creepin' with the Cats (Ace CDCHD 325) 1991 (contains Ultra and Dig material, 1955–1957)

The Capitol Years (Capitol C1-92858) 1989 (contains Capitol material, 1957–1959)

Let's Life It Up (Charly CRB 269) c. 1980 (contains King material, 1961–1962)